DATE DUE

11-15 99			
NOO 08 '99			

DEMCO 13829810

D1153947

Understanding language

Roger Fowler

Understanding language
An introduction to linguistics

by Routledge & Kegan Paul Ltd
© Roger Fowler 1974
any form without permission from the

Routledge & Kegan Paul   London and Boston

First published in 1974
by Routledge & Kegan Paul Ltd
Broadway House, 68–74 Carter Lane
London EC4V 5EL and
9 Park Street,
Boston, Mass. 02108, U.S.A.
Printed in Great Britain by William Clowes & Sons Limited
London, Colchester and Beccles
and set in Monotype Times New Roman 10 on 11pt
ISBN 0 7100 7755 6 (c)
ISBN 0 7100 7756 4 (p)

Library of Congress Catalog Card No. 73-92982

To my parents

Contents

Contents

Preface

In the preface to his collection of essays, *Extraterritorial*, George Steiner claims that there has been a 'language revolution' (and, furthermore, that it is common knowledge that there has been a language revolution). Whether or not the language capacities and language values of the 'civilized' world were revolutionized around or after 1914 is a question of interpretation; and such a revolution ought in any case to be put into perspective. How much more resounding must have been the effects of that dramatic change, deep back in pre-history, when man, by what process we do not know, ceased to be a naked ape and became a language animal. Language is possibly the most vital and powerful of mankind's unique endowments: by means of it we regulate our social and interpersonal behaviour and build up and stabilize our intellectual engagement with the world. Language is therefore of central interest to anyone who is curious about the distinctive characteristics which make man the peculiarly gifted and successful organism that he undoubtedly is.

The study of language is **linguistics**. There have been several revolutions in linguistics, among which the most significant recent ones are probably 1786, 1916 and 1957 (see chapter 2). Steiner's 'language revolution' includes the linguistics revolution of 1957, that is to say the publication of Noam Chomsky's *Syntactic Structures* which heralded the phenomenal success of a new style of grammatical analysis, 'transformational-generative' linguistics or 'TG' for short. TG is first and foremost a device for the display of syntactic structure in highly formal, abstract terms, and the professional journals of linguistics bear witness to the tremendous advances in the descriptive delicacy of linguistics which have been

ix

achieved since the transformational technique has been available. We now know vastly more about the structure of natural languages – particularly English – than we did fifteen years ago; and even where new *facts* are not revealed, we now have *explanations* for certain complexities of linguistic structure which traditional grammarians had noticed but had failed to explicate. In its descriptive aspect TG is often formidably difficult and technical. Some of its technicalities are expounded in the present book.

But the TG revolution was not merely technical or scholastic in its impact. It brought into fashion a whole new philosophy of language; or, as Chomsky expresses it, revived and substantiated traditional ways of looking at language which had been ignored in the earlier part of this century while linguistics was swept along with the tide of positivistic, empiricist feeling which dominated the physical and social sciences. Chomskyan linguistics, despite its formal and superficially forbidding symbols and rules, is built on an assumption of the essential naturalness of language, is so constructed that our discoveries about the way language is put together can be readily integrated with findings and hypotheses concerning man's social and psychological existence. As a direct result of Chomsky's work on grammar, psycholinguistics has thrived – particularly research into child language acquisition. At the same time, progress has been made in structural studies of the functioning of language in society. Whereas, twenty years ago, language was seen as an abstract code detached from human experience, it is now seen as a vital communicative system inseparable from other processes of living.

The present book is an introduction to language *and* to linguistics. It does not claim to be a textbook from which one might learn the entire methodology of linguistic analysis, still less a survey, historical or contemporary, of the vast range of activities that comprise the linguistic sciences. However, it alludes to most of the central aspects of the formal structure of language, as well as to the ways language integrates with the social and psychological existence of human beings. As the characterization of language unfolds, much of the conceptual and terminological apparatus of generative linguistics is inevitably invoked. I could have attempted to make the book neutral as to theoretical 'model'; but since the particular insights of generative grammar are presupposed by my generalizations about language, it would have been misleading and perhaps dishonest to conceal them. Now having chosen a generative model, I was faced with a major problem: TG has been in a state of continuous development since its inception in the late 1950s, and since about 1968 has been in violent fermentation. Disputes flourish, and new ideas, mostly challenging what Chomsky calls the 'standard grammar' (*floruit circa* 1965) continually erupt. Recently, the theory of meaning has been so developed as to stretch the powers of existing syntactic models to breaking point. It seems to me unlikely that a unified generative theory will be agreed upon in the foreseeable future; and I believe it is unnecessary for a book of the present kind to await a successful synthesis. The various sections of this book, then, lean on partial theories which are not always entirely compatible. In particular, specialists will recognize that the semantic analyses offered in chapters 3–4 and the ideas about syntax proposed in chapters 5–7 are drawn from different phases in modern linguistic theory, so that their compatibility cannot be absolutely assured. It would have been impertinent, or at least premature, for me to attempt a wholly integrated synthesis. Instead, I have tried to draw upon the insights of recent linguists who have written convincingly on the separate levels of linguistic analysis, acknowledging that discussion of these different levels has reached different degrees of refinement. I have been acutely conscious of the problem of 'drawing the line' chronologically, of deciding where to make pause while the science of linguistics is developing so rapidly. No cut-off point could fail to be arbitrary. My cut-off point is *circa* 1970; at that time the new 'generative semantics' was beginning to look very plausible. Now, reviewing the publications of 1971 and 1972, it seems that the syntacticians are making a come-back.

A word concerning the level, scope and mode of use of this book. It is intended as an elementary textbook, primarily but not exclusively for directed use in introductory courses in linguistics; it is written in response to my own feeling that there exists no comparable book which attempts to convey an impression of the importance and ramifications of language in our daily personal and social lives – thus, a suggestion of the range of heads under which language might be studied – and at the same time to provide a grounding in the formal techniques and concepts of scientific linguistics. It is difficult to avoid skimping on one or the other in a book of moderate length. So the majority of introductory texts choose one or other alternative: an informal evocation of the flavour of language, or an uncompromising onslaught on the methodology of some specialized aspect (usually syntax or phonetics) of linguistic science. The usual defect of books of the first type is that they tend to the enthusiastic evocation of a miraculism in language, and in the enjoyment of the wonders of language the essential systematicity, discipline, of the subject is dissipated. Usually, such books smooth over the controversies within the science of linguistics, making the whole thing seem gentler and less engaging and challenging than it actually is. The drawbacks of the second choice (introducing the student to the technique of one part of linguistic description) are twofold: first, other areas get left out; second, the text is bound to be severe, formal, and committed to one alternative in linguistic ideology. On both accounts, the student is left needing the informal, general, evocative and seductive text to supplement his specialized book – indeed, to lead him up to it ('a medicine of cherries', as Sir Philip Sidney said of another kind of book).

As a teacher of linguistics, I have generally been driven to an unsatisfactory solution: the medicine of cherries has consisted of a specialized text in syntax or phonology or semantics sweetened by one of the attractive 'classic' works dealing with language more generally, e.g. Bloomfield's or Sapir's *Language*. Dissatisfaction arises because of the chronological, ideological/theoretical and even *stylistic*, discord between the contemporary specialist and the classic generalist. Now I do not pretend that *Understanding Language* may join the ranks of those great books justly named *Language*: given the present disputatious state of linguistics, it is unlikely that anyone could maintain an acceptable consistency and generosity over all the branches of language-study that would have to be covered in the needed 500,000 words! I have attempted something much less ambitious: an introduction to language and linguistics which makes mention of most of the topics in linguistics, which aims at conceptual consistency, and above all which tries to be in tune with modern theory while at the same time minimizing disharmony with the more controversial innovations and with the great earlier theories which we may today neglect. I am conscious that the book presents an air of the 'fashionable' in linguistics today (or 'just-before-today', for safety): this is a deliberate strategy to facilitate students' access to more advanced and technical books of the last few years. At the same time, I have tried at all cost to bridle the contemporaneity of the book where it might have threatened to make earlier (specifically, pre-transformational) writings unreadable to the curious student.

At the end of each chapter, recommendations for further reading are offered, and the titles recommended are collected into a reading list on pp. 259–66. These bibliographical suggestions have been chosen with some care. Out of the enormously rich literature of linguistics I have picked those books and articles which fit most closely with the on-going chapter-by-chapter argument. I should caution the reader *not* to start with p. 259 and proceed through the reading list alphabetically. The suggestions for further reading are designed as a guide for the general reader who is working through this book on his own. In that situation he should pursue the 'further reading' in relation to my developing argument. In that way it is hoped that, without the guidance of a teacher or a formal course, the book may provide access to a broader linguistic science than can be covered in these pages. That is, the book may be used by the 'general reader' as his initial chart for linguistics.

Chapters 5–7 make brief use of material to be found more fully expounded in my earlier book, *An Introduction to Transformational Syntax* (Routledge & Kegan Paul, 1971). I have taken care that these two books should be as fully compatible as the present fluid state of linguistics allows.

The book has been developing for about a decade, and reflects my teaching of elementary language studies to undergraduates at the universities of Hull, East Anglia and California (Berkeley). The final version was written during 1971–2, and has benefited greatly from the comments of my colleagues, Veronica Du Feu, Gunther Kress and Sinclair Rogers, who helped me remove many errors, obscurities and infelicities of style. The defects which remain can be blamed mostly on my obstinacy, partly on the unstable contemporary situation in linguistics. I, like other writers in this field, have been forced to make the subject look a bit more settled than it actually is. If we did not take this liberty, such books as this one could never be written.

Roger Fowler

one

Language

When we need to speak, language usually comes to us with thoughtless ease; it takes social embarrassment, or intellectual incomprehension, or a severe fit of coughing, to render us silent when we need to speak – inhibitions which, we can readily feel, are quite removed from 'language itself'. That blocked word 'on the tip of the tongue' seems to be a rare case of a pure language failure; generally, speech flows freely. Whatever the real cause of our occasional verbal blockages, we *feel* them to be exceptional; conversely, we accept our normal power of language as a natural gift comparable to breathing, or balancing, or the process of digestion. We are quite right to do so. The first premise of this book is that language is an intrinsic aspect of our human inheritance. It thus differs in kind from such arduously acquired – and inessential – skills as chess-playing, bicycle-riding, calculus.

The first insight must be counterbalanced with a second. I expect that most readers of this book have attempted to learn a foreign language as adults, that most have experienced difficulty, and that few would claim to be anything like as proficient in their second language as they are in their 'mother tongue'. The problems of adult language-learners are interesting in themselves; but what is noteworthy here is the perspective we achieve, grappling with an unfamiliar tongue, of the structural complexity of language: we become conscious, perhaps for the first time, of the delicacy, depth and extensiveness of linguistic form. It cannot be true that 'all foreign languages are difficult' (although some languages may be particularly difficult – or easy – for speakers of certain first languages); it must be the case that language is a genuinely complicated kind of knowledge and behaviour. We do not normally realize this

1

fact, because we are not called upon, in the normal course of our day-to-day activities, to bring language structure to conscious attention. This consciousness is the preoccupation of the academic linguist (and of many of his scholarly near cousins): he is concerned to expound the structure of particular languages, and of language at large. His exposition is bound to convey the 'difficulty' of language, and in view of this he has a special responsibility to square the sense of difficulty with the fact of naturalness. His picture of the intricacy of language must be consistent with a further observation, and a rather spectacular one: babies begin to acquire this complicated skill of speech around their first birthday and are astonishingly articulate within a few months of starting to talk.

As we shall see in chapter 9, human infants seem to be naturally predisposed to talk. We refer to adults *learning* a language, children *acquiring* one: this terminological distinction is meant to suggest that children come to possess linguistic knowledge without formal instruction and, so far as we can see, without the conscious effort of drills, memorization and exercises associated with second language learning. Exposure to a language being used around them seems to be the simple prerequisite to set in motion some innate 'language acquisition device' which almost universally leads to proficiency within a short space of time. Children learn language quickly, and they learn it early – generally, the rudiments of speech are established before a child can draw a straight line, tie his shoe-laces or perform even more primitive motor skills. Furthermore, children very often acquire language against the odds: an impoverished linguistic environment (e.g. inattentive or uncommunicative or even speechless parents, or lack of siblings) does not seem to prevent acquisition of the formal bases of language, even though fluency and size of vocabulary in later childhood may be impaired. Congenitally blind children rapidly learn language. Those who are deaf or severely hard of hearing learn to speak only with great difficulty; but as soon as they can be taught to read and write they pick up a knowledge of language which may be perfect except in its phonetic manifestation. Retarding conditions such as mongolism often do no more than slow down the rate of acquisition and introduce slight deficiencies later on – poor pronunciation, occasional grammatical slips. Even babies who are so unfortunate as to suffer major brain damage can learn to use language, provided the injury occurs very early. It is only the most massive psychological handicaps (notably autism) which inhibit language totally.

If, then, a second language is hard to induce in an adult, the first language is nevertheless inordinately difficult to suppress in an infant. The rule seems to be: if you are human, you will in the natural course of events become a language-user very rapidly. It may be worth adding at this point that the rule applies irrespective of race or culture – we will see that there are no 'primitive languages' and this is because there are no (biologically normal) linguistically primeval babies. Language is natural in that it is **species-uniform.**

By 'language' I mean 'human language': it is not only uniform within the species, but also **specific** to the species. No other animal has command of language, at least not in the sense of 'language' utilized in linguistics. This is not to deny that other animals possess communication systems – of course, all social, reproducing organisms communicate with their kind. What is being denied is that any non-human species possesses naturally a communication system which is qualitatively like human language; and it seems that no other species can be brought to learn language. 'Talking' birds, for instance, cannot be said to know language, nor truly to use it. They mimic a limited set of phonetic signals; they cannot manufacture new utterances; and they betray their lack of understanding by producing their sham-sentences on inappropriate occasions. (Parrots notoriously lack tact.) Perhaps greater success might be predicted with species biologically closer to man. Chimpanzees, who are very intelligent, rapid and eager learners of tricks, have been perennial subjects in language-teaching attempts. Several experiments in which baby chimps have been lovingly fostered in human families have proved virtually complete linguistic failures. Sometimes the animals have been taught to react differentially to a small stock of commands (cf. dogs); one subject, Viki, was given intensive linguistic instruction and succeeded in learning to produce three words (*mama, papa, cup*) very indistinctly and in rigorously controlled standard settings (the inability to verbalize outside certain fixed contexts is revealing). But the vocal apparatus of apes is not well adapted to producing speech sounds, and perhaps this limitation was the source of the difficulty. On this assumption, the failure occurred for very trivial reasons. At the University of Nevada a chimpanzee called Washoe has been taught to communicate on a range of topics using American Sign Language ('deaf-and-dumb language'); however, it appears that she has no syntax – symbols, though used correctly, are put together in random order. It would be premature to allow Washoe's achievement to modify our overall assessment that chimpanzees cannot learn language as human babies do.

All animals communicate within their species and often with members of other species. Domestic cats address each other with obvious comprehension and make clearly meaningfully intended gestures and vocal signs to human beings; the same observation

3

applies to dogs. Most animals direct recognizable signs of, say, sexual receptiveness or territorial threat towards their fellows in appropriate situations and display behaviour indicative of warning or submissiveness to members of other species as the occasion demands. Depending on biological make-up and on the characteristics of the environment, the kinds of signs employed and the kinds of messages conveyed are quite diverse. Within one very broad and useful sense of the notion 'communication' (including language) there is substantial variety in the kinds, and degrees of complexity, of communication systems found in the natural world. For present purposes I shall give **communication** the following general definition: communication is the manifestation of an abstract message through the medium of a physical signal; particular messages being tied to a specific signal according to conventions shared by the parties to any communicative event. These conventions, or 'rules', allow a sender to encode a meaning in a proper signal and, provided the sender has obeyed the rules, permit a receiver to retrieve the intended meaning from the signal. Notice that I have said 'receiver' rather than 'hearer', for communication is not limited to vocal-auditory behaviour. In theory any medium by which energy can be transmitted can serve as a communication channel. Vocal (or other noise) is an especially efficient mode for transmitting signalling energy, since sound waves can travel round corners and over serviceably long distances and since the location of their source can be triangulated by an organism which has two ears (binaural, stereophonic, reception). In addition, use of the speech tract leaves the hands or feet free for simultaneous activity such as fighting or running. But vocal communication can be supplemented by, or replaced by, the use of other signalling modes dependent on any of the other sense-perception systems: visual, in all that makes up gesture – physical positioning, attitude of body, movement of peripheral limbs, facial expression, display of plumage, and, in humans, indirect manifestations such as style of dress; tactile, as in the many body-contact ways of indicating meaning, from the stylized duellist's slap to sexual caress; olfactory, as in the skunk's offensive signal to back off or in the human's use of artificial perfumes to announce 'come on'. (Notice, again, the *indirectness* of the human adaptation in this case; it relates to our tool-making capacity, the second important ability which distinguishes us from lower animals.) Combinations of media are frequent: the cat hisses and at the same time makes her fur stand on end to look larger and fiercer; the dog both whines and scratches at the door in a complex signal that he wants to go out; alarmed birds squawk and flap their wings; fish may erect their fins or change colour and simultaneously move so as to set up vibrations in the water.

Communication systems may, evidently, differ in respect of their media; in respect of the messages expressed or expressible; and in respect of the conventions for tying meanings to signals. And such differences are, obviously, very considerable as we move from system to system. At the level of the communicative medium, man's language is distinguished by the great intricacy and exactness of control of the vocal system. The respiratory system, the whole of the upper vocal tract and the musculature associated with the speech mechanism, all seem to be specially adapted to the complicated task of producing a rapid, virtually unbroken and constantly varying – but not random – succession of sound-waves. These sound-waves are completely distinctive: we can recognize a noise as unmistakably human linguistic noise, even if we hear a sample of some language we do not understand and have never heard before. The reason for this distinctiveness is the individuality of the human vocal apparatus. For example, the human larynx (voice-box) is of a structure which precisely determines the sounds which it can emit; and if we move from humans to the great apes, we find the same situation: their laryngeal structure is different, it has its own distinctive set of noises associated with it. The gibbon, for instance, has two sets of controllable vocal bands and hence emits a double, chord-like, call. The chimpanzee also has two sets of vocal cords, but he can vocalize with each pair independently, and can also 'speak' on an indrawn breath, an action which causes extreme discomfort in human beings. In man the secondary or 'false' vocal cords are not easily regulated and perform only a subsidiary phonetic function – perhaps in whispering; normally they are inactive. Thus in every case variations of physiological structure play a direct and deterministic role in the quality of the medium employed communicatively by the animal. Of course, the same principle holds for the grosser physical differences among species and the resultant signalling devices they have at their disposal.

The examples in the preceding paragraph concern a relatively crude, external, aspect of the speech-system: it is obvious that the noises which emerge from the human vocal apparatus depend on the physical structure of that apparatus! Just as obvious, however, should be the fact that this physical manifestation is only the tip of the iceberg. Human speech sounds the way it does because the vocal mechanism is structured as it is; and because the neurological system controlling the musculature is of a unique kind; and human *language* – not just its sounds – has its unique quality because of the specific character of the central nervous system. When we consider the meanings and the syntactic arrangements which distinguish human language, we are likely to come to the conclusion that these have the characteristics they do because they relate to a special kind of biological organism whose central nervous system is of a language-specialized kind. The meanings coded in natural language, the categories into which meanings are organized, reflect the way the human being's conceptual faculties dispose him to 'see' the world; the syntactic orderings of the surface of language are the ones which his cerebral organization requires; and so on. Language is part of man's essential character; he is an animal specialized to language. Every aspect of the communication system which he naturally employs is determined by the kind of organism he is. This is, after all, just what we would expect: that man, like any other creature, behaves communicatively in the way that his nature directs.

The variety of communication systems, and their intimate dependence on the species which utilize them, may be brought out by studying a different mode of communication in a different form of animal. This way we may learn something about the *general* features of communication too. Let us look at a form of communication which makes use of a medium quite different from vocal noise – the gesture system or 'dancing' of honeybees. Bee-dancing is one of the most sophisticated of non-human 'languages', and happens to be one of the best documented also. The Austrian, Karl von Frisch, has devoted a lifetime's study to the communal activities of bees. The most famous aspect of his research concerns the devices which bees use to signal to their fellows the whereabouts of sources of food. He found that if a single bee discovered a supply of nectar, this source would shortly afterwards be visited by numbers of other bees from the same hive; a sequence of events which suggested that there was some means of communication among the society of the hive. Observation of the behaviour within the hive of bees which had just returned from a food-source showed that they were able to convey the richness, distance and direction of the source of nectar by stylized movements which Frisch called 'dancing'. (Additionally, the odour of nectar from a specific kind of flower ingested by the bee and adhering to its body gives some guidance.) The vigour of the 'dance' correlates with the richness of the source: as the source dries up the dance becomes less and less enthusiastic. The distance of the flowers from the hive is indicated by the geometry of the dance and by the frequency of turns in the dance. Bees perform two distinct kinds of dance, a 'circling dance' which is used when the food is within a short distance of the hive (100 metres), and a 'wagging dance' or 'figure-of-eight' dance for greater distances. The wagging dance consists of movement forward in a straight line followed by a sharp 360° turn to the starting-point, repetition of the forward movement, and so on. The rate of turning, i.e. the rate at which the bee performs the complete figure, is proportionate to the distance of the food from the hive – the further away the food, the more slowly the bee does its dance. This measure gives a rough indication of the distance that needs to be travelled to reach the discovered food. Direction is indicated rather precisely. The bees dance on the vertical surface of the honeycomb, and the vertical dimension is taken to represent the direction of the sun (on a horizontal plane) relative to the hive. If the sun is directly above the source of nectar or pollen, the bee will indicate this by performing the straight part of the wagging dance along a vertical line with its head pointing up; if the sun is at 180° from the source, the straight part of the dance will again be aligned with the vertical, but this time with the head down. Other necessary angles of flight relative to the sun are translated into angles from the vertical. Of course, the orientation changes constantly through the day as the sun moves through the sky: it has no absolute value.

Linguists discussing the general characteristics of animal communication often refer to the bee example, not simply on account of the fascinating way the medium of gesture is employed, but because bee-dancing *as a formal system* possesses certain advanced properties shared with language but with few other styles of animal discourse. Considering these properties will lead us to think about the nature of language in a more abstract way than we have done up to this point. The two interesting characteristics I want to single out are what are called **displacement** and **productivity** (more accurately, 'one kind of productivity').

Displacement is a feature of some communication systems which enables their users to symbolize objects, events and concepts which are not present (in time and space) at the moment of communication. Thus, I can refer to King Alfred, or the State of California, even though the first has been dead for over a thousand years and the second is situated six thousand miles from my home. The honey-bee, in a more modest way, exhibits displacement: he can refer to a source of food which is remote in time and space when he reports on it. This ability is fairly remarkable among animals. Most animals respond communicatively as soon as they are stimulated by some occurrence of communal interest: a warning cry instantly announces danger, a food cry beckons as soon as discovery is made. We say that such animals are under 'immediate stimulus control'. The survival value of breaking the chains of immediate stimulus control is obvious: the power of communicative displacement allows an animal to go away quietly and report on a food source to his family or herd without announcing its whereabouts to competitors; similarly, detecting a threat to the herd, a lone animal who commands displacement can steal back to his social group and warn them, minimizing danger to himself and to the group by not

7

immediately announcing his presence. For man, displacement – again, an 'indirectness' of engagement with the environment, like tool-using and signalling by dress – brings immense conceptual power, as well as environmental control. Very little of our discourse takes place *in situ*, i.e. under the control of particular stimuli, in the presence of the referents of discourse. Certainly, the speech of very young infants tends to concern the 'here and now': to a large extent it consists of one-word utterances about single objects and processes which are physically present or going on at the time. But this phase passes very rapidly. By the time syntax is available to the child, he has the power of displacement (which is presumably a cognitive faculty separate from language yet expressed primarily in language). He modifies the names of objects, showing that he can 'locate' them spatially and temporally (*car garage*, *allgone car*, etc.). When he achieves a tense system associated with verbs, he shows that he can clearly distinguish between past, present and future time. Displacement is, of course, a prerequisite for thought. Language very early adapts itself to this faculty, and in so doing presumably accelerates the child's intellectual development.

For the adult, displacement is the enabling factor in his power to handle generalizations, abstractions. Since our words (*tree*, *house*, etc.) need not be used only in the immediate physical presence of particular houses and trees, and indeed in most cases *are* not used in such precise contexts, word-meaning, even in 'thing-words' (like *tree*), is a general latency for referential application. The meaning of *tree* is presumably some sort of general concept: and a generalization of this kind, a collecting term for things, is the essential step towards abstract discourse. If we can talk about things which are physically distant, we acquire the facility to manipulate concepts to which no 'things' answer: *truth*, *infinity*, *multiplication*. The real intellectual benefit of displacement to human beings is that it allows them to discourse (and hence, presumably, think) in abstract terms.

Before we consider 'productivity', another feature of language, related to displacement, is worth mentioning: this is what Joseph H. Greenberg calls **multimodality**. An animal which simply responds to a situation by instantly emitting a signal cannot be said to be making any particular *kind* of an utterance in relation to it. If an animal shrieks a danger cry on encountering a predator, what sort of thing is he saying? Is he merely exclaiming? or making a descriptive statement? or directing an imperative towards his allegiance group (*keep away!*)? Surely these alternatives have no relevance to animal communication: animals make no linguistic distinctions between commands, questions, statements, emphatic assertions, etc.: they simply respond vocally (or in other appropriate ways) to events.

But in human language such distinctions are important: imperative, indicative, interrogative, negative and the rest are contrasting 'moods' of utterance. Human beings express attitudes, degrees of commitment, curiosity, towards the subjects of their discourse. Displacement is a prerequisite for modality: you cannot take up a stance (chosen from a set of alternatives) towards a phenomenon unless you are free from its control. The freedom is an elementary one, but important: the freedom to choose between 'This is a dog', 'This *is* a dog', 'Is this a dog?' 'Beware of the dog!', etc. (Note that although modality presupposes displacement, the reverse is not the case: it would be nonsense to speculate on whether a bee-dance is a command or a statement or a request, for instance.)

We come now to 'productivity' (or, as it is sometimes called, 'creativity'). A productive communicative device is one which is capable of signalling an unlimited number of messages. Bee-dancing has productivity, in a sense. Bees can point the direction of a food-source, whatever the direction might be: the axis of the figure-of-eight dance may intersect the vertical (which, remember, symbolizes the position of the sun relative to the hive) at any angle. Similarly, the rate of execution of the dance answers proportionately to the distance of the source from the hive. Both of these indicators, direction and distance, move on continuous scales with infinite gradations, that is to say, there is an indefinite number of communicable messages. This might be called the 'speedometer' principle of linguistic structure: a continuous gradation in messages is correlated with a continuous gradation of signals. The device makes possible productivity *of a sort* – an indefinite number of meaning-differentiations, but within fixed limits and, one would suppose, all concerning one 'topic'. Bees, of course, can 'talk' only about nectar. Not unnaturally, the 'speedometer' relationship between messages and signals is not central to the creativity of human language. It is found, certainly: especially where emotional and perceptual states are communicated by sounds of varying intensity. The sharper the pain, the greater the rage, the louder and higher is likely to be the expressive cry. But this device of continuous variability of voice intensity is, as with the bees, semantically quite trivial. We must look elsewhere for the source of man's ability to produce and understand totally new sentences, to discourse on new topics: an ability he exercises all the time.

The 'speedometer' principle of symbolization is in any case inadequate to cope with the kind of conceptual universe inhabited by man. This is an ordered universe, as we shall see in chapters 3 and 4; but the ordering is not merely along continua – not merely degrees of emotional intensity, variations in distance or weight, progressions along continuous dimensions of that sort. Our world is seen as a structured collection of *discrete* phenomena: animals, people, trees, buildings, nations, rivers, flowers, apples, tools. A world of separate objects or concepts, provided that there are not too many of them, may be indicated by a set of separate signs. Primate communication is of this kind: the gibbon, for example, has at his disposal a finite repertoire of separate calls, each one unambiguously associated with a particular situation – anger, sexual arousal, friendliness, etc. An even simpler communication system of the same type is illustrated by two-state traffic signals: red means 'stop', green means 'go'; this little conceptual universe contains only two meanings, and only two signs. It is a primitive, explicit 'one-to-one' system.

Now all communication depends on the physical transference of energy for symbolization. This being so, communicative possibilities are restricted by the physical limitations of the mediating device. 'One-to-one' systems are in fact extremely uneconomical, since the number of messages cannot exceed the number of signs the medium is capable of indicating distinctly. A more efficient way of utilizing the capacity of a signalling device entails abandoning the one-to-one principle. Traffic lights in Britain, for instance, have only three distinct coloured lights (red, green, amber) but are programmed to emit four discrete signals. The extra capacity is gained by using the lights in combination: red means 'stop', green 'go'; amber means 'about to change to red'; red-and-amber-together means 'about to change to green'. (Still more capacity is available with further combinations, but to use it would introduce logical contradictions at the level of 'meaning'!) British traffic lights take a cautious step into a mode of communicative organization which, as far as I know, is not found in the sub-human animal world. The level of meaning and the level of signals are treated as absolutely separate: signals are not tied to particular concepts, and therefore may be combined to cover an inventory of discrete signs. This facility, which seems to be unique to language, is known as **duality of patterning** or **double articulation**. We can see how this works in language by looking briefly at the phonetic level. Although the human vocal apparatus is extraordinarily flexible and can be controlled fairly precisely, the number of sounds which can be enunciated separately so as to be perceived by a hearer as unequivocally distinctive units is strictly limited. English uses thirty to forty (depending on one's criteria for counting them), and the maximum reported for any language is about seventy. Without duality of patterning, human language could communicate only seventy separate concepts, assuming that seventy is the maximum for perceptibly discrete sound units. Suppose [æ] (the vowel in *act*) represented the concept 'house', [k] symbolized 'tree' and [t] symbolized 'man'; the symbolic potentialities of these three sounds would now be used up, and new concepts would demand quite new sounds. But under the duality principle, none of these sounds is uniquely monopolized by any one concept – indeed, sounds are quite meaningless in themselves – and so they can be put together in combinations, thus:

[æt]	'at'
[tæ]	'expression of thanks in some dialects'
[kæt]	'cat'
[ækt]	'act'
[tæk]	'tack'

etc. Not every combination of sounds is used to symbolize an English word. Some sequences are inadmissible on purely phonological grounds: [ktæ] for instance is not a well-formed sound-cluster in English (though it might be in some other language – it is not 'unpronounceable'); also there are 'accidental' lexical gaps: [kæ] is not an English word, although it is a permissible phonetic sequence. If all combinations of sounds in a language were used, the lexical resources would be enormous. Suppose a language possessed only ten sounds, could put them together in any order and tolerated sequences a maximum of four sounds long; a vocabulary of 10,000 words would be possible under this simple arrangement, given duality of patterning. English has in fact thirty to forty sounds, and there is no theoretical limit on the length of sequences.

'Duality of patterning' (Hockett's phrase) or 'double articulation' (Martinet's) receives its name in recognition of the separateness of structure of the semantic and phonetic levels. In a 'one-to-one' system, particular meanings and particular symbols are tied together absolutely; in a system which has duality, signs are freed from particular semantic functions. Sounds are semantically quite arbitrary. Together, the sounds of a language constitute an independent phonetic system, with its own rules for structure which are not influenced by meaning considerations (cf. the purely *phonetic* unacceptability – in English – of [ktæ], above). Similarly, the concepts expressible in a language make up an independent semantic system. We may thus speak of two separate **levels** of linguistic structure, semantic and phonetic; and we must propose a third level, syntax, a set of conventions for associating meanings and sounds in the formation of particular sentences. This notion of 'level' is of crucial importance in descriptive linguistics; and the three levels I have listed are the ones which are generally mentioned in traditional grammatical theory. I will discuss them further in the next chapter.

Duality explains how a very large number of meanings can be expressed by means of a very limited set of signals – in effect, it shows how a finite device or organism (e.g. a human being) with immense communicative needs can transcend the inevitable physical limitations of its own signal-making apparatus. But duality does *not* account for productivity in human language, productivity of a kind quite superior to that observed in bee communication, and perhaps meriting a different name: let us call it **creativity**. Modern linguists have repeatedly stressed the fact that mature human speakers can without conscious effort produce and understand an unlimited number of sentences which are quite 'new' to them. We know enough about the way children acquire language (see chapter 9) to be certain that they do *not* learn by rote an inventory of completely formed sentences, given to them whole by the community, building up a memorized stock from which individual utterances are selected one by one as occasion demands. Apart from being a psychologically implausible model of language learning (it would imply an inordinately inefficient use of brain 'storage space', for instance), this account is suspect in the light of certain empirical observations of children's language anyway. Very young children come out with sentences that they could not have picked up from adults (*allgone milk*, *I goed up*, etc.); the most likely explanation for these is that the infant *constructs* them on the basis of a set of provisional, un-adult, grammatical conventions which he has built for himself – if this explanation is accepted, a kind of creativity is evidenced from a very early age. At the same time, children seem to comprehend things which are said to them which they have most probably not encountered before. This capability is perfectly established by the time of linguistic maturity. There is a sharp division between strictly routine sayings (*Good morning, Thank goodness, You're welcome, I love you,* etc.) and the rest of our communication: the routine phrases are learnt as whole pieces of language, produced usually thoughtlessly, and are often semantically empty. They form a very small part of our linguistic behaviour: the bulk of our verbal performance is creative in a very important sense. We construct each next utterance as a new piece of language, tailor-making it to match the given situation and topic. It is extremely unlikely that you have ever previously encountered any of the sentences which you have read and understood so far in this book. Similarly, the next sentence you yourself produce is likely to be unique.

Of course, you have met sentences *like* the ones in this book. Naturally, the range of sentence *types* is limited – the grammar is ordered, finite; patterns recur. Some linguists claim that there is an infinite number of sentences in a natural language, but it is probably well to be more cautious and say that there are no bounds to the number of **utterances**, regarding utterances as 'tokens' of the sentence 'types'. If we take a given sentence-structure, there can be innumerable distinct realizations of that type. One interesting fact is that some constructions can be extended indefinitely by adding clause after clause:

1. John said that Mary thought that Tom had claimed that Richard believed . . .
2. This is the dog that chased the cat that killed the rat that . . .
3. She has eaten two hamburgers, a dish of salad, some pickles, several pieces of bread . . .

The syntactic facility guarantees that there is *no longest sentence* in a natural language, and thus an unlimited number of utterances, since for every utterance there is a possibility of a longer one. This is a largely theoretical observation, of course – in actual language use, the length of utterances is strictly limited by biological and psychological factors. However, it is a notable fact about the 'algebra' of language that it does – unlike other communicative systems – have this infinite potentiality.

More important than the variety and multiplicity of utterances, though, is the fact that we can talk about an infinite number of *topics*: a privilege not, apparently, shared by other animals. As our world of objects and ideas changes and expands, our linguistic representation of it is modified accordingly. This is true of society as a whole, as well as of the individual as he matures into his culture. The vocabulary is in a continuous state of change, all the time adapting itself to modifications in our material and conceptual universe. Words come and go, mainly come: *transistor*, *sputnik*, *television*, *morpheme*, *escalate*, etc., are added as the physical or intellectual need arises. Another process is modification of the values of existing words: the existing *record* and *disc* accommodated new meanings when the gramophone was invented, without destroying the old meanings; the twentieth-century entertainment world has also provided *star* with a new meaning which it carries without disturbing the old astronomical and astrological senses. In such ways a language extends its capability to say new things about new topics; and there is no reason inherent in the structure of language itself why this extensibility should be restricted: language appears to be genuinely and powerfully – limitlessly – creative.

Let us take stock of the argument so far. A human infant acquires, quickly and easily, a most sophisticated system of communication.

13

He seems to be innately equipped or predisposed to acquire linguistic knowledge, in just the same way that he is predisposed to walk upright, to perceive colours, to breathe in through his nose. There is nothing surprising in the notion of innate disposition towards certain forms of behaviour: it is for this kind of reason that dogs bark, let their tongues loll out to cool themselves, and so on. What is remarkable is the structural complexity, the flexibility and power, of the linguistic knowledge so acquired, and the fact that the formal system we call language is unique to man. A human being, controlling this ability, can express his thoughts on an unlimited variety of topics: signals are available for efficient communication about an extremely full and complex conceptual universe. Discourse may concern physical objects, imaginary objects (unicorns, Hamlet), impossible objects (the square root of minus one), abstractions. Discourse may exist in several kinds or moods: we can make statements, ask questions, issue commands, etc.

Further characteristics of this unique and powerful symbolic system will emerge in the course of the present book, the major preoccupation of which is to display the structure of language as an abstract, formal, systematic and highly regular communicative device. But it would be a mistake to restrict our perspective on language to the extent of seeing it merely as a formal, quasi-algebraic construct. In discussing the formal aspects of language I have found it useful to use words like 'device', 'system', 'efficient', 'structured', 'abstract', 'construct', etc. – words which perhaps suggest an excessive mechanization, even dehumanization. Because language is so complicated and, as I have suggested, profoundly regular, it is necessary to discuss its characteristics in an organized, explicit and, hopefully, systematized way. However, language is anything but mechanical or inhuman in its implications or in its use. At the same time as modern linguistics has striven to develop ways of representing language carefully, scientifically and formally, it has come to recognize more and more clearly that the object of representation is an object of profound psychological and cultural value. Descriptive linguistics describes, however methodically and coldly, linguistic *knowledge*: a psychological property, an aspect of the make-up of mature individuals. And this knowledge is shared culturally: what the individual knows linguistically is knowledge which is crucial to his social integration and to his working within, and in relation to, society. Perhaps we should remember that 'communication' is etymologically related to 'community'.

We may ask: what does a child gain by acquiring language? The starkest answer (but an essential one) would be something like 'a facility for associating sounds and meanings in an infinite number of sentences'. Going beyond this minimal formulation, we would want to add that this facility brings tremendous conceptual and cultural benefits. Whether or not language precedes thought is a futile chicken-and-egg argument, but it is certain that language is a primary instrument in the child's intellectual coming-to-terms with the world around him. As many writers have observed (from the author of *Genesis* onwards), the naming capacity of language allows us to impose order on a world which might otherwise appear anarchic, merely continuous and contingent. We learn the names which our society assigns to objects and simultaneously we learn the relationships that are felt to exist between them (Daddy and Uncle Charles are different by virtue of having separate names; similar through being classified under the same name, 'man'; knife, fork and spoon are associated in the vocabulary and together designate a self-contained sub-universe of things). As we acquire syntax, the basic principles of action and interrelation become stabilized: every time we employ a well-formed sentence we tacitly acknowledge that animate creatures perform actions, that changes of state come over things, that things may be in some permanent state, that events occur at particular times and places, that some situations are 'timeless', and so on. The child comes to recognize the conceptual, causal and spatio-temporal ordering which human beings find in their world, and it is virtually certain that the structure of language, in which this information is coded, is instrumental in enabling him to 'internalize' this structure. Equally, the mature speaker preserves his feeling for cognitive organization – his 'world-view' – as he maintains his competence in language. And since language is a shared ability, not merely a privately known code, we may learn by comparing world-views: by arguing with other people, by listening and reading. If logic is 'natural', it is transmitted and exploited through language. The world of ideas and of logical relationships is not independent of language: the extent of the intellectual deprivation of a person without language is unimaginable.

Such a person would be severely deprived culturally, also, for language is not simply a utilitarian means of passing information to another party (as our minimal definition of 'associating sounds and meanings' might suggest): it is a link between the members of a society. As the great linguist Leonard Bloomfield insisted, language has *instrumental* value, it is the main way, for human societies, of securing co-operation so as to get things done. Man is not a very tall animal, nor a very fast moving one, nor very strong; cannot fly; and cannot swim very well. He compensates for these deficiencies to a large extent by making and using tools (in a broad sense to include aeroplanes and fork-lift trucks, etc.) and also by employing language to give instructions (manifesting displacement) to his fellows in the interests of the efficient division of labour. Children rapidly discover the usefulness of this property of language (generally becoming more demanding as they become less helpless!); also they discover that language is an essential and productive short-cut in the transmission of experience. Their ceaseless requests for information, which parents may find tedious, are quite forgivable when we recall that language is the chief medium for preserving the continuity of tradition; written records of all kinds are the best means of ensuring that the experience of the past is not lost to us. And pre-literate societies employ oral poetic traditions for the preservation of experience.

Knowing about the values and preoccupations of a society is a qualification for belonging to it. Language serves to reinforce cultural identity, and in less intellectual, conscious, manners than that implied by 'knowing'. It is a means to conformity, a prime way of asserting 'I am like you; I can behave like you'. When a child learns to talk, he does not only acquire an information-transmitting, service-securing, communicative code; he acquires a code which approximates to the one which is employed around him. In the first place, he learns English or French or Swahili, not simply some neutral general form 'language'. Everyone knows that national languages are appealed to as expressions of large-scale communal identity. Lower down the scale, dialects and accents may serve the same function; assimilated automatically as a simple consequence of living in a certain geographical area or a certain socio-economic milieu, they may take on the additional role of proclaiming one's membership of the group. (They announce membership whether or not one actually wishes to proclaim it, of course.) Without conscious effort, the child growing into a community gradually accommodates his style of language to the norms of his immediate social group, and although in scientific terms these norms are completely value-free – mere patterns of sound implicitly agreed upon by a group – they inevitably acquire significance within the value-scheme of a cultural context. This is 'significance' of a different kind from 'meaning', the information content of language, but no less potent.

Finally, style in language is not merely group-style, not simply a matter of general identifying features added on to the linguistic form of sentences – a kind of dialect superstructure. That is there, of course, all the time: a constantly present layer of dialectal colouring. This is, as it were, a 'background' feature, a permanent signal of the group-membership of the language-user. Against that background, or, to alter the metaphor, within that framework, there are stylistic variations which correlate with the *use* to which a particular utterance is being put, its rhetorical function. We adjust the style of our discourse most delicately in response to the kinds of communicative situations we find ourselves in, to the speaker-role we assume on a particular occasion; in accordance with our status-relationship to other participants in a communicative event, and with our intentions and feelings towards them. Such stylistic adjustments are recognizably regular, conventional, and learnable varieties of spoken (or written) style, and are often called **registers**. The register selected by a mature, fluent and flexible speaker depends on a great variety of extra-linguistic factors, some of which will be discussed in chapter 10. If such a speaker is experienced and sensitive, he will possess, and employ appropriately, a large stock of registers, among which he will switch readily as occasion demands. Some hypothetical register distinctions might be: between the style and tone appropriate to command and that suitable for persuasion; the language used to address an interlocutor socially distant from oneself (either above or below), which will be relatively formal contrasted with the intimate and colloquial mode chosen for social peers and close acquaintances; between the register of prestige advertising and that of interpersonal persuasion; between learned and familiar topics of discourse. In general, the greater range of registers a speaker has at his disposal, the more effective will be his social dealings with the world at large: the height of skill in register flexibility is taken to be a sign of a highly cultured and socially relaxed person. Flexibility in register choice is in fact indispensable even within the most homogeneous social group. So the child must learn, not only the formal system which will allow him to pair sounds and meanings in an infinite number of sentences – a gift of nature realized concretely as he grows from an infant to a youthful member of society; but also a great range of sociolinguistic skills for fitting speech to situation. He must be able not merely to communicate, but to communicate appropriately. These skills can be gained only by sensitive and long engagement with other human beings who participate in the same social structure (more exactly, structure*s*, or 'network'). Thus language, as most other forms of behaviour, is finally the product of an intricate co-operation of nature and nurture.

Further reading

(Suggestions are offered at the end of each chapter. Full bibliographical details of the books and articles mentioned may be found on pp. 259–66 below.) Two classic books on language are Bloomfield, *Language* and Sapir, *Language*. Brown, *Words and Things*, is a readable and informative introduction to the characteristics of human and animal communication systems; see also Hockett, 'Origin of speech'. On bee communication, see Frisch, *Bees*; on ape and monkey communication, the articles by Bastian and by Marler in DeVore, *Primate Behavior*. See also Greenberg, *Anthropological Linguistics*. The first stages of the experiment with Washoe are reported in R. A. Gardner and B. T. Gardner, 'Teaching sign language to a chimpanzee'; cautious preliminary comments are offered by Brown, 'The first sentences of child and chimpanzee' and by several of the contributors to Morton's *Biological and Social Factors in Psycholinguistics* (see his index under 'Washoe').

Paperback collections covering many of the topics mentioned in this chapter are Lenneberg, *New Directions*, Lyons, *New Horizons*, Adams, *Language in Thinking*, Oldfield and Marshall, *Language*, De Cecco, *Psychology of Language*, Giglioli, *Language and Social Context*.

two

Linguistics

Linguistics is the scientific study of language. It is a recognized academic subject – a discipline which can be studied at universities, an area still with immense research potential, an enthusiasm of many thousands of devotees throughout the world, a scholarly 'industry' which produces scores of books and dissertations and hundreds of learned papers every year; its preoccupations are expressed in many specialized journals and at regular conferences. The justification for all this activity should be obvious from my first chapter: language is so valuable to the individual, so critical to the efficient functioning of human societies, and in itself so impressively intricate and profound in structure, that it is bound to attract a great amount of intellectual attention. And since this attention must produce studies which have *practical* importance (e.g. in speech therapy, education, techniques of translation and many more 'applied' concerns), linguistics is bound to be an academically and economically favoured pursuit. As an academic and technical subject, linguistics has enjoyed a 'boom' since the Second World War; as we shall see in a moment, its history is in fact much more ancient than that.

The complexity of language and the richness of its implications for the life of the individual and of the community ensure that any discipline devoted to its study must be extremely diverse and accommodating. Linguistics is in fact a considerable *cluster* of disciplines, not just one single scholarly technique. The syllabus of any university department of linguistics makes this fact clear: students and teachers are, characteristically, engaged in a multiplicity of studies, some of which bear little direct relationship to each other (e.g. phonetics and psycholinguistics). This chapter is designed to indicate

19

something of the range of activities subsumed under the general label 'linguistics'; perhaps the diversity should be asserted at the outset, by employing some such title as 'the linguistic sciences'. A 'linguist' may be any one of a considerable number of characters – some share very little except the commonalty of their subject-matter under the most general perspective: their analytic techniques and jargon may differ almost totally.

Before surveying the range of the linguistic sciences, I must indicate something of their history. The basic conceptual framework of modern linguistics was supplied by the philosophers and grammarians of ancient Greece and Rome and passed down to modern Europe and America by way of the rhetoricians and language scholars who have dominated our western educational structure for over two millennia. In this thumbnail history I must take that heritage for granted: it is well documented elsewhere and its insights pervade this book. The *methodological* ancestry of linguistics is just as ancient, and geographically more distant. It goes back at the very least to the grammarians who studied the Indian language Sanskrit centuries before Christ. These linguists, devoted to the preservation of Vedic religious texts of the latter part of the second millennium B.C., have much to say on theoretical as well as descriptive questions, and in the course of their work on Sanskrit provide very full and intelligent models for grammatical description. The best known and most influential of these writers, as well as the earliest known to us, was Pāṇini, whose remarkable grammar may be as old as 600 B.C. It was the 'rediscovery' of Sanskrit at the end of the eighteenth century which gave impetus to comparative-historical linguistics, the absorbing activity of the nineteenth century, and thus led to the establishment of descriptive language studies on a vast scale. On 2 February 1786 Sir William Jones, an orientalist and legal official in Calcutta, ventured in an address to the Royal Asiatic Society that Sanskrit bears to Latin and Greek

> a stronger affinity, both in the roots of verbs and in the forms of grammar, than could possibly have been produced by accident; so strong, indeed, that no philologer could examine them all three without believing them to have sprung from some common source, which, perhaps, no longer exists; there is a similar reason, though not quite so forcible, for supposing that both the Gothick and the Celtick, though blended with a very different idiom, had the same origin with the Sanskrit.

The notion that similarities between recorded languages could be a result of descent from a common and unrecorded original was, it seems, a new one. It was now possible to examine critically earlier explanations of linguistic similarity: that, for example, Latin was descended from Greek, a belief founded not on linguistic evidence, but on the assumption that in this, as in so many ways, the Romans learnt from the Greeks. Jones had, perhaps not with full consciousness of all the theoretical and methodological implications of his 'discovery', provided what was to be the main premise of nineteenth-century comparative linguistics, that the relationships between languages are susceptible of rational explanation in structural terms, and do not have to be attributed to chance or to accidents of historical contact. Much of the nineteenth century was taken up with the working-out of relationships between languages with observed similarities. There was intensive study of past and of contemporaneous manifestations of familiar European languages and of their more exotic, though true, kindred. During the nineteenth century such comparative and historical linguists as Rasmus Rask (1781–1832), Jacob Grimm (1785–1863), Franz Bopp (1791–1867) and August Schleicher (1821–68) accumulated a vast amount of information about the history, structure and interrelationships of members of the Indo-European 'family' of languages, a detailed demonstration of the rightness of William Jones's insight. They constructed a broad corporate grammar which encompassed the past and present structural facts of languages as apparently diverse as the Slavonic tongues, the Romance, Germanic (including Scandinavian), many Indian languages, Celtic, Persian. Nor was this a simple amassing of factual detail; in the process of building up their picture of the 'family tree', the Indo-European comparative philologists came to learn a great deal of the *principles* of linguistic change and correspondence. Regularities of phonetic relationship were observed and formal explanations for sound-shift were proposed. A famous example is 'Grimm's Law', which is an attempt to explain certain regular differences in consonant sounds between the Romance languages (Latin, French, etc.) and the Germanic (English, German, etc.). Where Romance has a voiced plosive – an explosive stop consonant uttered with the vocal cords in vibration, e.g. [d] – Germanic has the voiceless counterpart, e.g. [t]. So Latin has d*ecem*, English t*en*. A related correspondence is that, when Romance has a voiceless plosive – French t*rois*, in which the first consonant is a stop without vocal cord vibration – Germanic has (or had) a voiceless fricative: the English th*ree* preserves this sound, a voiceless 'hissing' sound. In order to explain these correspondences, 'Grimm's Law' proposed that systematic modifications of sound had occurred in the development of the languages concerned, leading to different distributions of consonants in the several cases. To give another example of the effects of 'Grimm's Law', French p*ied* begins with a

21

voiceless stop and ends with a voiced stop, whereas English *foot*, predictably according to the 'law', begins with a voiceless fricative and ends with a voiceless stop. 'Grimm's Law', postulating systematic sound-change involving a substantial part of the phonology of several languages, provides a good instance of the kind of broad structural concern which characterized the best of nineteenth-century linguistics. This particular sound-change was a continuing preoccupation for linguists. There are apparent exceptions to the rule, for instance the middle consonants of Latin *centum*, English, *hundred*: by Grimm's Law one would expect a voiceless 'th' sound ([θ]) where *hundred* has [d] – recall *trois*/*three*. These irregularities were not explained until 1875, when Karl Verner showed that the rule must be refined to take account of the position of stress ('loudness' of a syllable) in the word. Where, in the older language (here, Latin), stress falls *after* a middle consonant, the corresponding Germanic form is a voiced [d], not a voiceless [θ]. Verner's solution, taking account of stress, testifies to the growing precision with which, as the second half of the nineteenth century progressed, linguists noticed the sound features of languages.

Comparative philology marked the beginning of a *structural* approach to languages, one which took systematic notice of features internal to language, rejecting extraneous historical and cultural explanations of linguistic form and linguistic relationship. It evinced, for the first time in western linguistics, a care for method and for the scrupulous notice of linguistic fact. These attributes were inherited by twentieth-century 'structuralists' in Europe and America. But two qualities necessary to a fully developed science of linguistics were lacking: a general and abstract theory of the way language works and experience of the great variety of kinds of structure found in natural languages, experience which could be gained only by venturing outside the parochial world of Indo-European.

At the beginning of the nineteenth century linguistics had progressed when it began to increase the number of languages thought worthy of consideration: this was progress towards the comparative study of the whole of Indo-European. At the end of the century there was another very considerable step forward, a movement towards a much more inclusive linguistics made possible by the study of non-Indo-European languages. The Indo-Europeanists were intent on the *similarities* between languages; the features found over and over again in the members of the I-E family were confirmation of linguistic homogeneity, and their recurrence in such a large number of languages gave the impression that they were in some way 'universal'. There was little incentive to developing techniques of description, or to exploring models of linguistic form, which might be applicable to other types of linguistic system. Moreover, many of the linguistic characteristics which were institutionalized through the study of the Indo-European languages happened to coincide with those long discovered in Latin and applied blindly to other languages as if they were universals. Both of the main linguistic traditions, that of academic philology and that of Latin school grammar, converged to harden the categories of 'general linguistics'. When, however, familiarity with languages outside the Indo-European group grew, the inadequacy of existing general views of linguistic structure had to be recognized. Encountering impressively different grammatical systems, vocabularies and types of sound necessitated the formulation of a much more flexible theory and the invention of a new analytic methodology.

It was the intensive study of single non-Indo-European languages which broadened the horizons of the discipline. This came, at the beginning of this century, with the study of the indigenous languages of America by anthropologists with an earnest desire to set these Indian languages down in writing before they disappeared. (Additionally, the anthropologists found that they could not gain proper understanding of these exotic societies without learning the languages.) Pioneers in the Amerindian field, and in American linguistics as a whole, were Franz Boas (1858–1942) and Edward Sapir (1884–1939). The fruits of the work of these men may be seen in the introduction to Boas's *Handbook of American Indian Languages* (1911–22), in Sapir's *Language: An Introduction to the Study of Speech* (1921) and in the work of the many linguists trained by Boas and Sapir. The widened perspective on language study achieved by students of the American Indian languages was a product of the nature of the material. The grammarians of Amerindian discovered that the analytic tools and concepts which had been developed so efficiently for the revelation of the structure of Sanskrit and its modern and classical European relatives were inapplicable to the radically different forms encountered in Cree, Menomini and Iroquoian. The impact of this discovery on the techniques of linguistic description was considerable. It now came to be asserted that every language was potentially unique; analytic procedures had to be established which were flexible enough to apply to any language and which avoided the error of imposing the structure of one language upon another: of looking at Cree or Fox with eyes trained to the irrelevant qualities of English or Latin. As we shall see, these demands on analytic technique, this philosophy of diversity of linguistic structure, gave American linguistics a strongly methodological and pragmatic bent as the present century progressed.

Moving back to Europe for a moment, we find that the *theoretical* deficiencies of comparative philology began to be repaired with the thinking of the Swiss, Ferdinand de Saussure, whose views exerted the most powerful influence on structuralist approaches in both linguistics and anthropology. Saussure's *Study of the Primitive Vowel System of the Indo-European Languages* (dated 1879, actually 1878) had established him as a brilliant and learned comparativist. But he is best known for the *Cours de linguistique générale*, compiled by two of his pupils, Charles Bally and Albert Sechehaye, from students' notes of his lectures, and published posthumously in 1916. In the *Cours* Saussure departed from the exact study of linguistic detail to engage in a deliberately general discussion of the principles of linguistics, and in doing so provided some of the basic tenets of the discipline in its modern form. He examined the principles of language and of language study directly and methodically, partly by means of independent argument, partly by a critique of the views of his predecessors. His three headings under 'Subject matter and scope of linguistics' reveal his fundamentalist turn of mind:

(a) to describe and trace the history of all observable languages, which amounts to tracing the history of families of languages and reconstructing as far as possible the mother language of each family;

(b) to determine the forces that are permanently and universally at work in all languages, and to deduce the general laws to which all specific historical phenomena can be reduced; and

(c) to delimit and define itself.

(a) was, ostensibly, the overriding aim of the nineteenth century; (b) was ambitious and progressive in its hint of the possibility of a true general linguistics; (c) states an attitude most characteristic of modern linguistics: the compulsion to define the scope, aims, methods and validity of linguistic description and allied processes. Saussure's was the first of a long line of general theoretical books which set out to determine the very fundamentals of the discipline. His specific contributions to the theory of language are well known and have been summarized by many writers: his distinction between **langue** and **parole** – the essential separation between knowledge of a language and its concrete use (see pp. 37–9 below); his insistence on the idea of **system**, the complex orderliness of linguistic conventions; his discussion of the relation between the **synchronic** and **diachronic** axes in descriptive linguistics (p. 34 below); his conception of the nature of the linguistic sign, a union of 'signification' and 'value', which has analogues in the philosophical distinction between 'reference' and 'sense' and has exerted a profound influence on modern theories of meaning (see pp. 50–1 below); and his separation of the syntagmatic and **paradigmatic** planes of linguistic structure (see pp. 70–1 below).

The working-out of the principles of descriptive linguistics, or of what came to be known as 'structural linguistics', continued in America and Europe in the 1930s and 1940s. The dominant figure in America was Leonard Bloomfield, whose book, *Language* (1933), argued the need for a *science* of linguistics with its own rigorous methodology and properly defined terminology. Strongly influenced by the style of the emerging natural sciences of his time, he proclaimed a **mechanist** approach to language and rejected what he called **mentalism**, an attitude to language which, he believed, in its willingness to accept non-physical explanations of verbal behaviour, courted the danger of a degree of mystification inimical to scientific process. He maintained that linguists should restrict themselves to literally physical and observable explanations of language behaviour; that abstract notions such as 'mind', 'thought' and 'knowledge' must be avoided at all cost. As we shall see, contemporary linguistics, confessedly 'mentalist', has now come round to a reversal of this principle of Bloomfield's – a denigration of physical explanations and an espousal of abstract concepts. Under Bloomfield's influence, linguistics in America developed into a strongly empiricist kind of science, laying great stress on the accuracy of field observation of phonetic substance, on the evolution of mechanical procedures for the analysis of linguistic form on the basis of these observations of the sound-patterns of language. The aims of Bloomfield's linguistics were, for the time, admirable: it was useful that linguists should be reminded that acute, systematic observations in an experimental format must accompany theory, speculation, reconstruction. However, language does not exist all on the observable surface, and it is unfortunate that Bloomfield's followers extended his principles to the degree that they developed an inhibiting distaste for any mode of analysis which might depend on the assumption of unobservable entities. For example, it is a great problem – and fascination – in linguistics that the description of meaning cannot rely on a description of the manifest sounds and words which appear on the outer layer of language: what is presented to our eyes and ears in the form of letters and sounds spatially and temporally arranged is just a very poor guide to the meaning of sentences, and the linguist has the difficult task of explaining how speaker and hearers are able to link sound and meaning, given this disparity. Bloomfield realized this (though it is doubtful that he would have expressed the difficulty in just these terms) and he voiced some very cautious opinions on the problem of meaning (*Language*, pp. 139–40; cf. p. 96 below). He believed that linguistics must await the refinement of other sciences before it could have anything reliable to say about meaning. Bloomfield's attitude was that the description of meaning was out of reach at the time of writing. His followers went much further: where he had admitted the *difficulty*, they alleged the *irrelevance*, even *impertinence*, of allowing semantic considerations into linguistic analysis. Such influential scholars as Bernard Bloch, George L. Trager, Henry Lee Smith devoted their efforts (in the thirties and forties) to developing a mode of linguistic analysis which would be free of appeal to meaning, and this phase of structural linguistics reached its apogee in the early 1950s with Zellig Harris's *Methods in Structural Linguistics* (1951) and C. C. Fries's *The Structure of English* (1952). In the spirit of Bloomfield (and, indirectly, Saussure), these authors advocate a 'distributional' approach to linguistic analysis: the units on which language is built are to be discovered by examining the overt properties of utterances. Utterances are scanned for repeated segments (e.g. the *-s* on *utterances* and *segments*, the *-ed* on *scanned* and *repeated*); if it seems to a native speaker that such segments are significant, they are tentatively regarded as valid structural segmentations. The exact significance is said to be unimportant – the fact alone that *segment* and *utterance* share a common contrast with *segments* and *utterances* is noteworthy, and allegedly no speculation is called for on such questions as the nature of the concepts 'singular' and 'plural'. Distributional analysis calls for observation of the patterning of '-*s*' and 'no -*s*' and plays down the meaning of the pattern; quite clearly, the meaning of this pattern cannot be realized by observation, it has to be hypothesized. When the segments have been determined in this way, they are categorized. It may be predicted that this categorization is mechanical, not conceptual: segments are grouped together because they appear in similar positions in the linear sequence of sentences, not because they might have something 'deeper' in common. A classic example of this approach – a most valuable book and an influential one as far as the education of a whole generation of Americans was concerned – is Fries's *Structure*, mentioned above. Fries popularized the 'slot' technique of distributional study. His technique rests on the construction of almost-complete simple sentences with just one positional slot unfilled:

4. The——was good.

Whatever segments, drawn from the language as a whole, can be placed in this gap to yield an acceptable sentence, belong to the same distributional class: in the case of 4 above, *coffee, book, table, play, meal, programme*, etc. But what is the defining quality of the class? Fries will not say; he will only give the class an identifying tag 'Class I'. Traditional grammar knows that this is the class of **nouns**, but Fries has to avoid that term because traditional grammar failed to provide a definition of 'noun' which was acceptable according to modern structural criteria. Loose semantic definitions – 'a "noun" is the name of a person, place or thing' – must be rejected. Similarly, insights about the syntactic **functions** of words are eschewed (for instance, that a noun is typically a grammatical subject or object); positional characterizations are to be given priority, and functional definitions, if they are entertained at all, must be anchored to solid distributional observations.

We must, and with hindsight can, ask what is being left out, what is being dismissed, here. How do 'semantic' and 'functional' types of definition deserve banishment? Why does Fries (in a gesture absolutely typical of his generation) reject what I have called 'loose semantic definitions'? One reason for rejecting them would be that they were imprecise, and there is no denying that the schoolbook definitions of traditional grammatical categories are uninformative, inconsistent and vague. But Fries does not dismiss them only on the grounds that they are bad definitions of their kind: he dismissed definitions of that kind. What is being erased from the grammar is the traditional toleration of 'semantic' and 'functional' notions, while positional characterizations are substituted. The result is a notable advance in the observation of the superficial structures of sentences, but a neglect of abstract notions – 'noun', 'subject' – which linguistics positively requires. Abstract terms are required for the reason I have already given: all linguistic structure and meaning is not on the surface of sentences.

It must be said that, apart from an increased observational precision and an enhanced notational care in dealing with superficial matters, the gains of early structural linguistics were offset by losses. On the whole, we look back on a mechanical rather than imaginative style of linguistic science; a science which was mechanical, only shallowly theoretical, and uninquisitive – as well as 'mechanist' by principle and proclamation. The dismissal of semantic questions now seems unpardonable; and the neglect of psychological and – to a large extent – socio-cultural aspects of the subject led to a conception of language as a barren code improperly abstracted from the world of human experience. None the less, an overall judgment must pronounce that the achievement of the Bloomfieldian school was immense and invaluable to the development of linguistics as a secure and powerful discipline. The advances in some particular sub-fields were considerable – phonetics, phonemic transcription (especially the provision of alphabets for unlettered communities), some kinds of rapid language teaching, rudimentary mechanical translation, and so on. Phonetic, syntactic and morphological information (the last comprising facts about the internal structure of words) was gathered about a large number of unfamiliar languages, thus widening our knowledge of the types of organization to be found in the world's languages. Above all, there were two gains of a very general nature. First, linguistics was established, by the fifties, as a flourishing scholarly discipline and an academic profession, with departments and professorships in universities, specialist journals and monograph series, research grants, congresses, etc. If these institutions seem trivial, it must be remembered that they are prerequisites for intellectual development and the dissemination of ideas. Second, for all its defects, American descriptive linguistics in the totality of its efforts demonstrated the essential rightness of the structuralist assumptions upon which it was founded: linguistic descriptions which proceeded on the expectation of a systematic organization beneath the apparently fluid and informal surface of utterances worked well. Language was seen to be orderly, even if there were defects in the way the structuralists' grammars expounded this order.

The next significant event in the history of linguistics is so well known as hardly to need mentioning: the publication in 1957 of Noam Chomsky's *Syntactic Structures*, which was an attack on the whole fabric of American structuralism. According to Chomsky, modern linguistics was devoted to an attempt to construct a grammar of a kind which he called a **phrase structure grammar** (PSG). He proceeded to characterize the formal properties of a PSG more carefully than his predecessors had done, in order to specify exactly what it could and what it could not do; this scrutiny occurs as the central part of a comparative survey of several types of possible grammar, some simpler, and one more sophisticated, than PSG. It is important to note that Chomsky's purpose in undertaking this exercise was not merely historical, but formal and theoretical: he wished to determine the mathematical and logical designs of possible grammars, to evaluate their relative power, insightfulness and economy. The nature of Chomsky's enterprise required him to draw further away from the process of grammatical description than was usual – he achieved a longer perspective than most other modern linguists had done, was less bogged down in the mechanics of analysis and therefore freer to consider the general form and nature of linguistic descriptions. Chomsky's work heralded the beginning of a valuably 'metagrammatical', self-examining, phase of linguistics. Very few linguists had thought to ask the questions 'What is the nature of a linguistic description? What can a descriptive grammar achieve? How can competing grammars be evaluated?' These questions, once asked, were of course profoundly disturbing, particularly since they were asked at the high point of a settled and reasonably self-satisfied tradition. But ultimately they were very liberating questions.

To return to Chomsky's description of PSG: this is, he said, a mode of linguistic analysis which divides sentences into their constituent parts and then sorts these parts into classes (respectively, the processes of 'segmentation' and 'classification' illustrated above with reference to the work of Fries). Basically, this is the traditional school grammar activity of *parsing*; the American structuralists of the generation just before Chomsky called it **immediate constituent analysis** (IC). Chomsky acknowledged that these operations of segmentation and classification are an essential part of syntactic analysis. Sentences consist of structures of distinct **constituents**, and the constituents fall under recognizable types. We can show this with a simple example such as 5 below:

5. The young athlete set a new record.

Immediate constituent analysis will show, quite correctly, that the sentence breaks down into several components, of various 'sizes', and of types which recur elsewhere in the language. Thus 'the young athlete' and 'a new record' are phrases of the same type (cf. 'a blue flag', 'that dreadful winter'); 'a' and 'the' are related words, as are 'young' and 'new', and 'athlete' and 'record'; on the other hand, 'set' must be sorted into a different category from any other word in the sentence. Additionally, some partial sequences make up well-formed units, others do not: 'the young athlete', 'young athlete', 'set a new record', 'a new record', 'new record'; but not 'the young' (in this context), 'athlete set', 'set a', etc. We can show that the sentence comprises a hierarchy of structure based on the way these units 'include' each other:

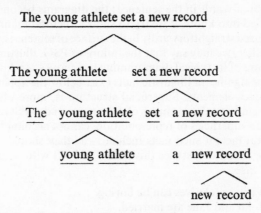

We can also show this information with brackets:

[[The + [young + [athlete]]] + [set + [a + [new + [record]]]]]]

Either of these diagrams, drawn on the basis of analytic techniques usual to PSG, shows the constituent structure of the sentence. A certain amount of important information about the sentence is yielded by this method. But Chomsky points out that constituent structure analysis leaves untouched many aspects of syntactic and semantic structure. On the one hand, it is incapable of dealing with some types of syntactic structure; on the other, it treats only the most superficial layer of syntax, and says nothing about meaning. As an example of a type of sentence which defeats PSG analysis, consider 6 below:

6. He put the book down.

A moment's reflection will show that this cannot be diagrammed by either of the methods we illustrated for example 5. This is because the words *put* and *down*, though separated in the linear arrangement of the sentence, actually form one single unit of meaning – cf. the word *deposit*. *Put* and *down* should appear as one constituent: in diagram form, they should depend from the same branch of a tree (the first diagram given for 5) or they should occur within the same pair of brackets (cf. the second diagram for 5). But if we were to put them together in a diagram, we would fail to do justice to the linear ordering of the words in the sentence; in fact, we would distort that ordering. We may say that the unit *put . . . down* is a **discontinuous constituent** and that the form of analysis reflected in the diagrams cannot cope with discontinuous consistuents. To put it another way, we may observe that the analytic method which produces diagrams such as those above is deficient because it is too dependent on the physical sequence of words in the sentence: the diagrams become impossible, or get tied into knots, if we try to show structural realities which are not realized straightforwardly in the surface of sentences. Generalizing still further, we may say that the failure of PSG, illustrated above by the failure of its typical diagramming techniques, is a failure to recognize that significant linguistic facts exist below the apparent ordering of sentence-elements. Superficial structure is, more often than not, a poor guide to the meaning of sentences; and a PSG, because it is so tied to superficies of representation, cannot account for important structural facts if such facts include – as they should – facts about meaning. We can instance this failure of PSG with a rather different type of case:

7. Visiting relatives can be boring.
8. John and Jane are married.

Once again, a description of the surface syntactic units would not account for the full set of properties of these sentences, because they are both ambiguous – in each case, one surface is underlain by more than one meaning: who visits whom? are John and Jane married to each other? Chomsky cites such examples as these, where PSG is inadequate because it cannot get 'below the surface', and also converse situations. Consider the pairs 9 and 10, 11 and 12, in which two surfaces amount to much the same underlying meaning:

9. Peter ate the apple.
10. The apple was eaten by Peter.

11. Dick's a politician and he's writing his memoirs.
12. Dick, who's a politician, is writing his memoirs.

A PSG must assign quite different analyses to 9 and 10, 11 and 12, even though the members of each pair are very closely related, and indeed have much the same meaning. Chomsky argues that a linguistic description must be capable of accounting for significant relationships between the sentences of a language, as well as of displaying the internal structure of individual sentences.

The way of dealing with such problems as these, Chomsky claimed, is to supplement a PSG with an additional kind of linguistic process; adapting an idea of his teacher, Zellig Harris, he proposed a **transformational** level of structure in syntactic analysis. Transformational rules will be illustrated extensively in chapters 5 to 7 so I will say little about them here. As just one example, we may re-consider 6:

6. He put the book down.

There is another version of 6:

13. He put down the book.

13 contains no discontinuous structure; and it is synonymous with 6. We might justifiably say that 13, in which *put* and *down* are side-by-side, represents more closely the intended meaning than does 6, on which argument it would be reasonable to say that 6 is in some sense 'derived from' 13, or, more probably, that both 6 and 13 are derived from a common underlying form, an abstract meaning-structure of which 6 is a less direct manifestation than 13. This indirectness can be seen as a consequence of the application of a transformational rule which concerns two-part verbs such as *put down*, *take away*, *keep up*, etc. and has the effect of shifting the particle (*down*, *away*, *up*, etc.) to the right of the noun which is the object of the verb. A similar transformational shifting-around of constituents (merely a bit more complicated) would relate actives to passives (9 and 10) and an extension of the principle can, as we shall see, account for many more constructions which are not adequately handled by a PSG.

We may now extrapolate from *Syntactic Structures* to the general implications of its insights. Transformational rules can be regarded in several different ways. They perform at least three functions. They relate sentences to one another, i.e. they explain how intuitively related sentences *are* related. They alter constituent-structure by shifting parts of sentences around, by deleting elements (the 'understood *you*' of imperatives is transformationally deleted), by adding constituents (the *-ed* on past tense verbs), by combining clauses in various ways (see 11 and 12). Finally – and perhaps most importantly – they form the bridge between what I called in chapter 1 'messages' and 'signals', 'meanings' and 'sounds'. In discussing examples 6 and 13 I suggested that both may be derived – by different transformational 'routes' – from a single abstract underlying semantic basis. A sentence is a pairing of a meaning with a phonetic (or graphic) signal. Meaning is abstract, a conceptual structure with no space–time existence. In the community at large, it is shared semantic knowledge; for the individual ready to speak, it is 'thought'. There is no reliable evidence for direct inter-person transfer of thoughts; communication invariably takes place through the mediation of a physical channel. Thus thought has to be rendered concrete, has to be endowed with a material manifestation. It seems that the purpose of transformations is to operate upon abstract semantic constructs and to impose a linear form upon them; to produce a syntactic arrangement with space–time potentialities, which can subsequently be acoustically realized by a speaker's sound-producing apparatus. In Chomsky this distinction between meaning and sound is later (1965) expressed as a distinction between **deep structure** and **surface structure** in syntax. The deep structure of a sentence consists of a complex of words in certain elementary functional relations with each other; these relations are given the traditional names 'subject', 'predicate', 'object', etc. The deep structure is said to be an abstract level of representation of a sentence containing all information relevant to its meaning. Transformations work upon this deep structure, ordering and altering its components – but, apparently, without changing meaning – to derive a surface structure, a linear concatenation of elements for concrete realization in sound or script. The deep structure/surface structure distinction provides a convenient way of talking about some of the sentence-relationships illustrated in this chapter. 6 and 13 have the same deep structure but are two distinct surface structures; similarly 11 and 12; perhaps also 9 and 10, but the question of whether actives and passives are synonymous is controversial. By contrast, 7 and 8 are both ambiguous; we can express the notion 'ambiguity' by saying that an ambiguous utterance is one surface structure which conceals two different deep structures. The transformations involved in taking the meaning through to surface structure have somehow 'neutralized' the deep structure contrasts.

The picture of Chomsky's transformational grammar which I have just drawn represents his modified position as argued in *Aspects of the Theory of Syntax* (1965) and related works. Since that time the new linguistics which he inaugurated in 1957 has been in a state of considerable turmoil (and still is). Chomsky has been attacked for not giving due priority to semantic considerations (it will be clear that his model of grammar is based on a *syntactic* core). Specifically, linguists such as Emmon Bach, Wallace L. Chafe, Charles Fillmore and James McCawley have pointed to the need to assume an independent level of semantic structure capable of showing meaning-distinctions much more delicate than those available in Chomsky's grammar. Some of the ideas of these linguists are reflected in my next two chapters, and so I will not present their arguments here. I would point out, however, that the current dispute among these linguistic theorizers is an argument between people who all subscribe to the same general framework – and a traditional one at that. All agree that any adequate representation of the structure of sentences in natural language must take account of three kinds of facts: facts about meaning, facts about sound and facts about the arrangements whereby meaning is converted into sound. Accordingly, a grammar is said to have three components: a **semantic** component, a **phonological** component and a **syntactic** component. The controversy rages around two aspects of this agreed three-part model: the exact structure of the semantic component and the nature of its relationship to syntax – in particular, which of these two components should be granted priority in accounting for the manner of construction of sentences.

The discussion has grown progressively more technical in the last few pages, particularly with my attempt to characterize disinterestedly a kind of grammar which is, in fact, employed in the central chapters of the present book. It may be advantageous to draw back for a while from the theory and principles of grammatical description, to attempt to set it in the perspective of the linguistic sciences as a whole. The brief history of linguistics sketched above has concerned itself primarily with descriptive linguistics, which is only one – albeit the most important – of four broad divisions in the linguistic sciences. There is first **general**, alias **theoretical**, linguistics, a study which seeks to illuminate the essential, recurrent and defining characteristics of human language as a universal phenomenon. The phrase 'general linguistics' is often employed as a catch-all to include all the particular researches which make up the totality of the linguistic sciences, but it is best preserved for this most rarefied of all the sciences devoted to language: the enquiry into the kind of thing language itself is. Of course, such an enquiry depends for its success not only on speculation and abstract reasoning, but also on inductive generalization from the facts revealed by individual grammatical descriptions, studies of particular languages: from the productions of **descriptive linguistics**, our second branch. Descriptive linguists construct complete or partial **grammars**, expositions of the structure of single languages or of selected facets (e.g. the verb system, the intonation) of single languages. I will discuss the extremely important term 'grammar' shortly. For the moment we will take its definition for granted: 'a description of the structure of the language'. Now the subject-matter of descriptive linguistics may be divided up in various ways; we may slice the cake of the world's languages along several different dimensions. On p. 24 above I mentioned Saussure's distinction between **synchronic** and **diachronic** linguistics: this becomes relevant at this point. A synchronic description takes a fixed instant (usually, but not necessarily, the present) as its point of observation. Most grammars are of this kind. If you take something called 'A Grammar of Modern Greek' from the library shelves, it will usually claim to be a synchronic (and contemporaneous) grammar; likewise 'The Structure of Shakespeare's English' claims to be a synchronic description of a single, past, state of the language. But of course synchrony is a fiction, for language changes as the minutes pass, and grammar-writing is a lengthy enterprise. A linguist describing even a single sentence finds himself at a great handicap, if he cares to think about it: the linearity of surface structure ensures that the linguist's attempt to capture the sentence as an instantaneous whole is doomed. However, the fiction of synchronic description is essential to linguistics. We must assume that at a given moment of time a community's command of its language is stable; that everyone knows the language in some perfect, single state. If we did not subscribe to this fiction, we would be hard put to explain how it is that speakers share the same linguistic competence and can communicate spontaneously at any particular moment.

Saussure's **diachronic** linguistics is the study of a language through the course of its history. Historical linguistics was a pervasive interest of the Darwinist nineteenth century; in the course of their historical researches into the development of the Indo-European tongues, the philologists instituted a firm tradition which has led to the production of much diachronic information about most of the culturally prominent, lettered, languages of Europe. The systematization and presentation of this information raises problems: a diachronic grammar is in principle a juxtaposed series of synchronic descriptions, and the intervals one chooses tend to have powerful effects on the historical picture presented (broad sweep or slow laborious muta-tion). As we saw earlier in this chapter, for the nineteenth century the historical and **comparative** methods were inseparable: compara-tive data from related languages provided the precipitating insights from which the vast imaginative hypotheses concerning the genesis and evolution of the Indo-European family depended. This kind of comparative study must be distinguished from a differently formed branch of descriptive linguistics, the **typological**. Comparative study of the kind indulged in by the Indo-Europeanists was preoccupied with correspondences of details of linguistic texture. The words *father*, *pater*, *Vater*, *père*, *pitar*, *faðir*, all meaning 'father', are found in languages as geographically and culturally widespread as English, Latin, German, French, Sanskrit and Old Icelandic (respectively); these words were almost certainly not 'borrowed' by one language from another, as, for instance, English has borrowed *scherzo* from Italian, French *weekend* from English. Thus a wholly linguistic explanation of the correspondences is called for: armed with a hypothesis about sound-change, the *comparativist* uses such material, and other facts of the same kind, to draw these languages together into one accommodating structure. Linguistic *typology* appeals to *contrasting* facts about languages in order to divide them off into structural groups which do not necessarily correspond to the genetic groups discovered by comparative study; moreover, typological linguistics deals in very general facts about language. For instance, Chinese employs variation of pitch level to make distinctions of meaning between words, English does not, even though intonation is regularly connected with other sorts of structural distinction in English: so Chinese is a 'tone language' (or perhaps 'group of languages' – a *comparative* question), English not. Latin and Russian are highly inflected languages in which word-order is not a particu-larly reliable indicator of syntactic structure; modern English dis-plays quite the reverse situation – word-order is the major signal of syntactic structure. This is a typological distinction, and one which is quite independent of the comparative perspective, which shows all three languages to be genetically related. English allows only one inflexional suffix to be appended to a noun or verb; many other languages tolerate a string of morphemes added to a word. Dealing in observations of this kind, typological linguistics clearly is equipped to serve the goals of general linguistics as defined above. If we have knowledge about the range of types of structure found in natural languages, we are well on the way to determining what is possible and permissible by way of organizing dimensions in language as a whole institution.

So far I have discussed only two of the four broad divisions in the activities of linguists: *general*; *descriptive*, with the sub-divisions of *synchronic*, *diachronic* and *comparative* depending on the perspective from which linguistic facts are observed, plus *typological*, which is one methodological bridge between descriptive and general. There is also an inclusive set of linguistic interests, our third branch, which as a whole has no special name but is concerned with aspects of language which join up with the subject-matter of other sciences devoted to human skills and behaviour: for example, **phonetics**, which is related to physiology and to acoustics; **psycholinguistics**, which joins forces with psychology and psychiatry; **sociolinguistics**, which has obvious links with sociology and anthropology. More information about these branches of linguistics will be found in later chapters, and I will return to general questions of the definition of their subject-matter in a moment. The fourth major branch of the linguistic sciences is **applied linguistics**, which is of course not a single discipline but a collection of more or less separate enterprises in which the descriptive findings, or the methods, of linguistics are put to practical use outside of linguistics itself. 'Applications' have proliferated since the Second World War – when there was a good deal of American government investment in rapid language-teaching programmes – and particularly with the high and evangelical, outward-going, spirit of confidence among American linguists in the fifties. Descriptive linguistics and psycholinguistics have made many contributions to language-teaching in all its aspects, particularly the theory and practice of second-language learning by adults. There have been similar benefits in speech pathology and speech therapy: linguistics has contributed considerably to our understanding of how speech defects arise and how patients may be trained to overcome them. (Conversely, linguists have learnt much about the biological bases of language, particularly the relation between linguistic knowledge and brain structure, by studying pathological states of language.) In recent years, linguists' interests in language education have extended to the native language of schoolchildren. Language learning does not stop when the young child has acquired the rudiments of the grammar of his language (as most children do before they enter school), but continues as the child is exposed to socializing forces which require the addition of the various 'stylistic' adaptations to his basic knowledge, as we saw in chapter 1. Education in fluency, articulacy, stylistic flexibility, is the aim of a number of recent language education programmes (e.g. *Headstart*, *Language in Use*). By 'style' in this context I mean style outside literature, of course (cf. pp. 16–17 above). A further application of linguistics, extensively illustrated and debated in the last twenty years, is in the study of literary style. Linguistics cannot replace criticism, for the aims of linguistic description and literary interpretation are very different; but it can provide valuable service of various kinds. There is a contribution to be made to literary theory – linguistics being an advanced theoretical discipline and modern criticism being strongly oriented towards language but without a well-articulated theory of how literary language actually works. There is a contribution to the practical criticism of individual literary texts, particularly where criticism demands a positive and delicate engagement with the more technical facets of literary form: a good example would be metrical analysis, which has recently been an absorbing interest for a number of linguists. Finally, I would claim that linguistics has a contribution to make to the education of students of literature. Linguistics, being a subject which encourages a clear and finely discriminating analysis of verbal form, surely cannot fail to encourage valuable virtues – perceptiveness, care of expression, analytic skill – in students whose subject-matter displays the most complex arrangements of language.

To end this chapter I want to return to the activity of *descriptive linguistics* – the central and fundamental branch of linguistics – in order to further clarify its aims and its relationships to the other divisions of linguistics. We must consider what is meant by the term 'grammar', which is obviously critical to our view of what descriptive linguistics describes and what the 'output' of its descriptive activity consists of.

The term 'grammar' is used in linguistics with systematic ambiguity. There are at least two important meanings, and more if we take in the semi-evaluative term 'grammatical'. The first definition of 'grammar' is reflected in an expression like 'He knows the grammar of English', by which we mean that he possesses certain knowledge which allows him to speak/write and understand English. We do not imply that he can bring the rules of English to conscious scrutiny as a linguist might; the knowledge is tacit knowledge of the kind found in every speaker from university professors of linguistics to uneducated, ordinary speakers. It is knowledge of the sort sometimes called 'performative knowledge': knowledge which enables one to do something. Riding a bicycle entails the possession of appropriate performative knowledge; yet one can do so without having conscious intellectual awareness of the laws of mechanics, by virtue of which one is able to balance. Performative knowledge may be contrasted with 'reproducible knowledge' – e.g. knowing the names of all the states of the USA so that one can repeat them in a list. Linguistic knowledge is clearly not of that kind. This performative knowledge corresponds to what Saussure meant by *langue* – a psychological property in the individual, but independent of the individual because culturally shared – the property of the speech-community, manifested in every person who can communicate according to the conventions of the community. Chomsky has re-christened Saussure's *langue* as **linguistic competence**: or, as I shall want to call it, **grammatical competence**. Competence is opposed to **performance** (roughly, Saussure's *parole*), performance being an occurrence of the employment of competence: speaking or listening and understanding, reading or writing, etc. Performance is a concrete instance of the use of language, competence the abstract knowledge which makes performance possible. To put it more exactly, gram-matical competence is one of the factors which underlie performance. It is obvious that, in any single act of speech, many more skills are in play than the simple ability to associate sounds and meanings. A striking demonstration of this fact is the disparity between the theoretically infinite potentialities of grammar and the strictly limited practicalities of actual speech. I showed in chapter 1 that there is no theoretical limit to the length of sentences in natural language. This was, of course, a purely theoretical axiom necessary to the argument that speakers encounter and deal with unpredictably 'new' sentences all the time. Since the ideal potentialities of a grammar are circumscribed by the necessities of physical existence, however, performance cannot match up to competence. People die, so there can be no sentence of infinite length. On a less dramatic plane, a speaker's ideal command of a language is not realized in performance, because he makes errors; he is distracted or his memory gives way halfway through a complicated sentence, so the structure goes awry. This is to say that extra-linguistic factors, factors which are external to grammatical competence, play a part in linguistic performance. A human being speaking (or, indeed, listening) employs a great range of competences, of which gram-matical competence is only one, and is additionally to some extent under the control of physical, situational constraints outside him-self. Lest it be thought that the speaker is at the mercy of all the environmental winds that blow, plus his own physical inadequacies, let us try to put the argument in more positive terms.

An act of speech is many things at once, the product of many skills and pressures working simultaneously. First of all, it is a pairing, productive or receptive, of a meaning and a graphic or phonetic signal. This aspect of language use is controlled by grammatical competence. The most obviously additional factor which is in play is the exercise of certain physical mechanisms. The speaker engages in a complicated motor activity, the control and co-ordination of the musculature associated with speech, his acoustic output continuously monitored by picking up vibrations passing through the air and through the bone structure of his head. The hearer decodes a speech signal only after it has passed through his auditory mechanism. Next, speech and comprehension depend on psychological processes, non-linguistic competences (and incompetences!) such as intelligence, memory, attentiveness, etc. Although the *possession* of language is, as we have seen, not debarred by any except the gravest deficiencies in these areas of non-linguistic psychology, the *exercise* of language is obviously all the time subject to the non-linguistic psychological properties of speakers and hearers. Also, language use is affected by all kinds of situational qualities over which speakers have varying degrees of control. At a crude level, noisy surroundings interfere with the production and reception of speech. More subtle influences obtain: all the stylistic adjustments to features of context of situation which we mentioned in the first chapter are dimensions of the speech act which depend not on a speaker's grammatical competence pure and simple but on additional areas of *sociolinguistic* knowledge which affect the output of the grammar. We may speak of **sociolinguistic competence** as an area of knowledge separate from, but working in co-operation with, grammatical competence (see further, chapter 10).

Our first sense of **grammar** (let us use a subscript numeral and call it 'grammar$_1$'), then, designates a psychological property, 'linguistic knowledge' of a deliberately restricted kind. Grammar$_1$ accounts, not for the whole complex of abilities which are exercised in linguistic performance, but only for the knowledge which controls the pairing of sounds and meanings in sentences – 'communication' in the narrow sense of the transmission of information by the medium of language. Grammar$_2$, the explicit description which the linguist constructs, is the representation of just the knowledge designated by grammar$_1$. Thus phonetics, psycholinguistics, sociolinguistics, etc. (see above, p. 36) are distinct from descriptive linguistics; collaborative sciences which together with descriptive linguistics explain the complicated activities of linguistic performance. The division of labour between linguistics, psycholinguistics (etc.) is marked by the definition of the term 'grammar'.

Let us say that a grammar (henceforth = grammar$_2$) is a device for **generating** all the sentences of a natural language, a set which is of course infinite. 'Generate' means simply 'enumerate' or 'describe', an abstract, formal and non-behavioural process. It is to be distinguished from 'produce', a term which must be restricted to talk about linguistic performance. Utterances are produced and understood in the realm of *parole*, but the grammar is a grammar of *langue*, which, considered synchronically, is a time-free, action-free, entity. A grammar generates a sentence by assigning to an utterance a **structural description**, a set of statements at semantic, syntactic and phonological levels which show how meaning and sound are associated in that particular sentence. An ambiguous utterance must receive two or more structural descriptions. Two synonymous sentences must be generated (described) in such a way that the equivalence of their meanings is obvious without appeal to informal, intuitive criteria. (They must enjoy comparable structural descriptions.) A generative grammar must be explicit and formal, so that each sentence of a language can be readily distinguished from all other sentences, while at the same time all *related* sentences can be *seen* to be related. Such a grammar must be capable of accounting for all purely linguistic knowledge (cf. 'grammar$_1$') which speakers have about their language, and that includes not only a feeling for meaningfulness but also perceptions of ambiguity, synonymy and all other structural attributes of sentences. Finally, a grammar must be able to represent speakers' feelings about the **grammaticalness** of the utterances of their language. It goes without saying that speakers can distinguish between sentences of their language and sentences which are not of their language, and that a grammar must reflect this distinction automatically by not including rules which will generate, say, French sentences when English only are required. Speakers can also distinguish the grammatical from the ungrammatical, and, moreover, make fairly fine discriminations between sentences which are *more* and *less* grammatical – they recognize, in effect, that there are degrees of grammaticalness. The following sentences are both ungrammatical, but 15 is more severely so than 14:

14. *I astonished the bookcase.
15. *I astonished.

(A prefixed asterisk is used to indicate deviant linguistic constructions.) A grammar of English must be arranged so that it fails to assign structural descriptions to such utterances and thus establishes them as ungrammatical. In the case of 14 this effect is guaranteed by a rule which prevents words denoting inanimate things following verbs like *astonish*; 15 is designated as gravely deviant because it affronts a rule which says that *astonish* must have an object.

In prohibiting utterances like 14 and 15 the grammar is being implicitly normative, and readers may wonder how a grammar can claim to be descriptive and nevertheless confess to being normative. A parallel worry may be raised by my use of the term **rule**. It must be stressed that a grammar is not, however, regulative or prescriptive: it is not designed to tell people how they must use language, although of course descriptive grammars may be, and are, adapted for instructional purposes, to teach foreign learners how a language is *used*. 'Rules' in descriptive grammars are notations for structural patterns in a language, acknowledgment of the existence of particular formal conventions. For some examples of 'rules' in this neutral sense, see chapter 6, examples 309, 313, 314. 14 and 15 are not well-structured English sentences, so the rules in which a grammatical description of English is couched must not provide for them. The principles according to which constructions are recognized or rejected must be purely linguistic: we must be careful to exclude considerations of extrinsic social judgment. Taboo words, for instance, are unacceptable merely for reasons of social etiquette: their prohibition has nothing to do with linguistic laws, everything to do with the sensibilities of the cultural group which, for linguistically irrelevant reasons, objects to them. A lexicographer who decides to exclude the terminology of excretion or sexual intercourse from his dictionary takes the decision on non-linguistic grounds. Similarly, judgments against usages such as 'ain't' or 'do it like I told you' or 'who did you see?' are social in origin. Taking the last example, both *who* and *whom* are nowadays grammatically warranted in the object position in sentences; the choice between them depends on formality of style of discourse, a matter of etiquette which is extrinsic to grammatical competence (though it is sociolinguistically interesting). To say that only *whom* is acceptable as object – that *who* is absolutely barred from that function – is to fly in the face of linguistic usage. A grammar is designed to represent linguistic facts, not to teach cultural tact.

Further reading

History of linguistics: Robins, *Short History*; Pedersen, *Linguistic Science in the Nineteenth Century*; Waterman, *Perspectives in Linguistics*.

Saussure's *Cours* is available in a good translation by Wade Baskin, but the passages containing the key terms (*langue, signification,* etc.) should be read in the original if possible. Roland Barthes, *Elements of Semiology* is a brief attempt to realize Saussure's ideal of a 'general science of signs'.

Two textbooks written from the American structuralist point of view are Hockett's *Course in Modern Linguistics* and Gleason's *Introduction to Descriptive Linguistics*. Joos's collection, *Readings in Linguistics*, is a comprehensive sampling of articles by linguists of the Bloomfield 'school'. The anthologies of Fodor and Katz and of Reibel and Schane do a similar job for transformational-generative grammar; but the student should also read the primary sources, Chomsky's *Syntactic Structures* and *Aspects*. John Lyons's little paperback, *Chomsky*, is useful as a guide to the development of Chomsky's ideas, but again is no substitute for the original.

Post-Chomsky and anti-Chomsky writings: Chafe, *Meaning and the Structure of Language*; articles by Bach, Fillmore and McCawley in Bach and Harms, *Universals*; Langendoen, *Essentials of English Grammar*, for a messy but readable amalgam of those authors' proposals.

Lyons's *Introduction to Theoretical Linguistics* is an eclectic, thorough and usually reliable introduction to the principles of general and descriptive linguistics (e.g. on distinctions like *generate* v. *produce*, *synchronic* v. *diachronic*). Various aspects of applied linguistics are touched on in Halliday, McIntosh and Strevens, *The Linguistic Sciences and Language Teaching*; for linguistics and literature, see Freeman, *Linguistics and Literary Style* or Fowler, *The Languages of Literature* and *Essays on Style and Language*.

three

Words and their components

In our ordinary, non-scientific thinking about language we tend to assume that **words** are the basic units of meaning; that our larger discourse is reducible to semantic building-blocks very much of the dimensions of the items which fill the columns of dictionaries. It is true that approximately word-size units play a prominent part in determining the semantic content of utterances, and for this reason – and also because words or 'lexical items' are comfortably familiar linguistic units – I will begin a pair of chapters on meaning by discussing the semantic structure of words. However, a preliminary caution is essential. The meaning of a sentence cannot be adequately represented as the sum of the meanings of its lexical parts. Lexical items are not really like building blocks, in that they cannot be merely juxtaposed to form a semantic whole. There are structural relationships *between* words in sentences which are indispensable to making up the meaning of the whole. The lexical items may quite plausibly be seen as conveying primitive 'blocks' of meaning, but the meaning of a sentence is more than an unordered heap of building materials: it is a construct which takes much of its semantic shape from compositional relationships which are external to the mere words. This fact is obvious if we consider one very elementary example of the reordering of lexical elements:

16. The napkin is on top of the fork.
17. The fork is on top of the napkin.

These sentences are very definitely not synonymous, even though they contain the same words. The justice of this observation that the meaning of a sentence is not fully specified by merely listing its component lexical parts may be tested by a simple experiment using a foreign language dictionary. Take a text in a language which you do not understand and, armed with a dictionary, look up every word in sequence. Even though the dictionary tells you the meanings of the lexical items, you can understand next to nothing of the text, because you do not possess linguistic competence which includes the *compositional* semantic structure of the language concerned. With this reservation in mind, we will explore some questions involving the semantic structure of lexical items.

The semantic component of a grammar is the part of it which makes it possible for us to form messages about the world outside language. It is natural, then, to enquire about the relationship of semantic units to material objects. The most common view of this relationship holds that 'words' are mere substitutes for 'things'. An extreme form of this belief is ridiculed by Swift in *Gulliver's Travels*. In the School of Languages at the Grand Academy of Lagado, Gulliver is introduced to 'a Scheme for entirely abolishing all Words whatsoever'. The proponents of this scheme argue 'that since Words are only Names for *Things*, it would be more convenient for all Men to carry about them, such *Things* as were necessary to express the particular Business they are to discourse on'. The gossips of the community rebel against this invention, but 'many of the most Learned and Wise' employ it. Gulliver comments that the scheme 'hath only this Inconvenience attending it; that if a Man's Business be very great, and of various Kinds, he must be obliged in Proportion to carry a greater Bundle of *Things* upon his back, unless he can afford one or two strong Servants to attend him'. Many other disabling 'inconveniences' spring to mind – in particular, all the facility for displacement and abstraction is lost in the Lagadoan 'thing-language', every benefit which normally accrues from the **symbolic** nature of language. Additionally, the relational structure of messages would be reduced to simple space–time juxtapositions, putting one 'thing' next to another, or producing one thing after another. However, the Lagadoan scheme does recognize one important property of language: its capacity to refer to material objects. We must give serious consideration to this quality of 'reference'; and we must ask how much of semantic structure is accounted for by this quality.

That words are 'names' is one of the most deeply rooted of all assumptions in semantics. The term *noun* is derived from Latin *nomen* 'name', and so the naming function of at least a major part of the vocabulary was very early emphasized in grammatical terminology. In traditional semantics, this naming function has been generalized, doubtless inappropriately, to non-nominal grammatical categories. Its popularity as a fundamental semantic principle reflects a feeling that proper names (*Sally, Cicero, Mickey Mouse*) present the simplest case of words having meaning, and that they can therefore be invoked as a model for semantic processes in general. The proper names which we have at our command are just those to which we can attach meanings unambiguously. I understand the meaning of the name *Peter Fowler* because that is the name of my elder son, and since I know no other Peter Fowler I am naturally inclined to believe that the name is unambiguous. When I use this phrase, I use it to refer to a particular, specifiable person. If someone asks me 'Who is this?' I can answer 'Peter Fowler'; or if someone asks me 'Who is Peter Fowler?' I can reply simply by pointing at the person to whom the name correctly refers.

It is at this point that the analogy between names and words which are not names appears to become impressive. Names – which, we are led to feel, are the simplest case of meaning – seem to throw some light on the mode of meaning of less straightforward bits of language. If someone asks me 'What's that?' I can reply 'A tree'; if I am asked 'What's a tree?' I can point to one. If I utter a sentence containing the words *Peter Fowler* or *tree*, I am referring to Peter or to a tree. The analogy seems to be exact: in both cases the linguistic unit is a sort of label for an object, and to use that label meaningfully is to refer to that object. The 'naming' theory of meaning entails commitment to the idea of 'objects' outside of language, and it invokes the notion of reference to explain the relation of words and things.

This account of meaning, under which words are said to be the names of things, is very familiar as the **referential** theory of meaning. The properties of 'standing for' and 'referring to' are natural qualities for a sign-system to possess: signs are substitutes for experience and they may be used in communication to refer to experience and to objects. But the referential theory of meaning is not adequate to delineate all aspects of meaning, and, moreover, it has inherent characteristics which cause great difficulty when we try to express the theory and its implications in formal scientific terms.

The referential theory exists in two versions. The simpler, and more pernicious, version states that the meaning of a word is that to which it refers. The error of this equation of 'meanings' and 'things referred to' can be shown very quickly: the theory breaks down unless the meant objects actually exist. The implication is that words which refer to objects which are no longer in existence are meaningless (or that sentences in which such words occur are meaningless): *Socrates, the dodo, Byzantium*; by the same argument, the names of fictional objects are meaningless since such objects have no 'real' existence: *Mr Micawber, unicorns, Middlemarch, Kellynch-Hall*. But all the words and phrases I have just cited are clearly meaningful, so this

45

version of referential theory is obviously to be rejected. (And for a second reason: a theory which equates meanings with existent objects cannot accommodate abstract terms, which would be by definition meaningless.) The second, more sophisticated, wording of the theory of meaning as reference focuses not on the thing symbolized but on the *relation* – the referential tie – between name and object. This version of referential theory, though still inadequate to account for all but a small number of semantic processes, does contain some important observations on the nature of linguistic signs.

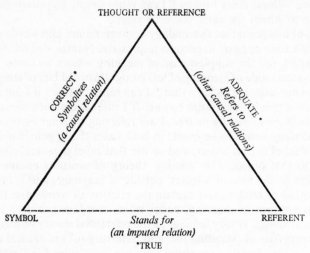

Figure 1

(*CORRECT, ADEQUATE and TRUE do not concern us here.)

Modern referential theory usually takes as its starting-point the famous 'triangle of reference' of C. K. Ogden and I. A. Richards, first published in 1923 and since reproduced with modifications many times by other writers. Figure 1 is the diagram, in its original format.

One major terminological benefit offered by this diagram is **referent**: 'that which is referred to'. *Referent* is an etymologically and philosophically neutral word, and it frees us of all the pheno-menological confusion caused by using words such as 'object', 'thing' in discussions like this. Note, however, that referents are outside the scope of semantic description. If the referent of the word *tree* is a tree, description of the physical characteristics of trees is the concern of botany, not of linguistics. The referent is not the meaning, and so semantics is not called upon to describe referents. Thus semantics is not forced, as Leonard Bloomfield thought it was, to wait for a full scientific description of the physical universe before making any statements about meaning.

If we employ the term *referent* in connection with some words, we are not committed to accepting that all linguistic expressions have reference. 'Referent' must imply the notion of physical existence, and although much of our discourse concerns concrete objects (books, tables, trees) and imaginary objects (unicorns, gnomes, yeti), much of it does not. Semantics must, if it is to be at all adequate, be capable of accounting for the meanings of words like *abstraction, process, imagination, good, true, happy*, etc. Some of the greatest confusions in semantics have come from the futile search for referents for words of this kind: for instance, the attempt to link words such as *happy, sad, angry* to physically describable biological states. Evaluative adjectives and abstract nouns will simply not yield to referential theory, and we must resist all pressures to generalize referential theory to the vast number of expressions which do not have referents. Even words which appear to have definite physical implications (e.g. *colour, loud*) cannot be provided with referents. Is the referent of *colour* some common property of the light-waves reflected from all objects which we call coloured? Can *loud* be defined in terms of decibels, and for any kind of noise? Even if such referents could be established, it is obvious that they would be quite different in character from the referents of *Peter Fowler* and *tree*, for instance. Such examples remind us that we must not try to force all meanings into the referential mould. If reference is a kind of meaning, it is not the only kind of meaning, and very probably it is not the typical kind of meaning. And even in cases where the notion seems appropriate, its application must be handled carefully. When the word *tree* is used in a particular sentence, it quite often refers to a particular tree, and that tree is the referent. But the referent is not the meaning of the word *tree*, if 'meaning' is considered as a stable property of the word itself rather than a temporary association in a particular communicative use of a word. To describe the meaning of the word *tree* we need to state what semantic features English speakers conventionally associate with it which, in turn, allow them in linguistic performance to relate it to a particular objective referent. Referentiality is, it appears, a latent quality: there is something in the character of many lexical items which allows them to be *used referentially*; 'making reference' is an aspect of linguistic performance, a part of the *use* of language. We must discover what quality in linguistic competence enables successful reference to occur.

47

The second notable aspect of Ogden and Richards's notion of the sign is the insight symbolized in their broken base line: the fact that the relation between symbol and referent (where there is a referent) is arbitrary and indirect. The phrase 'an imputed relation' at the foot of the diagram is explained as '[not] real' (p. 12). The Saussurean term is 'arbitrary', and this means conventional or non-natural: there is no intrinsic connection between the physical shape of a word and its meaning. Words do not picture the universe directly, but relate to it indirectly, by way of semantic conventions. This conventionality is a necessity in the nature of the communi-cative mode concerned. Because of the limitations of the physical media associated with language, the possibilities for direct repre-sentation are severely constrained. Our channels for language are restricted to sounds and letters, but our topics of discourse embrace much more than noises and visual images. Even 'onomatopoeic' words (*splash, whisper, ding-dong*, etc.) are conventionalized differ-ently in different language-communities – the community intervenes by placing a conventional link between symbol and referent, although its members may *believe* that onomatopoeic words are naturally representational. If the 'conventional link' is found in onomatopoeic words, it ought to command our attention even more forcibly in the case of that much greater part of the vocabulary which makes no pretence at direct portrayal of referents. Now this conventional link probably answers to the 'thought or reference' at the apex of Ogden and Richards's triangle, the mediating term between symbol and referent – at least, in so far as 'thought or reference' is a knowledge communally shared. But rather than attempting to get at the facts of semantic conventionality by further exploration of Ogden and Richards's ideas, I shall shift my perspective and introduce some new terms used by other semantic theorists.

Words in natural languages have associated with them certain conventional semantic properties which constitute their meanings. *Book*, for instance, has an underlying semantic structure which is in principle independent of the objective circumstances of any single use of this word. Although *book* is a referential word, its meaning is not determined by its referents (otherwise it could not refer to books of all shapes, sizes and colours) but by the position which it occupies in the vocabulary of English, in relation to other words in the same semantic field: *magazine, newspaper, pamphlet, paperback*, etc. As another simple example, an important part of the meaning of *hot* is that it is the opposite of *cold*. As we have seen, the physical realism of strict referential theory does not help us to define the meaning of words like *hot* and *cold* (cf. *loud*, above p. 47): speaking of the same temperature (air temperature, bathwater temperature), one person may say that it is cold, another person that it is hot. Yet these two people can agree that *cold* and *hot* are antonyms: the semantic relation between the words is a more stable indication of their meanings than are the conditions of their referential use.

We need, then, to investigate the relations between words and words, as well as those between words and things. This necessity is recognized by Stephen Ullmann, a proponent of referential theory who nevertheless warns against 'an atomistic view of language, in which each word would be regarded as an isolated and self-contained unit' (*Semantics*, pp. 62-3). Relations between lexical items take priority over relations between lexical items and 'the world', for three very important reasons. First, unless we assume that words have inherent semantic features not tied to the perceptual features of referents, we cannot explain how it is that one word can refer to a perceptually highly disparate set of objects (all the multiply various instances of tree, book, etc.). Second, not all words have referents (*believe, wonderful, associate, idea, transformation*, etc.). Third, in the case of referential words, a residue of meaning is always left over when we have identified the referent.

It was to cope with this third problem, the incompleteness of a referential statement even for referential words, that philosophers posited a dimension of meaning additional to (and, from the linguist's point of view, prior to) reference: the purely linguistic dimension of **sense**. The distinction between sense and reference is usually attributed to the philosopher and mathematician, Gottlob Frege, who pointed out that there are linguistic expressions which make the same reference but differ in meaning. The classic examples discussed by philosophers are 'the morning star/the evening star' and 'Sir Walter Scott/the author of Waverley'. In cases such as these the meaning cannot be given simply by stating what the expressions designate (their *Bedeutung* in Frege's terminology); we must also notice certain distinctive properties of the words chosen to do the designating (their *Sinn*, 'sense'). In the example of 'the morning star' versus 'the evening star' it would be all too easy to explain the variants *morning/evening* by simply relating them to the times of day at which the planet Venus is observed. This explanation would miss some important facts about the senses of the words. *Morning* and *evening* relate to each other formally within a highly structured system of terms concerned with 'natural' time-divisions. If we think carefully about the 'natural' structure of the day, we will be convinced that it is organized in a far less systematic way than is that part of the vocabulary which chops it up into sections. On to the simple progress of light and darkness the English language projects a pattern of oppositions and groups of terms:

18. night : day
    dawn : sunset
    morning : afternoon : evening
    midday : midnight.

In turn these groups interrelate, in various configurations, with other systems of vocabulary items – the terms for light and darkness, calendar terminology, social occasions (e.g. the names of mealtimes) and so on. The senses of *morning* and *evening* in the two expressions from which we started are established by the places which these words occupy in the vocabulary-system of English. One very simple structural factor which contributes to their sense, for instance, is that they fall into a three-term sub-system, and if there were no term *afternoon*, the senses of *morning* and *evening* would be different from their senses in the three-term system. It is knowledge of structural facts such as this which defines an English speaker's grasp of his vocabulary: that is to say, vocabulary competence can be represented as knowledge of senses. The sense of any word is an internal property of language structure. In the spirit of Ullmann's caution against 'atomism', we are led to view the vocabulary as a whole as a structured system the characteristics of which give meaning (sense) to each vocabulary item; and away from the approach which takes one word at a time and focuses on the way it relates to the world of non-linguistic referents.

The linguist's notion of 'sense' depends on a view of language as a structured system. We have seen how Ferdinand de Saussure stressed the idea of system in language. Fittingly, it was he who developed the concept of system in such a way as to map out a framework for the scientific study of the facts of semantic structure. He does not use the term *sense*. His basic semantic distinction is between **signification** and **value**. His 'signification' does not coincide exactly with 'reference', but 'value' corresponds well with our requirements for 'sense'. Signification in Saussure's approach is a property of individual signs: and a sign is an indivisible union of a **signifiant** or *acoustic image* and a **signifié** or *concept*. The *signifiant* is an abstract psychological representation of the phonetic level of a word; *signifié* is an abstract psychological representation of some part of the subjects of human discourse – of a referent, perhaps, but not inevitably. So if one knows the signification of a linguistic sign – say the Latin *arbor*, 'tree', to take one of Saussure's examples – one knows how to pronounce it and how to associate it with the correct referent, and this is one *unified* piece of knowledge; over and over again Saussure stresses the indivisibility of signifier and signified.

Because signification, like reference, is deficient as an account of meaning-structure in language, Saussure introduces the notion of *value* to complete the semantic model. Suppose that I learn the signification of the English word *tree*: that a native speaker points at a tree and says to me 'That's a tree'. The signifier has been fused with a signified by the method of **ostensive definition** – saying the word and indicating its referent by gesture or other non-linguistic means. Having come to understand the signification of *tree* in this way, do I know its meaning? Not necessarily. I cannot know its full meaning unless I know how it relates to other terms in relevant sections of the vocabulary. Part of the meaning of *tree* is that it is not a *shrub* or a *bush*; that it may be part of a *wood*, or a *forest*, or a *grove, spinney, copse*, etc.; that it has a *trunk, bark, branches, twigs, leaves*, etc. Readers who find this example fanciful or simpleminded may like to consider their knowledge of terms in technical areas in which they are not expert; if one cannot imagine not knowing the full meaning of *tree*, what about *laser, pulsar, quantum, algorithm, phoneme, watt, neuron, ionization*? I think it would generally be conceded that one does not properly know the meaning of an isolated scientific term unless one also knows the meanings of adjacent terms in the semantic field: that is to say, one must know its sense or value, which is derived from the relation of one term to others – in fact, ultimately from the relation of one term to *all* others in the vocabulary. Saussure's general statement of this thesis is as follows: 'Language is a system of interdependent terms in which the value of each term results solely from the simultaneous presence of the others . . .' (p. 114). He offers an analogy which explains the co-operation of signification and value in determining the meaning of signs:

> To determine what a five-franc piece is worth one must therefore know: (1) that it can be exchanged for a fixed quantity of a different thing, e.g. bread; and (2) that it can be compared with a similar value of the same system, e.g. a one-franc piece, or with coins of another system (a dollar, etc.). In the same way a word can be exchanged for something dissimilar, an idea; besides, it can be compared with something of the same nature, another word (p. 115).

Saussure makes it clear that 'value' is not a property of lexical systems alone: units at the syntactic and phonological levels, as well as the semantic, derive their value from their participation in systems. 'The value of a French plural does not coincide with that of a Sanskrit plural even though their signification is usually identical; Sanskrit has three numbers instead of two . . .; it would be wrong to attribute the same value to the plural in Sanskrit and in French;

its value clearly depends on what is outside and around it' (p. 116). But it is the value or sense of terms in lexical systems which most concerns us here. A final example of Saussure's may be quoted:

> Modern French *mouton* can have the same signification as English *sheep* but not the same value, and this for several reasons, particularly because in speaking of a piece of meat ready to be served on the table, English uses *mutton* and not *sheep*. The difference in value between *sheep* and *mutton* is due to the fact that *sheep* has beside it a second term while the French word does not (pp. 115–16).

The point is that the meaning of the words concerned is not given by their individual referential ties with denoted objects, but by their relationship to each other: their co-membership of a lexical set the members of which reciprocally define one another. We must now examine more closely the systematicity of the vocabulary of natural language.

When we are studying a foreign language, we are often given the task of learning by rote groups of words, sometimes a group of words each day or each week. Progressively we accumulate (hopefully) a stock of many thousands of words connecting with a vast range of potential topics of discourse. The lexical competence we so acquire may add up to something of the kind which might be represented in a formal dictionary. But a conventional, alphabetically listed dictionary has a format which is not strictly appropriate to the lexicon we have internalized. There is no psycholinguistic evidence that, when we are presented with a new sentence in a language we know, we perform a kind of mental alphabetical scan, looking up the words in turn in some conveniently arranged lexical store. Certainly, the lexicon which forms part of our linguistic competence is structured, but not by the mechanics of alphabetization. The *Oxford English Dictionary* is a poor analogue (but was never meant to be a model of known semantic *structure*); a better one would be a production like *Roget's Thesaurus*, which is an attempt to represent the conceptual structure of the lexicon in a consultable format. We are not concerned with matters of consultation and consultability here – those questions are for psycholinguistics, not descriptive linguistics – but we are concerned with structure. Perhaps, in this respect, the way many language-teaching programmes require us to build up our lexicon *is* significant. One day it is the vocabulary of the kitchen, the next day the set of lexical items connected with rail travel, then the lexicon of weights and measures. On each occasion we learn a set of words connected with some single area of experience; the learning procedure recognizes that the vocabulary of a language can be seen as a collection of **lexical sets** or **lexical systems**, each one communicating what we shall call a **semantic field**. A semantic field reflects a coherent inventory of human experiences; yet 'inventory' is perhaps the wrong word, because it does not do justice to the organization of semantic fields: the word 'system' is again appropriate.

We will refer to the vocabulary content of a speaker's linguistic competence (grammar₁), as the **lexicon**, then; by a familiar terminological ambiguity (cf. p. 39 above), we must say that a 'grammar₂' must contain – in addition to other sorts of semantic device – a lexicon. The lexicon is an overall structure of lexical sets; and each set comprises a formally organized and therefore mutually defining collection of lexical items. If a visual image is helpful, the lexicon could be pictured as a network of partly overlapping circles, each circle covering a particular semantic field, as in Figure 2.

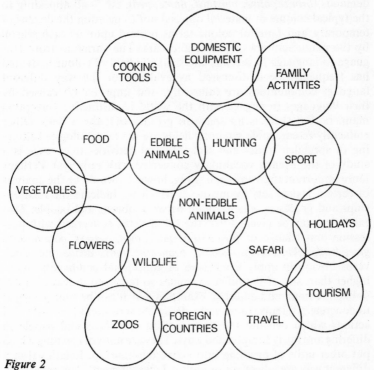

Figure 2

Very few semantic fields have so far been investigated, but it is clear that there are many thousands of them and that the lexical sets which map them out are organized to many different kinds of principles. Anthropologists have studied some of the more obviously structured sets such as kinship terminologies (which differ interestingly from language to language while preserving the same overall framework); taxonomic (classifying) vocabularies for plant life; colour terms, which again differ, perhaps surprisingly, from language to language. Differences include the number of basic terms which divide up the spectrum, the physical dimensions of the complex phenomenon 'colour' appealed to in the basic classification – difference of *hue* may be important in one language, *luminosity* in another, *saturation* in another. There may also be variations in the relationship between basic terms (*red, orange, yellow*, etc.) and subsidiary terms for finer discrimination (*crimson, scarlet, vermilion, gold, amber, azure, turquoise*, etc.); and in many cultures the basic stock of colour terms may be augmented by many more or less impermanent words and phrases to denote 'new colours' as fashion demands (*bronze, olive, mustard, flame, peat*, etc. – all appealing to the typical colours of material objects) not to mention the dozens of temporary and fanciful colour terms pressed upon us each season by the manufacturers of paints and cars. The variation from language to language in the way the semantic field of colour is treated has frequently been discussed as evidence of the way different language-communities are (allegedly, and improbably) caused by their languages to engage with the world in distinctive perceptual manners, but there is no space to go into that thesis here. Other eminently researchable semantic fields are the terminologies belonging to specialist trades and technological activities (e.g. there is a study of the French vocabulary connected with railways). Perhaps more important than any such study, however, would be the analysis of certain lexical sets by means of which we indicate the relationships and processes which obtain between objects and people. Two examples may be given. First, the set of verbs concerned with possession and change of possession: *have, own, possess, obtain, lose, give, lend, take, borrow, donate, bequeath, share, divide*, etc. Such verbs obviously imply a measure of conceptual complexity much higher than any of the other examples so far given in this chapter: unlike the noun and adjective examples which can be simply tagged to concrete referents, these verbs designate states and processes and actions which demand the participation of objects and people in differing and fairly complicated ways. They are units of meaning which put other units of meaning into active relationship. Relational in a different way are adjectives of physical measurement: *big, small, tall, short, long, wide, narrow, deep, shallow, fat, thin, broad*, etc. These are implicitly relational because they are implicitly comparative: when we say that something is tall or long, we are saying that it is tall or long by comparison with a norm for objects of the appropriate kind. The above two sets of relational terms are examples of lexical sets which are peculiarly important in language. Since they sort things into classes, put things into regular juxtaposition, they are of great conceptual utility to us, helping us to order our experience, to handle it linguistically as a meaningful pattern, not as a mere list or jumble of facts and perceptions.

Before we look more closely at the semantic structure of lexical sets, two brief points of a general kind need to be made. First of all, in each of the sets referred to so far, all the example words belonged to the same part of speech – all nouns, or all adjectives, etc. Community of syntactic category is not essential to the notion 'lexical set'. We would agree that all the following lexical items belong to one set, the set corresponding to the semantic field of heat and heat variation: *hot, cold, warm, freezing, icy, boiling, tepid, heat, warmth, chill, snow, ice, steam, burn, freeze, melt, roast, refrigerate, warmly, icily,* and so on. It is immaterial that the 'parts of speech' differ.

Second, as the simple diagram of overlapping circles (p. 53) suggests, lexical sets are not exclusive. Lexical items characteristically belong simultaneously to more than one set: *roast* and *refrigerate* belong to the vocabulary of cooking as well as to that of temperature, *snow* and *ice* are part of the diction of meteorology as well as that of temperature.

Because the lexical sets I have offered so far have been very informally presented, I have been able to get away with invoking a referential criterion in assembling and discussing the sample lexical sets: 'connection with a single area of experience' of course makes appeal to a referential tie between sets of lexical items and the sets of things and perceptions they designate. I do not deny that language is referential, and thus it is to be expected that lexical sets will to a large extent correspond with experiential fields. However, large areas of language are non-referential, so we cannot depend on a referential criterion to explain all meaning in language, and, as I have said, it is not a very reliable criterion anyway. It is necessary to devise what might be called a 'language-internal' approach to the definition of lexical sets and of lexical relationships in general: that is, an approach which can offer explanations of semantic patterning and which is not dependent on appeal to factors outside language. Is it possible to break down the meanings – the *senses* – of words into units, linguistic units, which show what it is that certain words have in common, and what causes others to be thought of as distinct? Are there semantic components of lexical items? If so, how do we get at them? One analytic procedure would be to divide up words into their linear constituents or **morphemes.**

Evidently, *blackboard* and *hardboard* divide up into *black, hard* and *board*, and *tigress* and *actress* yield the morphemes *tiger, actor* (itself segmentable) and *-ess*. These segmentations do tell us something about the meanings of the words concerned – that a blackboard is a board which is black, hardboard is board which is hard, a tigress is a female tiger and an actress a female actor. But the next thought that we are bound to entertain is that these descriptions of meaning are pretty uninformative. We still have not achieved any kind of insight into the meanings of *black, board, -ess*, etc. If meaning can be broken down into components, the analysis must reveal the components of simple as well as complex words. It is clear that the minute analysis of meaning cannot be achieved by simple linear segmentation; if words possess internal structure, it is structure more abstract than linear structure, and not at all observable. The prevalent attitude nowadays is that a lexical item is a complex cluster of **semantic components,** the components being selections from among features which are present latently in the semantic structure of the language as a whole, and the specific lexical item being a convergence of components selected from that wider network of meaning. We would, then, propose a process of 'atomization' of meaning or 'componential analysis': instead of looking for signs of meaning on the surface, we suppose the existence of covert semantic entities. The nature and relationships of these entities can be hypothesized by abstract comparisons of the meanings of lexical items.

A preliminary note on terminology: various linguists speak of 'semantic components', 'semantic features', 'semantic markers'. I will try to make a systematic terminological distinction between **semantic components** and **semantic features**: the former will designate the atoms of meaning in actual lexical items, the latter atoms of meaning considered from the point of view of the overall structure of the language in abstraction. Thus, a particular word-meaning may be said to be the sum of a number of semantic components; and the semantic structure of a whole language may be said to be a patterned network of semantic features. A component will be viewed as a 'value' of a feature: for example, the structure of language contains the feature [ANIMATE], and a particular lexical item will, when relevant, be marked with one of the two available values of that feature, the value [+ANIMATE] or [−ANIMATE].

The character of semantic features and components can best be shown by some examples. Compare the following lists of words:

19. fancy, truth, component, psychology, beauty, system
20. table, stone, mug, house, pen, carpet, knife
21. tree, peach, dahlia, vine, weed, yeast

22. giraffe, fish, elephant, cat, snake, ape, animal
23. girl, cousin, man, woman, grandmother, student, politician.

The lexical items in 19 contrast with all the others in 20–3. One way of expressing the distinction would be to say that all the words in 20–3 denote physical objects, whereas those in 19 concern abstractions. But we have determined to avoid that kind of explanation, involving as it does referential considerations. Instead, we might say that the words in 19 contain the component [ABSTRACT], the rest [CONCRETE]. However, it seems that 19 and 20–3 are contrasted in respect of a *single* feature (not, by one component in 19 and another in 20–3), and so it may be misleading to employ two separate words to capture this contrast. Accordingly, we will assign plus and minus values to one feature, marking every lexical item in 20–3 [+CONCRETE], those in 19 [–CONCRETE]. This +/– notation is not simply a terminological economy, but, as we shall see, recognizes the fact that binariness of opposition is an important principle in semantic structure. (In fact, it is one of the chief principles of organization in language in general, and so the +/– feature notation will be found in the chapters on syntax and on phonology, too.)

Now setting aside 19, we see that the lexical items in 20 differ from all of those in 21–3: they must be marked [– ORGANIC], all the items in 21–3 containing the plus value [+ ORGANIC]. Then the [± ORGANIC] set breaks down into [– ANIMATE] (21) versus [+ ANIMATE] (22, 23). (A rival analysis would ignore the dimension [+ ORGANIC] and label both 20 and 21 [– ANIMATE], contrasting with the [+ ANIMATE] 22, 23. But this is evidently an insensitive oversimplification, failing to acknowledge a crucial intuitive difference between 20 and 21, and not noticing the close relationship between 21 and 22–3 which is dramatized by such difficult borderline cases as *bug, amoeba, chrysalis*.) Next, 22 and 23 obviously divide on the feature [± HUMAN], 23 taking plus value, 22 minus. The whole network of componential relationships may be shown as in Figure 3 overleaf. Invoking only four semantic features, we can reveal a lot of information about the semantic contrasts found in 19–23 (and many more lexical items which could be added to those lists). However, there is still a lot of semantic information which needs to be formalized. Let us look again at 23, which is repeated here, with additions, as 24:

24. girl, cousin, man, woman, grandmother, student, politician, boy, daughter, baby, brother, aunt, nephew, foreman, chairman.

All are [+ HUMAN], but the set displays systematic internal differentiations. (An additional complicating factor which I will not discuss here is that some of the terms are available in [– HUMAN]

57

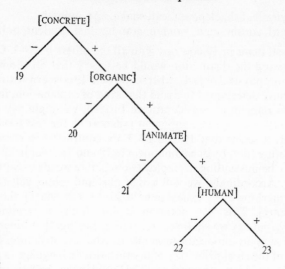

Figure 3

usages: *our cousins the apes, baby panda*, etc.) Of the several new features necessitated by this set, we will notice only [± MALE] and [± ADULT], which yield the following arrangements:

[+ MALE]   man, boy, brother, nephew, ? foreman
[− MALE]   girl, woman, grandmother, aunt
[+ ADULT]   man, woman, grandmother, ? student, politician, foreman, ? chairman
[− ADULT]   girl, ? student, boy, baby

Note that some doubtful cases inevitably arise. I do not know whether a foreman must be a man – are lady foremen called *supervisors* or some other distinctive term? Chairmen, on the other hand, may be male or female; perhaps children may be chairmen, too, in (e.g.) pretend parliaments. The query on *student* in relation to [± ADULT] does not reflect the possibility of disagreement through political prejudice, uncertainty over the legal age of majority, or any other extrinsic questions of that kind: it is a query about linguistic usage. American schoolchildren are called *students*, while in British usage the term is reserved for those engaged in higher education. For the British meaning, we would mark the term [± ADULT], whereas the American sense would be unmarked for [± ADULT] and would therefore have a semantic structure like the similarly unmarked *cousin, daughter, brother, aunt, nephew*. (The biological facts that aunts are often mature and nephews usually juvenile do not

58

impinge on the *semantic* descriptions of these words.) Notice that some of these words are unspecified in respect of the [+ MALE] feature: *cousin, student, politician, chairman*. These lexical items are not intrinsically either [+ MALE] or [− MALE], even though any objects designated by them must be either male or female − further confirmation of the independence of semantic and extra-linguistic facts.

Our new features do not fit neatly into the diagram given for the first four. They apply to both 22 and 23, so the diagram would have to duplicate branches uneconomically at the lower end. Moreover, [± ADULT] and [± MALE] are logically independent of each other − for instance, the first applies to some items in 21 (cf. *sapling, bud, seedling*) but the second, as far as I know, does not. It is not clear how the diagram could be modified to accommodate these new facts: is the primary division of humans governed by sex or by age? Even greater classificatory problems arise as more features are added − as they must be. Although some features, particularly the very general ones first illustrated here, are logically related, it seems that the majority are not; or at least, that any single lexical item is likely to contain components which are not logically linked. This observation leads us to view the lexical structure of a language as comprising a set of distinctive semantic features linked in sub-sets, but the sub-sets not necessarily joined together in one overall network. Then each individual lexical item can be regarded as a 'bundle' of components, each component being a particular value of some general semantic feature; the presence of each individual components linking the item to a particular system of features; and various components in the bundle relating the item to other lexical items, and hence securing its participation in different lexical sets. Moreover, the *kind* of features which relate lexical items componentially will determine the *kinds* of sense-relations holding among the members of lexical sets.

The branching diagram (Figure 3), which is, as we have seen, too demanding logically, professing a neat hierarchy which cannot be maintained in the face of the facts of cross-classification, may conveniently be replaced by a distinctive-feature table (see Table 1, p. 60). The terms in small capitals represent semantic features (not real words); the words along the top are lexical items. Where a feature is relevant to a lexical item, its value is marked as + or −, or ± if either value may obtain. Where a feature is irrelevant, the box is left empty. The semantic components of a particular lexical item are simply the list or 'bundle' below the item in question.

The idea of a lexical item as a 'bundle' of semantic components − values of features − leads naturally to a mode of representation − a

	truth	stone	weed	elephant	man	woman	boy	girl	cousin	nephew	niece
CONCRETE	−	+	+	+	+	+	+	+	+	+	+
ORGANIC		−	+	+	+	+	+	+	+	+	+
ANIMATE			−	+	+	+	+	+	+	+	+
HUMAN				−	+	+	+	+	+	+	+
MALE				±	+	−	+	−	±	+	−
ADULT				±	+	+	−	−	±	±	±

TABLE 1 (NOTE: This is only a cursory illustration. Many more features than the ones mentioned would be necessary to completely distinguish the words in question.)

format for **dictionary entries**. We can simply list the components within square brackets:

25.

man		woman		girl
+ CONCRETE		+ CONCRETE		+ CONCRETE
+ ORGANIC		+ ORGANIC		+ ORGANIC
+ ANIMATE		+ ANIMATE		+ ANIMATE
+ HUMAN		+ HUMAN		+ HUMAN
+ ADULT		+ ADULT		− ADULT
+ MALE		− MALE		− MALE
⋮		⋮		⋮
F_n		F_n		F_n

baby		cousin		nephew
+ CONCRETE		+ CONCRETE		+ CONCRETE
+ ORGANIC		+ ORGANIC		+ ORGANIC
+ ANIMATE		+ ANIMATE		+ ANIMATE
+ HUMAN		+ HUMAN		+ HUMAN
− ADULT		⋮		+ MALE
⋮		F_n		⋮
F_n				F_n

60

The symbol [. . . F_n] at the end of each lexical entry means 'and, in addition, all other components which are necessary to identify the lexical item, down to the nth component'. Obviously, many more components must be listed to make an adequate lexical entry. For instance, we need a component to distinguish the meaning of *grandmother* from that of *woman*; another one to differentiate *nephew* from *uncle*, since both of them, with the minimal componential apparatus we have at our disposal so far, would receive an identical representation; and we need a component showing exactly what kind of a familial relationship is indicated by *cousin*. It is not currently known how detailed this componential analysis might become, how far we might have to go in proposing features of very narrow, perhaps even unique, application. It is clear, though, that a *dictionary entry* is more schematic than a descriptive article in an encyclopaedia: we can know the meaning of the word *elephant* without knowing everything about the anatomy, feeding habits and reproductive mechanism of its potential referents.

One guess about the number of components necessary to define a word, however, is that this will vary in inverse proportion to the generality of reference of the word concerned. Relatively general words like *material, thing, animal, liquid* probably contain few components; more specific words such as *clavichord, kangaroo, paperweight* presumably require a greater number of components for their identification. This prediction rests on assumptions similar to those of logicians who distinguish the **extension** and **intension** of a term. A lexical item of inclusive referentiality (great *extension*) is defined by few criterial attributes (small *intension*); and vice versa.

Before we leave the question of the number of components to be included in a lexical entry, we must notice that, whatever essential components are, through our ignorance, omitted from the representations 25, nevertheless several too many are included. The component [+ HUMAN] implies [+ ANIMATE], [+ ANIMATE] implies [+ ORGANIC], [+ ORGANIC] implies [+ CONCRETE]; so it is necessary to specify [+ HUMAN] only. Wherever components in this sort of logical hierarchy of features occur in a lexical bundle, only the lowest in the hierarchy need be mentioned. This principle is known as a semantic **redundancy rule**: in this case, it reduces the first representation in 25 to 26 (and the others similarly):

26.
$$\begin{bmatrix} \text{man} \\ + \text{HUMAN} \\ + \text{ADULT} \\ + \text{MALE} \\ \vdots \\ F_n \end{bmatrix}$$

Since there is no logical hierarchy among the remaining components, no further reduction is possible.

At the conclusion of this chapter I wish to present various sense-relationships, or kinds of sense-relationships, between lexical items; and we will see that the componential specification of the individual word and the semantic relationships between words are two inter-related aspects of semantic description. Before looking at the various kinds of sense-relation, I should allude to two further questions concerning the status and nature of features and components. So far I have mentioned only features with +/−, either/or, value choices: [+ANIMATE] and [−ANIMATE], etc. I think it is fair to say that, throughout structural and generative linguistics, linguists have been particularly conscious of binary oppositions in language – IC analysis worked by progressive binary segmentation, and such dualities as Subject *versus* Predicate, Singular *versus* Plural, are indeed quite traditional. Linguists have tended to assume that binary structure is an important quality of language in general, of communication and even social structure in general. But there is no absolute reason to expect that all semantic features should have their values structured on a +/− choice. We might suspect that some features have multiple values. For example, multiple values might be needed to differentiate the meanings of whole numbers, or strictly closed sets such as the names of the four seasons, or words arranged on graded scales (e.g. *hot, warm, cold*). My second point concerns a special kind of relational feature, the type of feature which governs the acceptability of certain *combinations* of words in sentences. For instance, *mild* is applied to atmospheric temperature, *tepid* and *lukewarm* to liquids; in addition to establishing that all three words mean 'slightly warm', we must specify their different privileges of co-occurrence. Even more important is the need to specify which types of noun are required by which verbs: it is odder to say 'This stone is growing' than 'This water is mild'. Verbs exercise a stringent control over semantic structure elsewhere in a sentence (e.g. the verb *grow* has a component which demands that its subject be a [+ORGANIC] noun).

Equipped with the above explanations of the nature of semantic components and of lexical entries, we can proceed to explore certain sense-relationships – links and contrasts between lexical items which determine the internal structure of lexical sets and the distinctions between lexical sets. It now appears that a semantic field is defined by a set of lexical items *having components in common*: all the lists 19–24 illustrate (parts of) semantic fields. Note, however, that 'semantic field' is a term of variable scope, like some other linguistic terms (e.g. 'dialect'): a semantic field may be more or less inclusive. We cannot, of course, declare that all the items in 19–23 belong to one single semantic field, since 19 differs from 20–3 at the level of the very general feature [± CONCRETE]. But 20–3 could reasonably be said to form one lexical set, the set of words containing the component [+ CONCRETE], although this may be less convincing, certainly less useful, than some more specific and compact sets:

20 versus 21–3 together, or
20 versus 21 versus 22–3 together, or
20 versus 21 versus 22 versus 23.

In fact, semantic analysis is likely to be concerned with smaller fields still – that is to say, with lexical sets the members of which share a large number of semantic components (have great intension). Some interesting sub-fields of 20 might be

27. drill, lathe, press, hammer, rivet-gun, welding-torch, wrench, spanner, screwdriver
28. racquet, golf-club, billiard-cue, cricket-bat, hockey-stick (plus many other derived words formed with *-stick* and *-bat*).

And some divisions of the field partially illustrated in 23:

29. plumber, electrician, joiner, bricklayer, decorator, gas fitter, motor mechanic
30. captain, manager, leader, boss, director, headmaster, superintendent, president.

Here I can only appeal to the reader's intuition of the relatedness of the items in these lists (and of the distinctiveness of the lists one from another); but these divisions are certainly formalizable in terms of the componential principles outlined above.

As soon as we come down to relatively exclusive lexical sets like those illustrated in 27–30, we find that most lexical items belong to more than one lexical set. The explanation for this multiple membership is obvious: each lexical entry is a bundle of many components, and any one of these components, or more usually a set of components, may be selected as the criterial indicator of a semantic field. For instance, the word *woman* is included in list 23 because it contains the component [+ HUMAN]. If we ignore [+ HUMAN] the word falls into a set containing the following items, among others:

31. woman, cow, ewe, vixen, mare, doe, bitch.

The criterion for the set 31 is common possession of the bundle of components [+ ANIMATE, + ADULT, − MALE]; if we reduce the intension by dropping [+ ADULT], the list can be expanded to include also *girl, lass, daughter, princess*, etc., words which either specifically exclude [+ ADULT] or do not demand it. (The number of words which demand the combination [− MALE, − ADULT] or [+ MALE, − ADULT] is quite small, since immature animals are rarely distinguished for sex, cf. *cub, baby, piglet, chicken*, etc.)

The list of words in 31 may be almost symmetrically matched by a complementary list 32:

32.　man, bull, ram, fox, stallion, buck, dog.

The symmetry is not quite complete because *man, fox* and *dog* may be either specifically [+ MALE] or unmarked for sex. In symmetrical usages, a particular kind of sense-relationship is exhibited:

33.　ram : ewe.

We must now consider the various kinds of sense-relationship found between particular lexical items; here are some more pairs:

34.　girl : lass
35.　red : smooth
36.　red : green
37.　red : crimson
38.　wet : dry
39.　tall : short
40.　buy : sell.

The pair 34 is intended to illustrate the lexical relationship of **synonymy** or sameness of sense. Synonymous pairs of lexical items are notoriously difficult to find, and many linguists have denied that synonymy is a real characteristic of natural language. It is alleged that the exact meaning of a word depends on its context, and that all contexts are unique; that differences of tone, dialect and so on inevitably cause differences of meaning (*lass* would occur in a different dialect situation, etc.). But a *definition* of synonymy is available, in terms of the above componential framework: two lexical items are synonymous if their lexical entries contain the same components and no distinct components. Furthermore, we have a reliable test for synonymy which depends on the presence of certain implicational relationships between sentences which differ only in that one has one of a pair of suspected synonyms as a constituent, the other the other:

41.　John is a bachelor.
42.　John is an unmarried man.

If 41 is true, then the truth of 42 cannot be denied; and vice versa. Symbolically, $41 \supset 42$ and $42 \supset 41$ – the sentences imply each other reciprocally, and in such cases of bi-directional implication we may say that the sentences are synonymous and that therefore the lexical items which distinguish their surface structures are synonymous.

I shall say no more about synonymy at the moment. But the apparatus of logical implication which has been introduced by way of this concept will serve us further in distinguishing between the other kinds of sense-relationships exemplified in 35–40.

The pair 35 (*red* : *smooth*) provides an instance of mere difference of sense. Componentially the two items have virtually nothing in common – they both communicate perceptual qualities, but in very different perceptual modes. Implicationally, the two statements 'X is red' and 'X is smooth' (where X = X) are compatible (something may be both red and smooth), but the two items are not synonymous because they are not *necessarily* both applicable to one X. Now compare 36 (*red* : *green*) with 35. If X is red, it cannot be true that the same X is green (and vice versa). *Red* and *green* are componentially incompatible: *red* ⊃ not-*green* and *green* ⊃ not-*red*. These two words are not merely different in sense, their senses are mutually exclusive. The same sense-relationship holds between the members of the set 29 (*plumber, electrician*, etc.). If X is appropriately described as a plumber, he cannot be designated an electrician, at least if 'plumber' is offered as a *sufficient* characterization of X; and the same lexical incompatibility holds between any two members of the set 29. Now there is one difference between 29 and the set of colour-terms from which *red* and *green* are taken, i.e.

43. red, green, blue, orange, violet, brown, purple, white, etc.

All the words in 29 are special instances of a general category for which there is a superordinate term: *craftsman* or, archaically, *artisan*. The set 43 does not have a superordinate. *Coloured* will not do, since it is possible to assert that X is e.g. brown or white but deny that it is coloured; whereas you cannot assert that X is a joiner and simultaneously deny that he is a craftsman, at least in the descriptive, non-evaluative sense of *craftsman*. Where a set of terms is provided with a superordinate, they are said to be **co-hyponyms** of that superordinate; and a special implicational link holds between a superordinate and any one of its hyponyms. 37 (*red* : *crimson*) is a pair of terms linked in this way. If X is crimson, it is red; but if X is red, it is not necessarily crimson (it may be scarlet or vermilion, etc.). Implication works only one way: a hyponym implies its superordinate, but not the other way around. To repeat, if X is a joiner, it is implied that X is a craftsman; but to say that X is a craftsman is not to commit oneself to the necessity of labelling him a wheelwright, or a french polisher, etc.

The pair 38 (*wet* : *dry*) is more like 36 (*red* : *green*) than anything we have cited so far, but it differs from the examples discussed up to this point, including 36, in that *wet* and *dry* are 'opposites' semantically. So are the pairs 39 and 40, but in each case the 'oppositeness' is of a distinctive kind; again, the distinctions appear in the implicational relationships between propositions containing the terms concerned. Recall that in the case of 36, the proposition 'X is red' implied 'X is not green', and 'X is green' implied 'X is not red'; similarly with 38 'X is dry' implies 'X is not wet', while 'X is wet' implies 'X is not dry'. But additional implicational tests may be applied. Whereas 'X is not wet' implies 'X is dry', and 'X is not dry' implies 'X is wet', it is not the case that 'X is not red' implies 'X is green' (it may be blue), nor does 'X is not green' imply 'X is red' (it may be yellow). *Wet/dry* is one instance of a semantic relationship between two-term lexical sets which between them exhaust the descriptions which are available in a particular semantic field. Other examples are: *well/ill*; *married/single*; *male/female*; *full/empty*; *on/off*; *dead/alive*; *broken/unbroken*, etc. In all these cases, if the judgment is at all appropriate to an object, that object *must* be in one or the other state – there are no intermediate terms. Such pairs exhibit the sense-relationship called **complementarity**; it is quite different from 'difference of sense' (35), from incompatibility (29, 36) in which the set has more than two members – and, indeed, no natural limit to the number of members – and from **antonymy**, a further kind of 'oppositeness' which is exhibited by 39 (*tall/short*) and by many other such pairs. The implications which hold between the members of antonymous pairs are distinctive. If X is tall, he is not short; but if he is not tall, it is not necessarily the case that he is short; if he is not short, it does not follow that he is tall, although if he is short, he cannot be described as tall. There are many other examples of antonymous pairs, mostly concerned with the measurement or evaluation of experiences: *wide/narrow*; *good/bad*; *loud/quiet*; *hard/soft*, etc. The characteristic of antonyms is that they are **gradable**: X may be moderately soft, quite narrow, of medium height, and so on. Moreover, the terms in antonymous pairs do not designate absolute values, but make implicit reference to a conventional norm for the class of objects to which they are applied. Thus sentences such as the often-cited 44 below are not self-contradictory:

44.   A small elephant is a large animal.

'An elephant which is smaller than the size-norm for elephants is nevertheless larger than the size-norm for animals in general.' This paraphrase brings out the fact that the terms of antonymous pairs are implicitly *comparative*; those of complementaries are not – a light switch may not be more or less 'on'; it must be either 'on' or 'off'.

(However, many complementaries may have special usages imposed on them in which they are made to serve as antonyms: in certain contexts we might want to say that 'X is more married (more alive, etc.) than Y'. This fact does not undermine the criterion of non-gradability of complementaries: it means only that some pairs are *either* complementaries *or* antonyms, the latter characterization recognizing a 'special' secondary use of terms which are primarily complementaries.)

Finally, the pair 40 (*buy* : *sell*) represents yet another kind of 'oppositeness':

45. John bought the car from Harry.
46. Harry sold the car to John.

Buy and *sell* (likewise *give* and *receive*, etc.) are called **converses**. They are a very interesting class of 'opposites' – actually, it is rather misleading to regard them as 'opposites' like *tall* and *short*, *wet* and *dry*, etc. Converses might well be thought of as being synonymous. *Buy* and *sell* actually contain the same elements – the changing hands of goods and (in the reverse direction) of money, and two participants one of whom is recipient with respect to the money and parts with the goods, while the other parts with money and receives the goods. Typically, converses allow the description of a single event or process from two different angles, focusing on the participants in different ways. They are thus like the active–passive correspondence, where the same verb is used in conjunction with a varying syntax; cf.

47. John was sold the car by Harry.

(and consider other possibilities provided by these terms). The changes of syntax signal a kind of semantic difference which we have not so far encountered, not a semantic difference between words but one involving the different **roles** of participants in an action. This aspect of meaning will be a major preoccupation in the next chapter, in which componential meaning will be included within a broader semantic framework as we consider the meanings of propositions, not just simple lexical items.

It must be confessed that the current state of semantic research is more speculative than formal. Very few lexical sets have been explored carefully and in detail, and those which have been studied have usually been sets of words with self-evident and simple systemic connections: kinship terminologies, plant taxonomies, and so on. Once we stray outside these rigidly formalized bounds into the general vocabulary of a language, we are forced at the moment to offer semantic features of an *ad hoc*, and therefore sometimes less than plausible, character. Idiosyncratic features would be justifiable in a referential theory of meaning, where a suggested component could answer to some particular referent: we could tolerate components such as [+ LEFT HIND LEG OF A ZEBRA]. A semantic theory which spawned such components would obviously be trivial and anarchic. The best protection against such arbitrariness is to propose wherever possible semantic features which (a) relate to each other in a systematic way (e.g. the features [± ANIMATE, ± ORGANIC] which are hierarchically related); (b) allow lexical items to be associated in a systematic way (e.g. by providing grounds for a formal conception of *antonymy, complementarity*, etc.); (c) make available relationships which are discoverable in more than one language. The last of these criteria is particularly important. Contemporary semantic analysts assert that semantic features are abstract, reference-free, and universal: if they represent anything, they represent categories of conceptual disposition fundamental to the human mind. Thus we ought to be peculiarly attentive to whatever evidence issues from comparative language study that different speech-communities tend to structure their experience in comparable ways.

Further reading

An excellent collection of important papers which supplements my chapters 3 and 4 is Steinberg and Jakobovits, *Semantics*. See especially Howard Maclay's 'Overview', pp. 157–82, a historical account of recent linguistic theory (with emphasis on semantics), which will supplement the latter part of chapter 2, above.

No mention is made in chapter 3 of traditional accounts of meaning-changes, for which see Bréal, *Semantics*; Stern, *Meaning and Change of Meaning*.

Ogden and Richards, *Meaning of Meaning*, is worth reading not only for the 'semantic triangle' but also for their discussions of the general nature of signs and of the terminological confusion surrounding the term 'meaning'. Stephen Ullmann's *Semantics* is the most sensible modern discussion and adaptation of referential theory.

Frege's paper on *Sinn* and *Bedeutung* is translated as 'On sense and reference'. Some other important papers on semantics by philosophers are to be found in Parkinson, *Theory of Meaning* (which contains a clear and informative editor's introduction).

Componential analysis was initiated by anthropological linguists in the 1950s, but restricted to specialized, and obviously highly schematic, taxonomic lexical sets. An attempt to extend the principles to the study of less specialized vocabulary is Bendix, *Componential*

Analysis. Katz and Fodor's 'Structure of a semantic theory', followed by several papers by Katz, was a controversial but influential attempt to accommodate componential analysis within the transformational-generative framework. See Weinreich's critique, 'Explorations in semantic theory'. My observations on the structure of lexical entries follow Chomsky's in *Aspects*. More recently, Manfred Bierwisch has offered some excellent papers based on the Katz–Chomsky model; see, for instance, his chapter in Lyons, *New Horizons*.

My account of sense-relationships draws heavily on the ideas of Lyons, to be found in his *Structural Semantics* and in chapters 9 and 10 of *Theoretical Linguistics* – probably the clearest and most reliable introduction to the general tenets of semantic theory. Another stimulating work which explores componential relationships within the general framework of logical implications among propositions is Leech, *Towards a Semantic Description of English*.

On p. 54 above (discussing colour terms and perceptual distinctions) I referred briefly to the *linguistic relativity hypothesis*, the theory that the structure of our language determines the perceptual and conceptual discriminations available to us. Since I will not take up this fascinating thesis elsewhere in this book readers may appreciate some references. The theory is advanced by Benjamin Lee Whorf in several of his papers collected in *Language, Thought, and Reality*; for some level-headed discussion, see Brown, *Words and Things* and Carroll, *Language and Thought*.

four

Words within sentences

I began chapter 3 by pointing out that although words, or 'lexical items', are of major importance in determining the semantic content of sentences – as speakers feel them to be – nevertheless they are not the sole determinants of the meaning of sentences. Other kinds of semantic factor collaborate with words in endowing sentences with meaning: further 'dimensions' of meaning and also compositional processes, modes of relating words in sentences. By the end of chapter 3 we had seen that words are not even semantic primitives, not even for that kind of meaning ('sense') which is given by words: that they may be 'atomized' into abstract components, values of semantic features; in turn, these semantic features map out the structure of the vocabulary as a whole. The technique of atomization (componential analysis) ignores the links between words and things, studying instead 'the relations between words and words' (p. 49 above).

So far we have studied only a limited range of inter-word relationships. We now have to recognize that such relationships are found on two axes, which we shall call **paradigmatic** and **syntagmatic** or 'vertical' and 'horizontal' respectively. The previous chapter was concerned ostensibly with paradigmatic relations only: ties between lexical items seen in the context of the vocabulary as a whole, ignoring the links between words found on the horizontal plane in actual sentences. (The term 'paradigm' is almost equivalent to our 'lexical set'; the notion derives from syntax, and will be familiar to readers who have learnt foreign languages from formal printed grammars where the inflexional forms of noun and verb declensions and conjugations are set out in vertical paradigms on the page.) In this chapter we will concentrate on the other, i.e. syntagmatic, relationship, the horizontal link between lexical items in fully formed sentences. As we study syntagmatic forms of organization, however, we must remember that paradigmatic and syntagmatic facts are interdependent. This interdependence may be illustrated by the sentence-types which logicians call **contradictory, tautologous** and **analytic**. In each case we will see that the characterization as a certain kind of sentence depends on a particular (syntagmatic) coupling of lexical items which, outside the sentence, enjoy a particular componential (hence paradigmatic) relationship. For instance, the words *nun* and *grandfather* belong to the same lexical set, that defined by the component [+ HUMAN]. This paradigmatic kinship is reflected in their free interchangeability in many contexts:

48. The patient was a $\begin{Bmatrix} \text{nun} \\ \text{grandfather} \end{Bmatrix}$

But they are distinguished within the paradigm by containing components which are mutually exclusive values of the feature [+ MALE]. So certain syntagmatic couplings produce contradictoriness:

49. The nun was a grandfather.

Now consider the words *grandfather* and *man*. Because they are not divided on any contradiction-producing feature, 50 below is a perfectly grammatical, and logically non-anomalous, sentence:

50. The man was a grandfather.

But 51 is tautologous:

51. The grandfather was a man.

The predicate *man* adds nothing to the meaning of *grandfather*, since all the components of *man* − [+ HUMAN, + MALE, + ADULT] − are already present in *grandfather*. These components are redundantly duplicated by the predication of *man*. But in 50, predicating *grandfather* of *man* does not produce a tautology, since new components are added which are not intrinsically present in the subject *man*. The explanation of the syntagmatic difference between 50 and 51, we see, has to take account of componential factors. *Grandfather* is a hyponym of *man*, so it seems that one form of tautology at least can be described as 'the predication of a superordinate term of one of its hyponyms'. Notice that the definition makes combined reference to a paradigmatic relationship (superordinate-hyponym) and a syntagmatic structure (predication).

In fact, the definition needs to be made a bit more complicated than this. 52, which would be tautologous by our definition, is not actually so:

52. A grandfather is a man.

Here a superordinate is predicated of one of its hyponyms without tautology. This is an analytic sentence: one which is self-evidently true by virtue of the meanings of the words as they are joined together in a particular syntagmatic fashion. An analytic sentence is one way of providing a 'definition' of a hyponym term. (Other kinds of sentences, which may or not be definitionally useful, are **synthetically** rather than analytically true, i.e. true by virtue of empirical fact rather than linguistic structure:

53.   An elephant has four legs.)

Clearly the characterization of a tautology is deficient if it fails to capture the distinction between 51 and 52. We can mend the definition by taking notice of further dimensions of linguistic structure which affect meaning and sentence-type. First, there is a difference of **quantification** between *the grandfather* of 51 and *a grandfather* of 52. In the former a particular individual from the class of referents designated by *grandfather* is being talked about; in the latter the proposition applies to any instance and all instances of grandfathers. Connected with this difference of quantification there is a difference of **modality** between the two sentences (on modality see pp. 8–9 above, pp. 118–21 below). 51 refers, presumably, to an actual state in the past; but 52 is a generic proposition, a universal truth applicable to any time (it would be misleading to consider the word *is* in 52 a simple marker of present tense – in relation to universal quantification, it conveys much more complex information than that). Factors such as these have to be taken into account in describing the meanings of sentences, and in classifying them into types, as well as componential content and syntagmatic structural relationships such as predication.

Analyticity, contradiction and tautology would be regarded normally as territory of the logician rather than the linguist. But they are certainly semantic properties of sentences, as well as logical properties of ill-formed propositions – a judgment which is not intended to steal these properties from the logicians, but to suggest that logic and linguistics coincide in their interest in one aspect of semantic ordering. When we talk about 'sentences', we might most conveniently refer to the whole semantic–syntactic–phonetic complex as described by the linguist; and ideally, I should have chosen some less inclusive term in the title of this chapter, which is concerned with only the semantic part of this complex. In the latter part of the chapter I will be treating syntagmatic patterns in semantics using a method which recalls the philosopher's analysis in terms of **predicates** and **arguments**. Contemporary semantics – in one of the most impressive recent 'schools', anyway – suggests that the elementary semantic syntagms may turn out to be the same as the logician's **propositions,** or at least that propositions play a nuclear role in semantic structure. Additionally, researches such as those of Geoffrey Leech and John Lyons (see p. 69 above) demonstrate that logical considerations are relevant to determining certain types of sense-relationships between lexical items. For my immediate purpose, analyticity, contradiction and tautology serve to illustrate the intersection of the paradigmatic and syntagmatic axes in semantics, and to move us from the former to the latter: the 'horizontal' dimension of semantic structure is the concern of this chapter. The logical combinability of lexical items is one topic in syntagmatic semantics, but we will look at other aspects of the linear structure at the semantic level and consider wider questions of meaningfulness and meaninglessness.

On p. 62 above I mentioned that there are co-occurrence rules which specify the acceptability or non-acceptability of combinations of lexical items. I instanced the oddness of locutions such as 'This stone is growing' and 'This water is mild', pointing out that the first is more deviant than the second, or deviant in a different way. I now return to this question for more detailed discussion. Examples 54–62, listed below, are either nonsensical or semantically odd to some lesser degree. This is not to say that they would not occur in real linguistic performance – indeed, many of them exhibit semantic effects which are common in poetry, ironic discourse and some kinds of joke. When such sentences do occur (where they are not simply mistakes), they are deliberate constructions whose rhetorical impact depends on the audience's recognition of their oddity and on its skill in making something out of the oddity.

54. The cake is slightly delicious.
55. John constructed.
56. The truck weighed a politician.
57. This desk has eaten three mushrooms.
58. Peter frightened a stone.
59. Water does not mix.
60. The dog scattered.
61. The dog shattered.
62. John smashed a piece of paper.

I have included 54 (taken from Weinreich) for the sake of continuity with our earlier discussion. It is a contradiction, but the contradictoriness has a different kind of origin from that of 49 (*The nun was a grandfather*). 49 is a contradictory assertion because the two nouns contain incompatible values of the same semantic feature. In the case of 54, an absolute quality (*delicious*) is predicated of the subject (*the cake*); but the assertion is subverted by the quantifying adverb *slightly.* A more dramatic example would be *slightly frozen solid. Delicious, frozen, square, wooden, destroyed,* etc., share some semantic quality which makes them decline quantification or modification. Contrast *salty, warm, rough, flexible, deformed,* all of which can be modified by words such as *quite, very, rather, slightly.* It seems as though there is some regularity here which ought to be captured in a semantic description, by marking each of the two classes of adjectives with an appropriate feature showing whether or not it accepts quantification. If we were to look at more examples of adjectives, we would become increasingly impressed with the regularity of the semantic facts involved – and their complexity, for we would realize that there is not just one distinction relevant to this data, but several: note that *tall* accepts *rather* but not *slightly*; that colour terms are ambiguous as between absolute and relative senses: *red* ought to be like *delicious* – something is either red or not – but we can also say *very red, quite red,* etc. As we bring more and more material to this set of distinctions, we realize that what at first appeared to be a peculiarity of *delicious* is the outcrop of a systematic regularity in the semantics of adjectives.

My use of the ill-formed sequences 54–62 is meant to provoke the sort of reflections which I have briefly illustrated with 54. We are to enquire into the conditions which make each particular example deviant, what changes would restore its well-formedness; at the same time, it is helpful to think about further examples to which the same observations pertain. Since the examples 54–62 illustrate a quite diversified range of problems and solutions, this procedure will allow us to survey several distinct facets of semantic structure.

The fault with 55 (*John constructed*) is that the verb lacks an object: you cannot just *construct* (as you can *sleep, laugh, die,* etc.); you must construct *something.* So the verb must contain, not only whatever components are needed to define its semantic content – *construct* as opposed to *build, destroy, plan,* etc. – but also a component which dictates that a noun phrase must follow. Such a component might be symbolized thus:

[__NP]

The lowered dash __ (*not* a minus sign) indicates the place where the verb goes in a syntagm; 'NP' to the right of the dash symbolizes the necessity of a noun phrase after the verb. This notation is included in the lexical entry for every verb of the traditional category 'transitive'. Its omission indicates 'intransitive' (*sleep,* etc.). (There is a third category of verbs which may be followed by objects or may have the object deleted: *read, eat,* etc.; the lexical entry must contain the component [__NP] and a *further* component indicating that the *NP* may be deleted – thus true intransitives such as *sleep* are distinguished from pseudo-intransitives such as *eat*.) The error in 56 (*The truck weighed a politician*) involves more complicated syntagmatic constraints. *Weigh* here means 'determine the weight of'. We can tell that it has this meaning because the *NP* after the verb is not a unit of weight; cf. *the truck weighed three tons*. Only humans can perform the action of weighing: thus the verb must contain, in addition to the components which specify its lexical meaning, a component which requires a particular kind of noun phrase as subject – symbolically, with the lowered dash meaning the same as before, [[+ HUMAN]__]. The other meaning of *weigh*, 'have the weight of', tolerates a subject designating any kind of physical object; both *The truck weighed three tons* and *The politician weighed 200 pounds* are fully grammatical. So the subject-specifying component, for this sense of the verb, is [[+ CONCRETE]__]. But in this case the *object* has to be specified exactly within the verb: [__[UNIT OF WEIGHT]]. Now the verb in 57 (*This desk has eaten three mushrooms*) is less demanding than the first 'weigh', more so than the second: its subject must be animate, but can be either human (*boy*) or non-human (*dog*). The selectional component for kind of subject incorporated in *eat* must be [[+ ANIMATE]__]. Similarly, the evidence of 58 (*Peter frightened a stone*) and of such sentences as *Peter frightened a boy* and *Peter frightened a dog* is that *frighten* contains an object-restricting component [__[+ ANIMATE]]. This component of course rules out not only 58 but 63 also:

63.   Peter frightened imagination

where the object is [– CONCRETE] and the selectional component [__[+ ANIMATE]] necessarily implies [+ CONCRETE].

59 (*Water does not mix*) and 60 (*The dog scattered*) exhibit failure of another kind of selectional link between words. The predicate *mix* in one of its senses (like *collide, meet, unite*, etc.) demands a subject with two or more nouns denoting objects or entities engaged in some joint process or action entailing combined participation. (Notice that negation of a proposition containing a 'combine-type' verb which is anomalous conjoined with a single subject does not mend the anomaly.) 60 (*The dog scattered*) is slightly different, but its fault falls under the same general kind of explanation as does that of 59. Here, the verb *scatter* requires, not a conjunction of nouns acting, or being acted upon, in combination, but a noun phrase denoting a simple plurality of objects engaging in a multiparticipant action or process which does not, however, entail co-operative participation (cf. *gather, assemble, disperse*, etc.). The interesting difference in the selectional requirements of the predicates in 59 and 60 from those of 56–8 is this. In 56–8 the semantic components of the verbs clash with those of specific nouns (or, more accurately, with instances of specific sub-categories

of noun). If the noun alone is changed in the required way (*This boy has eaten three sandwiches*, etc.), the sentence becomes acceptable. In 59 and 60 it is not the semantic character of the actual subject nouns which is at fault but the **quantification** imposed on the nouns. Quantification (about which more will be said in the next chapter) is the addition to nouns – all nouns, compulsorily – of non-lexical semantic components which modify their meaning in various ways. The nouns in the subjects of 51 and 52 (the sentences about the grandfather p. 71 above) were quantified differently: the first is understood as denoting a particular grandfather, the second as applying to all grandfathers. We may formalize this distinction by adding to the nouns the distinct components [+ DEFINITE] and [+ UNIVERSAL] respectively (*the grandfather* in 51 being implicitly [– UNIVERSAL] also). Another difference in quantification underlies the distinction between the ungrammatical 60 and its well-formed counterpart:

64. The dogs scattered.

Evidently the verb *scatter* requires its subject to be quantified [+ PLURAL] (and it is also [+ DEFINITE] here, incidentally). *The dog*, or *the grandfather*, is marked [– PLURAL] and therefore should not appear as subject of *scatter*. Now if we look at 59 (*Water does not mix*) again, we see that *mix* also demands a multiple subject; but we remember that the objects designated by the subject are in a semantic relationship of a kind more intimate than is conveyed by the notion of 'plurality' which is appropriate to 64. In recognition of this, we might assign some component such as [COMBINED] to the noun(s) associated with *mix*. It appears from these data that the English language possesses a number system which is more complicated than appears on the surface. It is too early to do more than make tentative suggestions at this stage, but an analysis somewhat as follows seems called for: a noun must be either singular or plural; if it is plural, its *denotata* are in either a 'combined' or a 'simple plural' (which might be called 'disjunctive') relationship. (The componential notation above does not quite convey this arrangement.) This quantificational difference between kinds of plural is relevant to interesting ambiguities of the type concealed beneath surface structures such as

65. The students bought the new book

which means either 'each of the students bought a copy of the book' or 'the students clubbed together and bought one copy of the book between them'.

One final observation which emerges from this digression on quantification concerns the status of the term 'noun phrase' (*NP*) which was introduced on p. 74 above. 'Noun' is a lexical category,

or part-of-speech in traditional wording. We have now seen that
nouns do not appear in sentences as mere lexical items, simple
bundles assembled by selecting from the semantic components
provided by the lexicon: in sentences, they are attended by non-
lexical components also. This non-lexical element is obligatory:
all nouns must be quantified. This is true even where no overt sign
of quantification appears in surface structure; for instance, the subject of

66.   Man is mortal

though showing no article before the noun and no suffix tacked on to
it, is none the less quantified: this is a general statement about men –
'all men and any man'. In analysis the word would have to be
assigned an appropriate component, or be accompanied by an
additional abstract constituent, to make this meaning clear. A
display such as the following would be suitable:

67. $\begin{bmatrix} - \text{PL} \\ + \text{UNIV} \end{bmatrix} + \begin{bmatrix} \text{man} \\ + \text{HUMAN} \\ \vdots \\ F_n \end{bmatrix}$

This analysis makes it clear that, since *man* in 66 contains a quantificational element as well as a lexical element, it is an *NP*, not a
simple *N*.

Our final examples of deviant sentences in the list on p. 73 –
61 and 62 – will allow us to return our focus to verbs. I will repeat
the sentences here for ease of reference:

61.   The dog shattered.
62.   John smashed a piece of paper.

The verbs in these examples make very exacting demands on the
nouns associated with them. Both convey the sense that a change of
state from 'whole' to 'destroyed' is suffered by some physical thing.
So a selectional component [__[+ CONCRETE]] at least is required.
But more delicate discrimination is needed, for *shatter* and *smash* are
relatively fussy about the things they apply to, in contrast to the
more general verbs of destruction *destroy* and *break*. Only a rigid,
brittle substance such as glass can shatter – certainly not a soft
organic body like a dog. Thus the lexical entry for *shatter* must make
reference to the kind of substance which is subject to that form of
destruction. A similar criterion – the kind of material destroyed –
is applicable in the componential representation of the verbs *melt,
burn, dissolve, crumble*, etc. By contrast, the shape or style of construction of an object, rather than the material out of which it is

formed, seems to be criterial for the meaning of *smash*. Manifest three-dimensionality is called for: to suffer the fate of being smashed, an object must have reasonable extension in all three dimensions (e.g. be cube-shaped), must be not very densely compacted (e.g. not a solid block of metal), and perhaps be constructed from many parts (e.g. a car). To smash something is to deform its shape and upset the integration of its component parts. A piece of paper does not have characteristics which would permit its destruction or deformation to be described appropriately as 'being smashed'. In particular, a piece of paper is very thin in relation to its other two measurements: sheet-like objects of this kind are more commonly described as *torn*, *cut* or *ripped* (especially cloth).

For *smash* and *shatter*, then, we must devise lexical entries which specify very precisely the kinds of objects which may suffer these processes. At the same time, noun specifications must include components which indicate in some considerable detail their shape, mode of construction, physical constituents and density. Readers may imagine just how various the demands of these change of state verbs are, and what corresponding precision is required in the lexical entries for nouns, by working out informally the semantic expectations of the following assortment:

68.   slice, crush, shred, flatten, splinter, fragment, crumple, bend, fold, twist, warp, atomize, solidify, crack.

With examples of the kind listed in 68 we have come to consider semantic facts of a very delicate nature. It will be realized, I hope, that units of meaning can be characterized at different levels of generality: the selectional restrictions proposed in the last few pages have been very specific; other components which are necessary to identify particular lexical items may be of more particular application still; and at the other extreme, semantic components must be entertained which are very generally applicable, very inclusive. For instance, the list 68 can be regarded as a gathering of verbs with *similar* properties as well as a collection of items with distinctive, perhaps even idiosyncratic, characteristics, as they were first offered. What do they have in common? I labelled them 'change of state' verbs, and it is that kind of highly general semantic characterization which must now receive our attention. (*Note*: the discussion which follows is more speculative than anything else in this book, since it reports, no doubt imperfectly, on issues which are at the heart of current controversy in theoretical linguistics. Also, it is heavily dependent on the ideas of Chafe, Fillmore and Lakoff – ideas which are themselves admitted to be very tentative – expounded in the works cited at the end of this chapter.)

In the last few pages **verbs** have been increasingly the focus of attention. These items do seem to have a special status in semantic structure. For one thing, their senses seem to be determinable largely in terms of the nouns which are expected to accompany them: *shatter* is 'a mode of destruction which is suffered by objects made of rigid, brittle materials'. In other words, the syntagmatic associations of verbs are more important to the sense of verbs than are their paradigmatic positions; by contrast, the senses of nouns were discussed in chapter 3 from an almost exclusively paradigmatic perspective. The verb seems to be the really essential element in the semantic syntagm: we have sentences (e.g. imperatives) consisting of a verb only – *Go!, March!*, etc. – but sentences consisting of, say, a noun by itself would seem very odd indeed. Another interesting pointer to the centrality of verbs is that they are inflected for aspects of meaning which seem to concern the sentence as a whole, not just its verb: for instance, 69 below is apprehended as a whole statement about past time; it would be ridiculous to assert that only the verb is 'past', the *NP*s not:

69. I listened to the radio.

The 'pastness' of the proposition seems to radiate from the verb and take in the whole of the sentence. But the inflexional information in particular *NP*s is restricted to them alone, and is not a general property of the sentence, as is evident from the fact that two *NP*s in the same sentence can be quantified quite differently without contradiction:

70. Many children have profited from this course.

Finally, verbs seem to exercise a considerable influence over our interpretation of the nouns which occur with them. Suppose we were asked to make some sort of sense of the anomalous 61 (*The dog shattered*). We would not search for a metaphorical meaning of *shatter* which might be appropriate to dogs, but would rather devise a meaning for *the dog* which would allow the utterance to be interpreted: a model dog made out of china, a dog in a Tom and Jerry cartoon. More serious evidence for the influence of verbs on our interpretation of sentences comes from sentence-pairs such as the following:

71. He's reviewing the book.
72. He's writing the book.

We understand from 71 that the book exists; from 72 that it still has to come into existence. Traditional grammatical theory was conscious of this difference and explained it by positing two different kinds of syntactic object manifested in what was only superficially the same phrase (*the book*); but it seems more true to the linguistic facts to attribute the difference to expectations controlled by the verbs. That which is being reviewed is reasonably expected to exist, whereas that which is being written cannot be construed as yet existing.

The above examples lead us on to scrutinize our usage of the term 'verb' further. The remarks on the full sentence 71 apply equally to the phrase *his review of the book*. Since *review* here is, in part-of-speech terminology, a 'noun', not a 'verb', it seems that my comments on the semantic status of 'verbs' in sentences do not, strictly speaking, apply to verbs as such: in fact, they concern abstract, very inclusive, semantic units which are most typically, but not inevitably, realized in surface structure as verbs. These deep structure units are often called **predicates** or **predicators**. The term 'predicate' has been used a number of times above; at this stage we must try to develop its precision in order to indicate a crucial concept in our development of semantic theory.

The term 'predicate' is used in both linguistics and philosophy, and in both disciplines it appears in two distinct senses. First, it is applied to the whole of a simple sentence except the left-most *NP*:

73.   The three terrorists *hi-jacked the airliner*.

Alternatively, its application may be restricted to the 'verbal' part of a sentence only:

74.   The children *broke* the window.

(My definitions are phrased to apply to English, of course; details need to be changed for other languages, but the principle can be preserved.) In recent linguistics it is coming to be realized that semantic analysis is more revealing if it builds on the second use of the term. The fact that the object (*the airliner, the window*) is more closely linked to the verb than is the subject lends support to the first analysis; this closeness is reflected in sentences like

75.   The three terrorists did

(in reply to a question *who hi-jacked the airliner?*) where *did* replaces the whole of the verb-object sequence, not just the verb. But we can quite properly claim that predicate-phrases such as *hi-jacked the airliner* are constructed on the basis of simple predicates serving as nuclei.

Every sentence communicates a state of affairs in which a set of objects, or concepts, are found in a certain relationship. For instance, a thing may be described as in a particular location (*The book is on the table*); an event may be said to take place at a certain time (*The demonstration occurs at eleven o'clock*); one person may do something to another (*Bill kicked Peter*); something may undergo a change of state (*The flowers wilted*); and so on. It is predicates which are responsible for delineating the various relationships which obtain between objects or between concepts – these objects and concepts being symbolized by the nouns in a sentence, of course. So we can propose a classification of predicates according to the kinds of relationships that they impose on the nouns which may be syntagmatically linked to them. In a formal grammar this classification would be expressed in terms of components included within the lexical entries for individual predicates; but since the analysis is bound to be very tentative, in our present state of semantic knowledge, I shall not suggest components here, but merely mention some informal categories of predicate.

Some predicates indicate that an associated noun is in a certain **state**:

76. John is tall.
77. This coat is dry.
78. Peter was weak.
79. The house smells.

The stative character of these predicates can be confirmed by submitting them to certain transformational tests. They do not take the imperative mood (**Be dry!*); they are not appropriate answers to questions of the form *What did X do?* or *What happened to X?*; in general they cannot be turned into progressive aspect (**John is being tall*). The failure of the imperative, the progressive and the *do*-question tests reveals that these predicates do not communicate **actions**. Action predicates are a separate class:

80. She laughed.
81. The children were being aggressive.
82. The animals scattered.

The predicates in all the above three sentences pass the imperative, progressive and *do*-question tests – including 81, underlining the point that the verb is not the only word-class which can function as a predicate. But, like 76–9, these sentences fail the test which requires adequate answers to questions containing *happen*. A third type of predicate, indicating **processes**, fulfils this criterion:

83. John became tall.
84. The coat dried.
85. The road widened.
86. Churchill died.

Notice that each *state* predicate has a process corresponding to it. This correspondence is manifested in double service by the same lexical item (*dry/dry*) or in an adjective paired with the same lexical item plus a process-forming suffix (*wide/widen*) or in a pair consisting of an adjective and an adjective with *become, grow* or *get* (*tall/grow tall*). The existence of the productive suffix *-en* in English (and of similar suffixes such as *-ize*, *-ate*) suggests that process predicates are regularly *derived from* states. This dependence of processes on states is quite understandable in semantic terms: logically, if a state S is possible, it must be necessary that objects should come to be in that state S; so 'state' implies 'process'. The 'change-of-state' verbs discussed above can now be seen as process predicates: *shatter* means 'come to be in the state of being shattered', and so forth.

Clearly processes and states are incompatible, in the sense that an object X cannot simultaneously be in a state S and coming to be in that state: they are mutually exclusive semantic components of predicates. Similarly, X can be simultaneously in a state S and perform an action A only if S and A are indicated by distinct, co-ordinated, predicates – and even so the resultant sentence suggests a succession rather than a co-presence of statements:

87.   John was afraid and ran.

To my knowledge, there is no single predicate which can at one and the same time contain the components which signal actions and states. However, *action* and *process* may co-exist in the same predicate, as is witnessed by the following sentences:

88.   John shattered the mirror.
89.   I dried my hair.
90.   The Senate rejected the proposal.

In each of these sentences, the predicate is an *action* in respect to the first noun, a *process* in relation to the second. John performs an action, and the mirror undergoes a process (i.e. comes into a certain state). The type of predicate illustrated in 88–90 may be dubbed **process-action**.

Now consider the following sentences (as before, the asterisk indicates ungrammaticalness):

91.   The window broke.
92.   John broke the window.
93.   The window was broken.
94. *John broke.   (*i.e. non-metaphorically*)

91 shows the predicate *break* as a process; in 92 it is a *process-action*. 93 is ambiguous: it either indicates a *state* (cf. *the broken window*) or a *process-action* (cf. *The window was broken by John*)

82

in the surface structure realization of which the noun phrase designating the instigator of the action has been deleted or is simply not
specified. Finally, 94 – which is intended to be viewed as a sentence
like *John laughed,* not like *The window broke* – is ungrammatical
and thus demonstrates that *break* cannot be an *action*. The most
economical way of displaying these facts is to postulate the existence
of just one lexical item *break* and to include in its componential
representation all the permissible alternative kinds of predicate of
which it may be the exponent. (A convention for symbolizing
alternativity of components must be added to those introduced
on p. 60 above.) The lexical item will be prohibited from serving as
an action predicate because no 'action' component appears in its
semantic representation. Note that this omission of any mention
of 'action' provides a much neater and more revealing explanation
for the ungrammaticalness of 55 (**John constructed*) than does the
preliminary proposal advanced on p. 74 above: saying that *construct*
must be followed by an *NP* tells us nothing about the meaning of the
word; characterizing it as a process-action and not a pure action
tells us a lot. *Construct* may also be a state (*The house was constructed*), but unlike *break*, not a process (**The house constructed*).

The analysis of predicate types is only just beginning, and doubtless needs to be considerably refined. Additional types may emerge:
for instance, Chafe has proposed the types **state-ambient** and **pro-
cess-ambient** to cover the predicates of sentences such as *It's hot*
and *It's raining* respectively. Probably some of the categories are
too coarse – for instance, actions may be distinguished, as the
philosopher Kenny has suggested, as 'performances' and 'activities'.
But even if the details of the analysis sketched above turn out eventually to need considerable overhaul, the semantic principles upon
which it is based seem broadly acceptable and likely to survive
further testing.

We now turn from predicates to the nouns associated with them.
When nouns occur in sentences, they carry not only their lexical
meanings as provided by the lexicon, but also structural meanings
derived from the functions they perform in sentences. Traditional
grammatical terminology recognizes this fact in words like **subject,
object, indirect object**. *John* in 92 is the subject, *the window* the
object:

92.   John broke the window.

In describing English these structural notions are usually applied in
accordance with the positions occupied by *NP*s in the left-to-right
ordering of sentences. As a consequence of this procedure, *the window*
must be called 'subject' in 95 and in 91:

95. The window was broken by John.
91. The window broke.

If we compare 92 and 95, we see that they have the same, or virtually the same, meaning. This being so, the concept 'subject' – applied as it is in radically different ways to 92 and 95 – seems to be a very weak, uninformative notion from a semantic point of view. This difficulty was recognized by the transformational-generative grammarians, who suggested a way out of it by a distinction between 'subject in surface structure' and 'subject in deep structure' (a more traditional wording is 'grammatical subject' and 'logical subject'). *John* is deep structure subject as well as surface structure subject in 92; it is still deep structure subject in 95, but *the window* is subject in surface structure. The value of this distinction is that it allows us to show that *John* is in the same semantic relationship to *break* in both sentences. However, the notion 'deep structure subject' remains semantically relatively unhelpful. Presumably *the window* in 91 is simultaneously deep and surface subject of *break*, as *John* is in 92. But, knowing what we do about the nature of *break* as a process-action predicate, we must realize that *John* and *the window* relate to *break* in two quite different ways, and the distinction is obscured by any such common label as 'deep structure subject'. In both 92 and 95 *the window* is affected by a process, and *John* is responsible for the initiation of the process. We are entitled to attribute different semantic functions to *John* and *the window*, despite the syntagmatic appearances of 91 and 92. These functions must be defined quite independently of syntactic order, of course, so that they may hold for 95 as well as 92. We will say that *John* is **agent** and *the window* is **patient**; and that 'agent' and 'patient' are examples of semantic **roles** (or **cases**).

'Subject', 'object', 'indirect object' and the like are now reserved for purely **syntactic** use; that is to say, for labelling classes of *NPs* revealed by the analysis of patterns of surface structure. When they are invoked again in this book, they are intended to have no semantic force.

To return to agents and patients; here are some examples, with agents *italicized*, patients printed **bold**:

96. *He* has visited **Spain**.
97. *Peter* laughed.
98. **Peter** is tall.
99. **Plants** grow quickly.
100. **These apples** were cultivated by *small farmers*.
101. **Organic things** die.
102. **Stones** are hard.

Roles are of course not shown in the lexical entries for nouns: they are functions which nouns assume only in sentences. Furthermore, roles are to some extent independent of componential character – 'John' can act, or he can be acted upon so as to change in state. Either 'a stone' or 'a dog' can be in a state (and hence subject to a state-changing process). But there are some restrictions, the most important of which is that only a noun containing the component [+ ANIMATE] can serve as an agent; breach of this condition leads to a common type of metaphor, personification:

103. The clock laughed.
104. Faith triumphed.

But how do we characterize perfectly well-formed sentences such as the following?

105. A wrench loosened the nut.
106. A cricket ball smashed the window.
107. The wind blew down the tree.
108. An explosion wrecked the factory.

In each case the right-hand *NP* is patient, and in each case the left-most *NP* fails the test for agent, since *wrench, cricket ball*, etc. are all [– ANIMATE]. No predicate can have more than one patient, except in the case of conjoined patients (*John and Mary were ill*). So the left-hand *NP*s must perform some role or roles additional to the two identified so far. *A wrench* and *a cricket ball* are in fact both instances of the role **instrument**. In 109 below we have all three of the roles identified so far – in left-to-right order, agent, patient and instrument:

109. The plumber loosened the nut with a wrench.

The preposition *with* usually signals the presence of an instrument, at least in sentences where an agent also is syntactically present, as 109; where no agent is identified, the instrument *NP* is moved to the beginning of the sentence and its attendant preposition is lost. This reordering and deletion, exhibited in 105 and 106, is a transformational (syntactic) operation. I mention it here because it is essential that we understand the nature of the 'absent' role in 105 and 106. Though missing from surface structure, the role 'agent' may be *conceptually* present – 'understood' in the same way that *you* is understood in imperatives. It is implausible that a wrench should loosen a nut without the control of some agent; so we may say that the role 'agent' is conceptually necessary, and implicit, but unspecified as to lexical content. I must admit that this analysis rests upon a merely plausible construal of 105; but since 105 can undoubtedly be construed in this way, we need to allow for conceptually present but syntactically unexpressed roles. As circumstantial support for this proposal, consider the probability of discourses such as 110 and the improbability, even anomalousness, of 111:

110. The plumber struggled for hours, and in the end a wrench loosened the nut.
111. A wrench loosened the nut, but no one wielded the wrench.

107 and 108, which look so similar to 105 and 106, have very different semantic structures from that pair. The *NPs the wind* and *an explosion* are not instruments (one might expect them not to be, since they are [− CONCRETE]). There are no non-metaphorical sentences corresponding to 109; both 112 and 113 below are odd:

112. X blew down the tree with the wind.
113. X used an explosion to wreck the factory.

Discounting such poetic explanations as 'God used the wind to blow down the tree', we must recognize that *the wind* and *an explosion* are more like agents than instruments, despite the fact that they do not contain [+ ANIMATE]. Yet 107 differs intuitively from, for instance 92 (*John broke the window*), so we do not want to say simply that *the wind* is an agent in just the same way as *John* is, i.e. to drop the requirement [+ ANIMATE] for agents. Presumably some special arrangement has to be proposed under which a certain sub-category of inanimate nouns can be employed as agents: I shall not attempt to pinpoint that sub-class here, although the general requirements seem clear enough – the sub-class of nouns concerned probably consists of members all of which denote phenomena which are felt to have some intrinsic, independent 'force': *thunder*, *gravity*, *electricity*, *the sea*, *magnetism*, *fire*, etc. It would be hazardous to try to guess the precise componential factor which makes these nouns distinctive, however.

Linguists discussing meaning from the point of view adopted in this book have already distinguished more roles – and detected more problems in their definitions – than I have space to consider; and I assume that many more will be proposed, and perhaps abandoned, during the next few years. I would like to mention four which are postulated by Chafe and which appear to be consistent with the suggestions of other contemporary semanticists such as Fillmore while at the same time remaining faithful to the intuitions embodied in traditional grammar: these he calls **complement**, **location**, **beneficiary** and **experiencer**.

Complements are nouns in object positions which are not patients; contrast 92, which has the semantic skeleton 'agent + process-action + patient', with 115 and 116:

92. John broke the window.
115. The choir sang a chorus.
116. The children were playing a complicated game.

The objects in 115, 116 have the same semantic function of 'completing', in the sense of narrowing down or specifying, the meanings of the predicates. *Game* is implicit in the meaning of the action *play* (contrast the semantic independence of *window* and *break*) and the object simply adds more information about the action of 'playing'. 'Song' is implied by the action predicate *sing*, so 117 below is semantically well-formed even without an object:

117. The choir sang.

'A chorus' merely attributes a species to the implicit song; it adds little new information. (Note: the predicate *eat*, discussed on pp. 74–5 above, might now be re-analysed as a completable verb like *sing*.)

States, as well as actions, may take complements; the typical examples are predicates of measurement:

118. This outfit costs $100.00.
119. The car weighed a ton and a half.

Note that completable state predicates, unlike actions (cf. 117), *demand* complements; there are no well-formed sentences on the pattern

120. *The car weighed.

The role 'location' occurs in sentences such as the following:

121. The choir occupied the stage.
122. The book is on the table.
123. They moved to their new house.

The nouns which act as locations in these sentences are easy enough to identify, but in 122 and 123 a problem arises over the status of the predicates to which they relate. If we ask 'what is the predicate of 122?' the readiest candidate is the word *is*. But this cannot be so. Sentences like 124 below seem to have semantic structures very similar to that of 122, but the adjective is the predicate:

124. The book is red.

Examination of other uses of 'be' and its inflected forms (*was, were,* etc.) will suggest that it has no real semantic function. It occurs in sentences where for one reason or another there is no verb to which semantic units such as tense can be affixed, and it serves as a root to which such information can be affixed. For instance, when a verb is in progressive aspect the morpheme -*ing* is added to it as a suffix. Only one inflexion can be attached to a single verb; we are not permitted to say *movinged* or *moveding*, so we employ a form of *be* to accommodate the past tense element: *was moving*. The case of 124 is similar: adjectives cannot receive verbal inflexions. Interestingly, there are languages (including Russian) in which tense does not have to be shown in constructions of this type, and in these the adjective simply follows its patient noun without an intervening 'copula'. Applying these analogies to 122, we see that there is no reason to suppose that *is* is the predicate: rather, it is present to signal tense and mood. It is much more likely that the predicate underlies the surface preposition *on* – an analysis which should not be difficult to accept given the fact (amply illustrated already) that a predicate does not have to be a verb. *On*, *in*, *under*, *near*, etc. all have clearly distinguished meanings and presumably easily describable componential properties, and there is no powerful argument against granting them the status of predicates compulsorily attended by location nouns. According to this analysis, example 123 must contain two predicates; that is to say, it is a complex sentence. The predicate *move* is a typical process-action: X moves, and his state changes in one respect – he comes to be in a different place. The predicate *to* introduces the noun phrase which specifies the location he finds himself in as a result of moving. Just how the relationship between the two predicates is to be shown in a formal analysis is a difficult question, but in general this account feels right and entails no great departure from the semantic principles which so far have seemed to work satisfactorily.

We look finally at two more roles which may be played by [+ ANIMATE] nouns. Since animate beings interact with their environment in a multiplicity of different ways, it might be suspected that a corresponding richness of roles is available to nouns containing the animate component. In addition to agent and patient, at least two more seem to be necessary, called by Chafe *beneficiary* and *experiencer*.

'Experiencer' is the role of a noun characterized as being in a certain 'mental disposition'. It contrasts with patient as patient occurs in such sentences as the following:

124. The book is red.
125. The cat is short-haired.
126. John is tall.

In each of the above cases the state predicate attributes external physical properties to a patient, which may be animate or not; but in 127 and 128 psychological or emotional tendencies are predicated:

127. The cat is fierce.
128. John is clever.

Experiencer may also contrast with agent, as in 129 and 131; in 130 and 132 the subjects are agents:

129. John knew the answer.
130. John learned the answer.
131. The barman needed a drink.
132. The barman mixed a drink.

'Know' and 'need' are not actions, 'learn' and 'mix' are: the distinction is reflected in the roles required of the subjects of these verbs.

Finally, beneficiary is the role of an animate noun which possesses something, comes to possess something or has something inalienably as a part of itself; it may be illustrated here without discussion:

133. Harry [*agent*] sold Max [*beneficiary*] a desk [*patient*].
134. Harry [*beneficiary*] owns a Rolls-Royce [*patient*].
135. The president [*beneficiary*] received a threatening letter [*patient*] from the committee [*agent*].
136. Our cat [*beneficiary*] has no tail [*patient*].

The final example, incidentally, yet again illustrates the independence of referential and semantic considerations. *No tail* is an *NP* with a perfectly clear sense, and is therefore entitled to play a role in sentences. The fact that it asserts the non-existence of a referent is immaterial to its linguistic analysis.

We should now look at some general implications of the model of semantic structure sketched above. In outlining it, I have adopted a view which is, I think, now gaining wide support: that semantics is a level of linguistic structure which is independent of, and prior to, syntax. This separation of levels has in effect been required even since the very informal presentation of chapter 1, and in this and the previous chapter I have tried to give it a progressively more formal expression. We have seen how the 'signals' in language are in several senses 'arbitrary' from the point of view of the meanings they are called upon to express, that the link between message and sound is indirect, conventionalized. The conventions alluded to here are syntactic conventions, for it is syntax which is responsible for processing semantic constructions, for transforming them into linear orderings of morphemes, words and phrases – what have been repeatedly called 'surface structures' – still abstract units, but units which can now be concretized as sounds (or, *mutatis mutandis*, letters) by the phonological component of the grammar.

The indirectness and complexity of the syntactic passage between meanings and surface structures make the latter non-isomorphic with the former. What this means is that semantic structure is not reflected in surface structure by any simple one-to-one representation. In general, surface structure is a rather poor guide to meaning, and we have already had several instances of this. A very obvious example was sentence 6 (p. 31 above), in which a single semantic unit, an indivisible predicate, was realized as the syntactically discontinuous verbal phrase *put . . . down*. Many other examples can be thought up very easily. In English the suffix *-s* affixed to nouns means 'plural'; attached to verbs, it means 'not plural'. Many words have two or more (synchronically) unconnected senses: *bank, wave, right, pound, crane, plane, novel*, etc. Imperatives must contain a semantic element 'command', but there is no sign of it on the surface. The past and present tenses of verbs like *cut, hit, put* are identical, as are the singular and plural forms of a few nouns: *sheep, fish*, etc. In addition to these, and many more, isolated evidences of the non-correspondence of the structure of messages and the form of signals, we have encountered hints of more general and perhaps systematic kinds of failure of surface structure to make manifest structure clearly and uniquely: I refer to the cases of **ambiguity** and **synonymy**. I have already touched on these processes several times (see examples 6 and 13; 7 and 8; 9 and 10; 34; 41 and 42; 45, 46 and 47; 65 and 93). We may now look at ambiguity and synonymy from the point of view of the predicate and role model of semantic structure offered in this chapter. Considering ambiguity first, it seems that instances of surface structures which are ambiguous as to role or predicate type are extremely plentiful. Here is a variety of such constructions (many more are given in the book by Langendoen cited at the end of this chapter):

93.		The window	was broken.	
	(a)	patient	state	
	(b)	patient	process-action	[agent]

92.		John	broke	the window.	
	(a)	agent	process-action	patient	
	(b)	instrument	process-action	patient	[? agent]

When 92 was first introduced (p. 82), interpretation (a) was assumed: John broke the window (using a hammer, a stone, etc.). But (b) is possible: instead of the agent-permitting component [+ ANIMATE]

being emphasized, the more general [+ CONCRETE] is foregrounded –
John's body broke the window, the agency being unspecified.

137.	The clerk	received	the rent.
(a)	beneficiary	process	patient
(b)	agent	process-action	patient

Meaning (a) is the one which is perhaps more natural to 137,
because *receive* is felt to imply a beneficiary. But it does not demand
that role, as (b) shows: 'receiving' can be regarded as a formal action
(cf. the illegal *act* of receiving stolen property): here the clerk is
pictured as, say, sitting in a rent office taking receipt of money.

138.	Tom	felt	the needle.
(a)	experiencer	process	patient
(b)	agent	process-action	patient

138 is an example from Chafe, who intends it to be taken in the sense
(a); but (b) is also possible, as when one puts a finger against the
point of a needle to test its sharpness.

139.	I	weighed	160 pounds.
(a)	patient	state	complement
(b)	agent	process-action	patient

(a) is the more likely interpretation – 'My weight was 160 pounds';
(b) attributes an action to 'I', weighing out quantities of some
unspecified substance so that the resultant weight of the substance
totalled 160 pounds. 139, if accepted, is perhaps of particular
interest because both roles are changed as well as the type of predicate. 137 and 138 are more typical: the predicate differs as between
(a) and (b), and one noun changes its role in consequence, the other
remaining the same. In 92 the predicate type is the same in (a) and
(b), while one role varies; the converse situation is found in 93. The
kinds of ambiguity, we see, are multiple. As a final – and common –
representative, consider this more complicated example:

140. The baby crawled under the table.

It is quite difficult to offer a notation for the two semantic structures here, but the following paraphrases will make the point: (a)
'The baby performed the action of crawling and the action of crawling occurred under the table'; (b) 'The baby performed the action
of crawling and the outcome of this action was that the baby came
to be under the table.'

Ambiguity can be amply demonstrated. The converse situation,
synonymy or **paraphrase** – two surface structures for an identical
semantic structure – is rather more difficult to argue convincingly.

The general theoretical framework adopted in this book allows for the possibility. Our separation of semantic structure from the syntactic level which is responsible for the formation of surface structures permits both situations: the concealment of more than one meaning under the surface of one utterance, as in the examples just discussed; and the manifestation of the same meaning in more than one utterance. The reality of the latter situation might be supported by such examples as the following:

6. He put the book down.
13. He put down the book.

141. The cat killed a bird.
     A bird was killed by the cat.

142. John opened the door with a key.
     John used a key to open the door.

143. Tom sold a car to Peter.
     Peter was sold a car by Tom.
     Peter bought a car from Tom,
     A car was bought from Tom by Peter.

144. We lost a daughter and gained a son.
     We gained a son and lost a daughter.

145. Arthur, the plumber, fixed the leak.
     Arthur fixed the leak – he's the plumber.

146. (a) The garage is behind the house.
     (b) The house is in front of the garage.

Some of these sentences are distinguished from their counterparts by differences in word-order only; others display differences in the choice of lexical items (142, 143, 146). The common factor throughout the list is that the paired or grouped sentences have the same truth-values: if one is true, then the truth of the other cannot be denied. If 146(a) is a faithful description of the state of affairs it concerns, then 146(b) cannot be said to be false, and the reverse relationship holds too: 146(a) implies 146(b) and 146(b) implies 146(a). Such a relationship does not obtain between, for instance, the sentences 'John is short' and 'John is fat' – although both states may be appropriately predicated of John, the truth of one does not guarantee the truth of the other, since there is nothing in the language which allows us to predict the applicability of one description merely on the basis of knowing the truth of the other.

The bilateral, or reciprocal, entailment which holds between 146(a) and (b), and between all the other matched sentences above, is the minimal condition for synonymy. Sentences which display it may be said to have the same **cognitive content**. Sameness of cognitive content is easy enough to demonstrate where pairs of sentences contain the same lexical items fulfilling the same roles, as 6/13, 141 and 144 do; 145 also seems to present no particular problem, since the two sentences concerned differ only in word-order and in minor morphological respects. But semantic theory must also be framed in such a way that certain kinds of lexical difference do not interfere with cognitive equivalence. The traditional sort of lexical synonyms – *large/big, house/home, twilight/dusk, baby/infant* – must be explained componentially, and also the converses of 143 (*buy/sell*) and 146 (*behind/in front of*). The ordinary synonyms can be accounted for by showing that they have the same semantic components; what is less obvious – though on reflection perfectly reasonable – is that converses too contain the same semantic components. This becomes clear as soon as we stop thinking of them, misleadingly, as 'opposites'. The meaning of both *buy* and *sell*, for example, can be paraphrased somewhat as follows:

147. '*Patient* leaves the possession of *agent* and comes into the possession of *beneficiary* as a result of monetary transaction.'

Selection of the surface form *buy* or *sell* depends on a *non-semantic* transformational choice, choice of the order in which the roles are to be mentioned. (Transformations, being post-semantic processes, do not change meaning; and surface differences, such as the alternative spellings 'buy' and 'sell', are not relevant to semantic interpretation.)

Linguists – and literary critics (particularly the American New Critics) – who dispute the idea of paraphrase claim that any change in expression involves a change of 'meaning'. It would be said, for instance, that the meaning of *twilight* differs from that of *dusk* because the two words have different 'overtones', or because they are typically used in different contexts; that 146(a) is a statement about the garage, 146(b) about the house; that the variants of 143 differ in meaning because in each one different aspects of the process-action are picked out for emphasis; and so on. It seems to me that such arguments depend on too inclusive a conception of 'meaning', which I would like to restrict to a compositional product of lexical content, predicate type and role functions, quantification, modality, tense, aspect. One justification for this position is, in fact, the conventional and deeply rooted cultural feeling of the reality of 'style' – the feeling, long recognized in literary theory and in the rules for linguistic etiquette in society, that it is possible to 'say the same thing in different words', to find alternative 'expressions' or 'forms' for the same 'content'. People can, and do, provide paraphrases of sentences when required to do so, and agree that the paraphrase preserves the sense. There is, apparently, some very real dimension of semantic structure which can stay untouched by changes in expression, and this is the level which semantics as conceived in this and the previous chapter must seek to explicate. In restricting the scope of semantics in this way I am not, of course, seeking to deny that there are linguistically interesting differences to be pointed out among the members of paraphrase-sets; I am simply arguing that these should not be regarded as differences of *meaning*, since so regarding them sets impossibly generous and vague goals for semantics. I would agree, for example, that there are most important distinctions between the sentences in 143 – distinctions of emphasis, subtle shades of difference between imputed degrees of 'activeness' in the participants, interesting psycholinguistic consequences of the differences in order of presentation of the constituent parts of the proposition. These are 'expressive' distinctions which we will be better off relating to transformational structure than to semantic structure.

Further reading

On the 'syntagmatic' and 'paradigmatic' dimensions of linguistic structure see Saussure, *Course*, part 2, chapter 5 (his word for 'paradigmatic' is 'associative'); Lyons, *Theoretical Linguistics*, pp. 70–81.

Katz and Fodor, 'Structure of a semantic theory', Katz and Postal, *Integrated Theory* and Weinreich, 'Explorations in semantic theory', debate the ways in which the meanings of lexical items are amalgamated syntagmatically. On 'selectional restrictions' see Chomsky, *Aspects*, pp. 75 ff., including some lists of examples of the type given as 54–62 (p. 73 above); Weinreich also has some interesting examples, pp. 414–15.

The semantic structure of predicates and roles has been explored by Fillmore, 'The case for case' and 'Lexical entries for verbs' and by Chafe, *Meaning and the Structure of Language*. Langendoen's *Essentials of English Grammar* is a stimulating if untidy textbook based on Fillmore's work and that of Emmon Bach, especially 'Nouns and noun phrases'.

Lakoff's pioneering article, 'Stative adjectives and verbs in English', should be consulted, and might be usefully compared with chapter 8 of Kenny's *Action, Emotion and Will* (referred to on p. 83 above). Some parts of Lakoff's *Irregularity in Syntax* are relevant, e.g. Appendix A. For other recent treatments of semantics, and of semantics in relation to syntax, see Steinberg and Jakobovits, *Semantics*, Fillmore and Langendoen, *Studies in Linguistic Semantics*, Jacobs and Rosenbaum, *Readings*, Katz, *Semantic Theory*.

For further discussion of the arguments glanced at in the last paragraphs of this chapter see Fowler, 'Style and the concept of deep structure'.

five

Simple sentences

One of the most frequently referred to parts of Leonard Bloomfield's great book, *Language*, is his comment on the difficulty of semantic description: 'The statement of meanings is therefore the weak point in language-study, and will remain so until human knowledge advances very far beyond its present state' (p. 140). Bloomfield's followers not only accepted the validity of this judgment, but went further, attempting to devise a form of linguistic description which explicitly eschewed semantic distinctions, claiming to concentrate instead on 'structural' patterns by which meaning was conveyed. As a result of the efforts of the American structuralists, meaning was almost totally neglected in the mainstream of linguistics until quite recently. Phonology, syntax and morphology (study of the internal structures of complex words) progressed: syntax notably in the work of Chomsky and his disciples after 1957, phonology continuously (though in very different styles) in the period from about 1930. Semantics remained immature until the 1960s, not because it was waiting for the requisite advancement of human knowledge, but because linguistics had developed a style which was radically antagonistic to the study of meanings. In fact, the necessary principles for the development of structural semantics were available from at least the time of Saussure; that they were not built upon was purely a result of various intellectual inhibitions – distrust of abstract entities, of unobservable components; erroneous belief that meaning depends on reference and thus that semantics demands extremely powerful observations in physical science, and so on. For such causes as these, my account of meaning in the previous two chapters has, in its insecurity, reflected the newness and instability of modern semantics. The present chapter and the following two are mostly, but not exclusively, about syntax, and here we tread on much firmer soil.

The distinction between syntax and semantics has already been touched on several times in this book. Meaning is abstract; syntax is the level of linguistic structure which is responsible for its concretization. We have seen that the surface structure of an utterance is not a wholly accurate guide to its meaning, hence the need for an independent level of syntactic structure to be recognized, reflecting semantic structure in only an indirect way. For instance, 148 and 149 below have the same cognitive content, differing only in the contrasted modes of syntactic ordering:

148. A knife cut the cake.
149. The cake was cut with a knife.

It seems reasonable to say that the same proposition is expressed in 148 and 149, the differences between them concerning only the words chosen (the insertion of *was* and *with* in 149) and the order of the words and phrases (the 'cross-over' of *a knife* and *the cake* between the two sentences). Granting that 148 and 149 have the same meaning, we can agree that the differences between them are syntactic (and, consequently, phonological, since a good part of pronunciation depends on syntax). In 148 the semantic role 'instrument' is signalled syntactically by the position of the first *NP*; in 149 this *NP* is in a different position, but its instrumentality is shown by the word *with*; other syntactic expressions are available for this semantic function, e.g. the word *use*:

150. A knife was used to cut the cake.

The differences among 148–50 are, then, syntactic differences: differences of words and differences of word-order, independent of meaning. They illustrate quite dramatically the fact that though syntax and semantics run parallel, they do not correspond exactly, and they provide a kind of illustration which helps us to a definition of syntax. Looking at another aspect of these sentences will help us still further. We noticed above (p. 77) that every lexical item of the class 'noun', when it is put into a proposition, must be attended by certain 'features of **quantification**'; features which signify the number of referents designated by a noun, whether they are unique, specific, indefinite, universal, etc. Such components are, of course, just as abstract as the semantic units (**senses**) which underlie nouns themselves. When *NP*s are realized in syntactic surface structure, quantifiers are manifested by conventional words and morphemes in set positions. Number takes the shape of a suffix on the noun, typically -*s* for plural and, as in 148–50, 'zero' for singular. Additionally, number has implications for the **articles** which occur before the nouns: *the* indicates either singular or plural, *a* or *an* singular only. The main function of articles is to signal facts about the universality, definiteness or indefiniteness of reference of nouns. From a syntactic point of view, articles always precede the noun in English, moving to the left if an adjective qualifies the noun: *a sharp knife.* All these facts about the manifestation and ordering of quantifiers are **syntactic** facts. There is no essential reason why, e.g. 'definiteness' should be shown by a word placed before the noun – it simply happens to work that way in English; other languages do it other ways. (The principal distinction between languages is syntactic, or, as we shall come to regard it, transformational.)

We may now attempt to refine our terminology somewhat. I have talked about 'lexical items', 'propositions', 'words', 'sentences'. With the normal tolerance granted to chapter headings I used 'Words' and 'Words within sentences' very informally for chapters 3 and 4. In fact, it is better to employ 'lexical item' for the basic compositional unit, the bundle of components, in semantics, and 'proposition' for the semantic construction built up in the manner sketched in chapter 4 (note that a 'proposition' is not necessarily an assertion or statement; commands, questions, etc. also have propositional content and structure). 'Word' and 'sentence' can now be reserved for syntactic elements. In this way the parallel, but not quite isomorphic, levels of syntax and semantics can be recognized as parallel-but-distinct by a paired terminology in which 'word' almost approximates 'lexical item' and 'sentence' in many cases answers to 'proposition'. Syntax then concerns the make-up of sentences in terms of words; it is the study of sentence-structure, a study which must always remain conscious of the fact that sentences merely *express* propositions, that they are not the same as propositions. For further precision, we can restrict the concept 'sentence' still more by introducing a third term, **utterance**. 'Proposition' allows us to take a semantic view of a piece of language; 'sentence' encourages a syntactic perspective; 'utterance' treats a section of speech or writing *as* a mere piece of language – any stretch of language between pauses: it carries no implications of structure. Utterances are physical, behavioural entities: people speak utterances and write them down. The sentence is a linguist's construct – people do not talk in sentences, for a sentence is what a linguist, engaged in syntactic analysis, *imposes* on utterances. 'Sentence' is thus a descriptive concept, a tool in linguistics, rather than a physical or behavioural notion.

I have suggested that syntax is the study of the *ordering* of elements in sentences; and nothing said so far hints otherwise than that these elements are **words** – the units which are separated from each other by gaps in conventional orthography and which correspond fairly closely to lexical items in semantic parlance. Certainly, words do have a degree of special status in syntactic analysis, for a sentence may be represented as a linear, left-to-right, concatenation ('chaining together') of words:

151.   We + believed + that + we + had + arrived + at + the + wrong + house.

The validity of the syntactic divisions marked by plus-signs can be verified by substituting other words, as in 152, 153, etc.:

152.   Ted + believed + that + we + had + arrived + at + the + wrong+ house.
153.   We + believed + that + we + had + landed + at + the + right + port.

However, the same substitution test suggests that there are also syntactic units intermediate in size between word and sentence:

154.   *The whole family* + believed . . .

The whole family is a unit capable of performing the same function as the syntactically indivisible unit *we* in 151. Similarly, *that we had arrived at the wrong house* may be replaced by a single word, thus showing that that string of nine words in some way combines to form one single syntactic whole:

155.   We + believed + *it.*

More evidence for the existence of sub-sentence syntagms larger than the word comes from our feelings about the ways of inserting divisions within sentences. Everyone who knows English would agree that, if 151 is to be divided into two parts, the cut comes between *we* and *believed*:

156.   We – believed that we had arrived at the wrong house.

Compare 157, which shows that the sequence *believed . . . house* is not an arbitrary string of words:

157.   We – laughed.

Furthermore, the right-hand part of 156 divides naturally into

158.   believed – that we had arrived at the wrong house

and further cuts may be made equally as naturally. Speakers of English will also agree that some segments are intuitively right while others are patently erroneous: compare *had arrived, the wrong house* with the quite arbitrary strings of words *at the, the wrong*. The triviality of these segments may be checked by trying to substitute single words for them; they are obviously not real constituents of the sentence.

Constituent-structure analysis, which is the technical name for this segmentation procedure, has already been referred to in chapter 2 (p. 29). Constituents of various sizes are revealed, and are shown to be nested within one another:

159.   [We + [believed + [that + [we + [[had + arrived] + [at + [the + [wrong + house]]]]]]]].

Each pair of brackets encloses a proper constituent: so *wrong house* is shown to be a syntactic whole, and also *we had arrived at the wrong house*, etc.; but not *believed that we, at the wrong*, etc. Typographically, bracketing-diagrams of constituent-structure, such as 159, are complicated and it is difficult to retrieve the relevant information from them; tree-diagrams such as 160 and 161 below are much easier to read, and provide exactly the same information:

160.

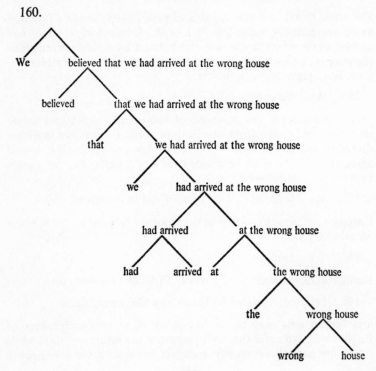

161.

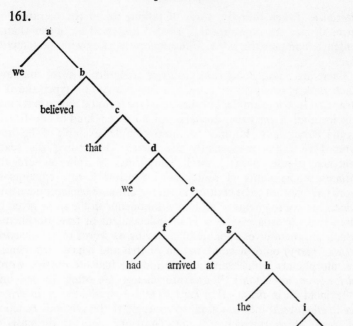

(The bold lower-case letters **a-i** in 161 are for ease of reference in the discussion below; they are not a standard convention in tree-diagrams.) Tree-diagrams provide a vivid portrayal of one fact about syntax which is not obvious from the equivalent bracketed arrangement: that syntactic structure is **hierarchical** and not (as pictured in 151–3) purely linear. Each intersection in the tree (called a **node**) links two units into one single constituent. Starting from the lower right-hand corner we can see that *wrong* and *house* are the constituents of a syntactic unit **i**; that in turn **i** and *the* are the constituents of **h**; **h** and *at* together make up **g**; **g** and **f** are the constituents of **e**; and so on. The highest unit in the hierarchy, here designated **a**, is the sentence itself, which is (by definition) not a constituent of anything, and which includes and dominates all lower-order constituents. The British linguist, M. A. K. Halliday, has proposed that the syntactic hierarchy be recognized by a set of terms on a scale of **rank**. So 'sentence' would be the highest-ranking unit, 'word' a constituent of a lower rank. The term 'rank' is useful since it permits us to avoid misleading size metaphors. It is unhelpful to call the sentence a 'larger' unit than the word, for syntax, including sentences, is an abstraction: physical concepts such as 'size' relate to the plane of *utterance*. Taken literally, ways of talking about the hierarchy in terms of size are nonsensical – a word may well be bigger than a sentence: compare the word *carboxymethylcellulose* with the sentence *Fire!*

There are not as many ranks as there are nodes in a tree-diagram. Each rank is occupied by a constituent of a certain type, and it is clear that in, for example, 161 the same type is found more than once. For instance, **h**, *the wrong house*, is not a different kind of constituent from **i**, *wrong house*, but merely a more complex example of the same type. Five ranks are usually recognized: descending the scale, **sentence, clause, phrase, word, morpheme**. Morphemes are the *ultimate* constituents of sentences, indivisible linear segments of words. (*Note:* not to be confused with the ultimate *semantic* elements, which are not segments at all but 'components' in the sense given by chapter 3.) Words may consist of independent or **free** morphemes which are themselves capable of behaving as words (*black + board*, *straw + berry*) or of a combination of free and **bound** morphemes, i.e. morphemes which can have no independent life outside words (*drive + -er, un- + fold*). Bound morphemes are often divided into **inflexional** (*-s* in *fires*, *-ed* in *herded*) and **derivational** (*-er* in *driver*, *-ee* in *employee*); inflexional morphemes mark the syntactic function of words, derivational morphemes form one word on the basis of another. It must be pointed out that, although the concept of the morpheme is useful for recognizing sub-word regularities of syntagmatic patterning, there are dangers and difficulties in the way of developing an all-embracing theory of morphological structure. The dangers concern the potential confusion of semantic and syntactic micro-structures, as mentioned before. The difficulties emerge when we attempt to subject some words to a complete morphological breakdown. What are we to say about awkward residues such as the *-ceive* of *receive, deceive, conceive*, etc.? or about morphological alterations which entail phonetic changes which cannot be expressed by separate segments – *man/men, mouse/mice, child/children*? Can we justify a 'zero' morpheme, which we might propose as the inflexion for the plural of *sheep*, the past tense of *hit*, the plural of *see*? American linguists who grappled with these puzzles seemed to find them insolubly perplexing or controversial. In this book, although the notion of the morpheme will be appealed to whenever clear-cut cases of sub-word structure need to be noticed, no assumption is made that all words can be decomposed neatly into morphemes; hence 'morpheme' is a marginal concept in the present grammatical model.

Probably no more needs to be said about the rank 'word'; we may pass on to **phrase**, which is a word-like unit whose constituents are themselves words. A phrase is not just any odd collection of words cut from a sentence at random – not *believed that we, at the wrong*, etc.; the qualification 'a word-like unit' ensures that only proper constituents are characterized as phrases: *the wrong house*, etc. A phrase is a sequence of words which as a group fulfils a single structural function, as a single word might do. The substitution test proves useful here. We can replace *large cats* in *large cats like fish* by the one word *cats*, hence *large cats* is a proper phrase; but since no such replacement is available for *cats like*, that is not a phrase. Just as a phrase is a single entity from the point of view of its external syntactic relationships, it is also hierarchically structured internally: this fact is demonstrated in the diagram 161 above, where the phrases dominated by the nodes **h** and **i** both have regular branching structure. Each of them is built up layer by layer on the basis of the word *house*. There is, however, a typological distinction to be drawn between the two phrases *at the wrong house* and *the wrong house*; though the first is an 'expansion' of the second, the addition of the word *at* changes the function. *The wrong house* is a phrase of the sort which is often called **endocentric**: the phrase as a whole is of the same syntactic category (here, noun) as its centre or 'head', the word on which it is based; this is not true of *at the wrong house*, an adverbial phrase built on a noun. This type is known as **exocentric**. Another example of an exocentric phrase would be *at times*; of an endocentric phrase, *three long books*.

Certain combinations of phrases make up the unit **sentence**: the minimal construction is a noun phrase followed by a predicate phrase, as in 162:

162.   The lion has escaped.

Why a sentence demands these minimum constituents should be obvious from the design for semantic structure outlined in chapter 4: a sentence is the expression of a proposition, and a proposition puts a noun and a predicate into a certain semantic relationship. Extra phrases will be present if more roles are to be communicated (*The lion has escaped from the zoo*); the noun phrase may not be given syntactic expression, under certain circumstances, although it is nevertheless conceptually present or 'understood' (*Escape!*). The predicate phrase, however, *must* be given expression: utterances such as *Lion!* (as a warning) or *The lion* (in reply to a question) are not to be regarded as full sentences – as *Escape!* is – but rather as exceptional truncated versions, made comprehensible only by implicit reference to wider linguistic and/or situational context.

The essential conjunction of a noun phrase and a predicate phrase defines the **clause** as well as the sentence. The term 'clause' appears in traditional syntactic description in recognition of the fact that many sentences – indeed, *most* sentences – consist of two or more sentence-like constituents. A **simple sentence**, such as 162 above, consists of one clause; **complex sentences**, like 163–8 below, consist of two or more clauses, which, as we can see, may be combined in a variety of ways:

163. The lion has escaped and the zoo is very worried.
164. John played the piano while Mary sang.
165. This tile, which is cracked, needs replacing.
166. The fact that you were drunk at the time makes no difference.
167. The lion has escaped and is roaming the neighbourhood.
168. Josephine and Alexander have passed the examination.

In most of these sentences two clauses each with its own noun-predicate structure can be detected. 167 and 168 show that parts of one clause can be deleted in complex sentences: *the lion* is present twice in the deep structure of 167, but needs to be expressed only once, while in 168 the same comment applies to the predicate *passed the examination*.

Chapter 7 is devoted entirely to the syntax of complex – multi-clause – sentences. One further observation which may be added at this point is that many complex sentences are not so easy to detect on the surface as 163–8. 169 and 170 are just two instances of complex deep structures heavily disguised by the transformational arrangements to which they have been subjected:

169. A ferocious lion has escaped.
170. Caruso's singing enthralled the audience.

169 contains two predicates: *ferocious* and *escape*. The noun *lion* is implicitly present twice: once as agent, in relation to *escape*, and once as patient in relation to *ferocious*. ('Patient' rather than 'experiencer', probably, because ferocity is seen from the point of view of an observer's experience, not the lion's.) In 170 *singing* is a predicate, as well as *enthrall*: it is a 'nominalized' form, but a predicate none the less; *Caruso* is its agent. A syntactic account of simple sentences must take care to exclude such examples from its domain. We will see, in the next chapter, how prenominal adjectives such as *ferocious* in 169 must be introduced transformationally by a particular kind of combining of two underlying propositions. (It seems inappropriate to talk of 'clauses' here.)

Remembering this caution concerning the deceptive character of many apparently simple sentences, we will now examine the syntactic structure of some typical elementary sentences associated with the kinds of one-predicate semantic structures discussed in chapter 4. Here are some actual sentences from that chapter, re-numbered for convenience of reference, supplemented by some new examples:

171. She laughed. (= 80)
172. The house smells. (= 79)
173. The dogs scattered. (= 64)
174. The window broke. (= 91)
175. John is tall. (= 76)
176. Peter was weak. (= 78)
177. The cat is fierce. (= 127)
178. John is clever. (= 128)
179. He's reviewing the book. (= 71)
180. The children broke the window. (= 74)
181. A wrench loosened the nut. (= 105)
182. This outfit costs $100.00. (= 118)
183. The book is on the table. (= 122)
184. We were in the house.
185. She's at a dance.

The sentences express a wide range of semantic structures (readers may care to revise their knowledge of semantic structure at this point by checking this statement against the discussion in the previous chapter). They fall under only four syntactic classes, however: (a) 171–4, (b) 175–8, (c) 179–82 and (d) 183–5. Group (a), semantically, manifests the constructions 'agent-action', 'patient-state', 'agent-action' and 'patient-process' in that order, but reduces to one syntactic syntagm: a noun phrase followed by a verb. (On 171, cf. p. 77 above where it is explained that what appears to be a lone noun in a sentence is always implicitly a noun phrase, since all nouns receive quantification – *she* is definite, singular, etc.) The common structure of these four sentences 171–4 might be expressed in the formula

186. NP + V.

Group (b), 175–8, is equally homogeneous syntactically despite semantic diversity, but the formula is different:

187. NP + Adj.

For (c), 179–82, we may generalize the construction as

188. NP + V + NP

and (d), 183–5, may be expressed as follows:

189. NP + Prep + NP.

(Notice the similarity of (b) and (d): neither contains a *V*, so an appropriate form of the pseudo-verb *be* has to be inserted transformationally to carry tense; cf. pp. 87–8 above.) Several more formulae must be proposed to cover the full range of English simple sentence-types. For instance, there is the construction

190. $NP + V + NP + NP$

exemplified in *John gave Mary some flowers*. There is the instrumental construction with *with*: *He opened the door with the key*. Among others, there is a most important structure – for simplicity's sake not mentioned in chapter 4 – in which an *NP* serves as a predicate:

191.   The widow was a teacher.
192.   Our dog is a terrier.

These are **state** predicates; processes can be expressed by forming a complex predicate with *become*:

193.   The widow became a teacher.
194.   John became a hippie.

Since there is no good reason to assume a sequence of two separate predicates in 193–4, it would seem appropriate to treat *become* as a pseudo-verb, like *is* in 191–2; then all four sentences can be represented in the same notation – recognizing formally their intuitively felt similarity:

195. $NP + NP$.

Our six formulae 186–90, 195 comprise a primitive constituent-structure analysis of the main types of elementary English sentence. The grammar must now be refined so as to show the hierarchical relationships among the constituents; this can be done in such a way as to relate the formulae to one another, also. Each formula has an *NP* on the left; and English speakers, invited to divide a sentence into two parts, will agree on a primary cut between this *NP* and the rest of the sentence:

196.   She – laughed.
       The house – smells.
       John – is tall.
       He – 's reviewing the book.
       This outfit – costs $100.00.
       John – gave Mary some flowers.

The 'remainder' on the right of this cut is the predicate or has the predicate as its centre, so we may call it **predicate-phrase**, abbreviated *PredP*. Every sentence, at the most abstract level of description, is an arrangement of an *NP* followed by a *PredP*; this is a general syntactic rule which can be captured in a conventional symbolic notation:

197.   S → NP + PredP.

'A sentence consists of a noun phrase followed by a predicate-phrase.' (The notation 197 is the standard style employed in phrase-structure grammars of the type devised by Chomsky – see pp. 28–33 above. The single arrow '→' asserts that the element designated by the symbol on the left 'has as its constituents' the elements symbolized by the letters on the right. A secondary meaning for the arrow symbol will be introduced below.) Next, both the *NP* and the *PredP* are analysable into further constituents. We saw above (p. 77) that an *NP* consists of a lexical item of the class 'noun' and a 'quantifying' element which in surface structure may be realized as, for example, an article (*the chair*), a demonstrative (*this chair*), or nothing (*John*). The quantifying constituent is usually called a **determiner**, abbreviated *Det*. Thus the rule for the structure of *NP*s is

198.   NP → Det + N.

We will return later to the components of the element *Det*. We must now examine the constructions associated with the predicate phrase; and it should be obvious that there is not just one of these, as there is for *NP*, but several. What is more, our formulae 186–90, 195 not only ignore some kinds of *PredP*, but also omit mention of an obligatory constituent which supplies the inflexional information vital to predicates. This information is carried in surface structure by a great variety of words and morphemes: suffixes, as the *-ed* for past tense, *-ing* for progressive aspect and *-en* or *-ed* for perfect and for passive; *can*, *will*, *should*, etc., representing the various **modal** forms. In the very general representation of syntax that we are building up, all the meanings reflected in these fragments of words are gathered under one symbol, *Aux* (not simply the 'auxiliary' forms *can*, *may*, etc., but verbal suffixes also, since all derive from the same complex of meanings). The meanings associated with *Aux* qualify the whole proposition; not just the verb is, say, past tense, but complete statements are. But since these meanings are, syntactically, expressed by morphemes which are affixed to the verb, and by words which are juxtaposed with it, it seems preferable to introduce *Aux* by the syntactic rule for expanding *PredP* rather than by the rule (197) which expands the symbol *S* into its lexical constituents. So the following rule gives the structure of one type of *PredP*, that found in sentences 171–4 (cf. formula 186):

199.   PredP → Aux + V.

The following rules describe the other kinds of predicate-phrase:

    200.   PredP → Aux + Adj   (cf. 187)
    201.   PredP → Aux + VP   (cf. 188, 190)
    202.   PredP → Aux + PrepP   (cf. 189)
    203.   PredP → Aux + NP   (cf. 195).

A more economical presentation which has the added advantage of showing the likeness between predicate-phrases is the display 204 below, in which braces { } indicate alternativity; 204 is a conflation of the five rules just given:

    204.   PredP → Aux +
$$\begin{Bmatrix} V \\ Adj \\ VP \\ PrepP \\ NP \end{Bmatrix}$$

Notice that two new symbols have been introduced – *VP* and *PrepP*. Their purpose is to acknowledge the fact of hierarchical structure within the predicate phrase, a fact not noticed by the representations 188–90. As *VP* and *PrepP* are symbols for sequences of segments, not single segments, their own internal structure must be shown by additional constituent-structure rules:

    205.   VP   →
$$\begin{Bmatrix} V + NP \\ V + NP + NP \end{Bmatrix}$$
       (cf. 188)
       (cf. 190)

    206.   PrepP → Prep + NP   (cf. 189).

(*Note*: the lower line of 205 actually needs revision to show hierarchical structure in *VP*s with two *NP*s. The relevant example is *John gave Mary some flowers* or *John gave some flowers to Mary*. I am not sure which of the trees given in 207 would be appropriate, so have not chosen between them.

    207.

The symbols introduced by our elementary syntactic rules can now be added to tree-diagrams to provide an explicit picture of constituent structure; 208 is an abstract representation of any of the sentences 179–82.

208.

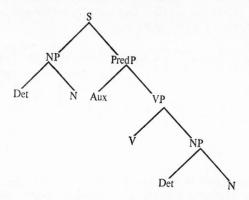

Alternatively, the syntax of a simple sentence can be described by attaching a **derivation** to it. A derivation is a sequence of lines, each in succession representing the structure of the sentence in finer detail. A line is derived from the preceding one by applying a phrase-structure rule to just one symbol at a time. We start with the grammar's 'initial symbol' *S* and 'rewrite' it as the sequence of symbols *NP + PredP* by application of rule 197 (hence the term 'rewriting rule': the arrow '→' may be regarded as the 'rewriting symbol', an instruction to rewrite whatever is on its left as whatever is on its right), and so on down the sequence as follows:

209. (i) S
     (ii) NP + PredP   (by rule 197)
     (iii) Det + N + PredP   (by rule 198)
     (iv) Det + N + Aux + VP   (by rule 201)
     (v) Det + N + Aux + V + NP   (by the upper line of rule 205)
     (vi) Det + N + Aux + V + Det + N   (by rule 198)

Each of the lines (i) – (vi) adds more information about the syntax of the sentence; they become progressively less general representations, approach surface structure more closely.

208 and 209 show only syntax. In a proper derivation semantic information would appear too. Let us see how this is arranged in a representation of sentence 180, *The children broke the window*. The *V* and the *N*s of this sentence are already, by application of a sequence of semantic rules, componentially specified, endowed with lexical meaning, predicate-type, role-types. The meanings selected under *Det* and *Aux* will have been chosen, too, and the whole complex mapped on to a syntactic structure which is a more detailed

form of 209 (vi). 210 below approximates the fuller representation, except that I have not detailed *Det* and *Aux*, which will be the subject of our discussion for the next few pages.

210. Det +
$$
\begin{bmatrix}
\text{child} \\
\text{agent} \\
+\,\text{N} \\
+\,\text{HUMAN} \\
-\,\text{ADULT} \\
\vdots \\
F_n
\end{bmatrix}
+ \text{Aux} +
\begin{bmatrix}
\text{break} \\
\text{process-} \\
\text{action} \\
+\,\text{V} \\
\text{DESTROY} \\
\vdots \\
F_n
\end{bmatrix}
+ \text{Det} +
\begin{bmatrix}
\text{window} \\
\text{patient} \\
+\,\text{N} \\
+\,\text{CONCRETE} \\
-\,\text{ANIMATE} \\
\vdots \\
F_n
\end{bmatrix}
$$

(Because this is assumed to be a line in a derivation, the hierarchical structure is implicitly known: 210 is only in appearance a crudely linear display.)

Although the meanings permissible under *Det* are to some extent dependent on the choices which have been exercised under *Aux*, so that *Aux* must be selected before *Det* in a proper derivation, I shall discuss *Det* first because it can be expounded with less difficulty. We have already seen (above, pp. 76–7) that every noun, when it is used in a sentence, is accompanied by non-lexical semantic components which tie down its mode of signifying referents or classes of referents. Restricting ourselves to words which actually have referents – the same principles apply, *mutatis mutandis*, to abstract nouns – we know that a noun may refer to just one object, or to a plurality of objects. If it designates more than one object, it may refer to a set of objects acting or being acted upon either separately or in some corporate manner. The subject-*NP*s of the following sentences illustrate these three possibilities in order:

211. The cat is an intelligent animal.
212. The cats ran away.
213. The trains collided.

In 180 *the window* is of course [– PLURAL]. It cannot be easily discovered whether *the children* is [+ PLURAL] or [COMBINED], for that is a semantic distinction which is not signalled by any difference of inflexion. Some predicates (*collide*, *meet*, etc.) impose a 'combined' interpretation on their agents or patients; *break* does not. I shall assume that its subject-*NP* is [+ PLURAL] here.

There is not a free choice of number for every noun. Most nouns may, indeed, be either singular or plural: in recognition of this fact, we call them **count nouns**. There are two classes of noun which may not be [+ PLURAL]: **names** or **proper** nouns (*John, The Hague*);

and **non-count** or **mass** nouns. Typical non-count nouns are words for substances which do not have any determinate physical outline (*wine, sand, oxygen*) and certain abstract nouns (*happiness, sincerity*). (Expressions like *the wines of France* or *the Joneses* are special usages, transformational shorthands for *the varieties of French wine, the people called 'Jones'*, etc.) To ensure that a noun does not receive an illegitimate determiner, it must be marked as [+ COUNT] or [− COUNT] or [+ NAME] in its dictionary entry.

As well as being assigned a certain number, a noun must be characterized as having particular or general reference. The primary distinction is between [+ UNIVERSAL] and [− UNIVERSAL] *NP*s. The subject-*NP* of 214 is clearly [+ UNIVERSAL]: the statement is true of any and all cats:

214.   The cat is a mammal

but the corresponding *NP* in 215 is [− UNIVERSAL]:

215.   The cat is a tabby.

Since the same surface structure may express either of these two opposed meanings, ambiguity arises. 211 is ambiguous as between 'any cat' and 'this particular cat'. Synonymous expressions exist, too. In addition to 214, we have both 216 and 217:

216.   A cat is a mammal.
217.   Cats are mammals.

The surface forms of *NP*s are quite misleading with regard to the [UNIVERSALITY] feature. However, the inflexion of the predicate usually determines what value of this feature to assign to a noun. From *broke* in 180 we know that *the children* is [− UNIVERSAL]; and since a specific action at one point of time is described, *the window* must be so, too. Having said that both of these *NP*s are [− UNIVERSAL] there is more to say, for we have to distinguish 180 from, say, 218:

180.   The children broke the window.
218.   Some children broke a window.

All nouns which are [− UNIVERSAL] may be either [+ DEFINITE] or [− DEFINITE], except names and personal pronouns, which are of course implicitly [+ DEFINITE] − they designate already identified objects. The *Det*s of 180 both receive the component [+ DEFINITE], those of 218 [− DEFINITE]. In the light of these observations on number and universality, the notation 210 may now be more fully specified as follows:

219.

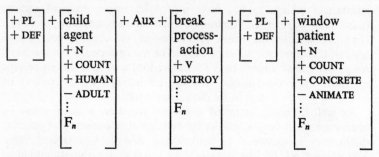

The *Det* segments of these two *NP*s are as simple as they could be: they merely obey the minimum requirements of containing one component selected from each of the systems 'number' and 'universality'. Several other meanings are optionally available under *Det*. For instance, if an *NP* is [+ DEFINITE], it may be further specified as [± PROXIMATE] – *this window* ([+ PROXIMATE]) or *that window* ([– PROXIMATE]). 'Proximateness' is an interesting semantic system, the classic instance of the **deictic** properties of language. **Deixis** (from the Greek, meaning 'pointing') is the facility for 'orienting' propositions and their parts in relation to the time and place of utterance: *this* and *that* (likewise *near* and *far*, *here* and *there*, etc.) set the topics of discourse in a particular spatio-temporal attitude relative to the reference-point provided by the act of speech. Tense also is a deictic quality: the fictional base-line 'present' is drawn by the speaker, or by the reader of a written document making an appropriate reconstruction, and the tenses associated with predicates 'locate' propositions in relation to this standard. Other features of the *NP* are deictic, for instance the **person** systems by reference to which pronouns are defined.

Apart from deixis, the semantic functions of *Det* extend to, for instance, counting devices beyond the outline provided by the number system. Cardinal and ordinal numerals (*one*, *two*; *first*, *second*, respectively) are based on components introduced under *Det*; so are the more relative shades of proportional quantification communicated by words like *all*, *many*, *some of*, *a few of*, etc. These optional systems of quantification have not yet been fully explored, and in any case there is no space to delve into their intricacies. Nor is there sufficient space to show in detail how the sets of abstract components like those found in the *Det* positions of 219 (the first and fifth segments) come to be syntactically rendered, turned into actual words and morphemes by the application of sequences of transformational rules. It must be remembered that formulas like

219 are only the input to the syntactic section of the grammar – complex processes of substitution and reordering occur between 219 and the surface structure 180.

We turn now to *Aux*. Like *Det*, this symbol marks the location, in the most abstract syntactic notation, of a collection of systems of deictic and related meanings; like *Det* again, it provides the basis of a very ragged-looking bunch of formatives in surface structure – while *Det* is the ultimate basis for, say, *many of the three Ns*, *Aux* underlies sequences as complicated as *would have been being Ved*. Because the surface structures of these non-lexical elements attached to nouns and to predicates are so complex – and, as we saw with *Det* (especially examples 214–17), such an unreliable indicator of meaning – it would be profitless to adopt the traditional approach of classifying the words and morphemes and then trying to attach meanings to them. In any event, that would be to put the cart before the horse, for the model of grammar argued here tries to assign priority to meaning rather than to syntax. Instead, a tight system, or set of systems, of meaning-distinctions is proposed; these meanings are expressed in features whose values yield components in terms of which the particular *Det*s and *Aux*s of individual sentences can be represented; finally, the components are realized as actual words and suffixes by the transformational section of the grammar.

Aux endows sentences with four kinds of inflexion: **tense, aspect, mood** and **voice**; these inflexions convey a mixed range of varieties of 'information' and whether all of these should properly be called 'meaning' is open to dispute. Here are some illustrations:

220.   I'm baking a cake.

Tense is 'present', aspect 'progressive', mood 'indicative' and voice 'active'. Compare

221.   Was she being coy?

which is past (T), progressive (A), interrogative (M) and active (V). 222 below is past, perfect, indicative, passive:

222.   He had been sacked by the firm.

We may now look briefly at each of these systems in turn, starting with tense. Although sentences can make reference to a variety of points of time, tense in English, from a formal point of view, has only two values: [± PAST]. A sentence is either marked 'past' or not marked at all. It is in fact misleading to speak of 'present' tense, as I did just now in the informal description of 220. [+ PAST] is a positive designator of 'before-the-present-time', but [− PAST] (which I shall prefer over 'present') has no such unequivocal reference: it doesn't mean simply 'present time'. 223, for instance, though technically [– PAST], is in actuality a statement about the past and present vocation of 'I', and presumably carries an assumption about his future employment: he was a teacher yesterday, is a teacher today, and believes he will be a teacher tomorrow:

223.   I am a teacher.

Non-tense systems convey temporal meanings. English has no future tense, but evokes future time by use of modal expressions (often reinforced or clarified by adverbs):

224.   I will go to London (tomorrow).
225.   I may return to France (next year).
226.   I could do it for you (next week).

Interestingly, 226 is marked [+ PAST], but clearly concerns future time. Tense does not correlate neatly with time and tense is not the only communicator of time. A definition of the system 'tense' in English cannot depend exclusively on a study of the literal time-relations expressed in sentences.

Aspect interrelates with tense, most obviously in that one particular morpheme (the *-ing* form of progressive aspect) can be used to express future time:

227.   I'm leaving for London on Tuesday.

A more systematic interconnection of tense and aspect is that aspect characterizes the manner, duration, repetition, etc. of an action or state relative to the temporal base-line set by the time of utterance. Some basic aspectual contrasts in English are represented by the following sentences:

228.   I closed the door. (One action in the past.)
229.   We're going to the library. (Either a continuing action in the present, or an action in the future.)
230.   I've finished my homework. ('and can now go out to play': a completed action relevant to the present.)
231.   I had opened the door. ('before I saw who it was': a completed action with relevance to subsequent, but deictically past, time.)
232.   I was walking down the street. (Continuous action in the past, not embracing the present.)
223.   I am a teacher. (Statement about yesterday, today and tomorrow.)
233.   Water boils at 100° centigrade. (A general truth.)

234. I had been reading *Giles Goat-Boy*. (A continuous activity
      up to a past point of time, when some subsequent activity
      occurred.)

Progressive and **perfect** aspects are the most obviously recognizable
in English, as they have distinctive morphological manifestations.
Progressive is realized as the *-ing* form of verbs – see sentences 229,
232, 234. It indicates ongoing actions or continuing states, and is
combined with either [– PAST] or [+ PAST] tense, depending on
whether the action continues through the present or stops short of
present time. Contrast 229 – on one reading – with 232. As 234
attests, progressive may combine with **perfect**, the aspect of a completed action or terminated state. Perfect is found in either [+ PAST]
or [– PAST], the distinction being one of 'relevance': [– PAST]
accompanies perfect when the action communicated by the predicate
has relevance to present time (see 230); [+ PAST] is employed when
the completed action had implications for a subsequent action occurring before present time (see 231, 234).

'Perfect' and 'progressive' aspects are clearly evident in surface
structure. One might be tempted to assume that any sentence which
is not overtly marked for aspect calls for no semantic statement
concerning that dimension of meaning. This would be a fallacious
supposition: English possesses at least three, perhaps four or more,
aspectual contrasts which are not obvious in the syntax. One of them,
momentary, is the aspect of simple, single, action or event, and is
readily discernible in many [+ PAST] predicates:

235. The plane crashed.
236. Charlton scored the first goal.
237. Dennis Brain played the horn.

Combination of momentary aspect with [– PAST] tense leads to a
distinctive 'commentary' or 'demonstrating' style of discourse:

238. I switch the cleaner on, thus.
239. Now Charlton moves down the centre of the field.
240. The referee starts the game.

237 and 240 are in fact ambiguous as between momentary and
habitual aspects. 237 may mean 'Dennis Brain was a horn player';
240 'It is conventional that the referee starts the game'. Habitual
is the aspect of 223 and of, say, 241 and 242 below:

241. I don't eat meat.
242. He drives a sports car.

In each case a permanent or quasi-permanent fact, disposition or
state of affairs is communicated. A variant of the kind of report

given by 'habitual' might be called **iterative**: this communicates a disposition to regular, but not continuous, activity. It is found in sentences such as the following – note that it is reinforced adverbially:

243. I go to London every Tuesday.
244. She washes her hair twice a week.

Perhaps parallel aspectual categories are needed to characterize other modes of action as they occur relative to the time-scale provided by tense.

For a final contrast of aspect, compare the following sentences:

223. I am a teacher.
245. I used to be a teacher.
233. Water boils at 100° centigrade.
246. (?*) Water used to boil at 100° centigrade.

223 conveys an only quasi-permanent fact, whereas 233 states an immutable truth: the situation described in 223 can change if 'I' takes on a new job, while the truth of 233 depends on a constant physical fact or at least on the acceptance of a physical definition. The distinction is reflected in the combinability of habitual aspect with [+ PAST], and the incompatibility of [+ PAST] with the aspect of 233, as witnessed by the absurdity of 246. A second difference between 223 and 233 is that the subject *NP* of 223 is [– UNIVERSAL], that of 233 [+ UNIVERSAL]: I assume that the [+ UNIVERSAL] of *water* in 233 is required by the aspect of the predicate. Chafe would call the aspect of both 223 and 233 'generic', but I shall reserve the term **generic** for 233 only. Examples of generic sentences in chapter 4 are 52, 53, 66, 99, 101, 102; of habitual, 79, 98, 122, 124, and 191, 192 in the present chapter.

The third predicate-inflexion which is subsumed under *Aux* is **voice**. This system – which varies considerably in its composition from language to language – provides alternative ways of treating the role 'agent' in sentences based on process-action predicates. English is usually said to possess only one contrast of voice: **active** versus **passive**, 247 versus 248:

247. Peter swallowed the medicine.
248. The medicine was swallowed by Peter.

(Notice that 248 is somewhat unlikely; occurring perhaps only in answer to equally improbable questions like 'Who swallowed the medicine?') Actives and passives are cognitively synonymous: if 247 is true, 248 cannot be false, and vice versa. Transformational-generative grammarians have made great play with this fact of cognitive synonymy – the active/passive relationship being regarded as the classic instance of two surface structures having the same deep structure. That active and passive equivalents have the same deep structure is doubtful, since there must be some distinguishing component in deep structure which 'triggers' the distinct transformations which lead to the radically different surface arrangements. But that is perhaps an academic point; what is more important is that we should ask why, granted the equivalence of content, two syntactic forms so utterly different should be available to the language-user. There seem, in fact, to be two very cogent justifications for the passive. One is that it allows the agent role to remain unspecified in certain conditions:

249. A hitch-hiker was murdered.
250. Dinner had been finished.
251. Sam was beaten.

Conceptually, the agent is present: if the hitch-hiker was murdered, it is inconceivable that he wasn't murdered by anyone, so the semantic structure must include an instance of the role 'agent'; however, the role may remain unfilled – a particular convenience if the identity or nature of the agent is not known to the speaker, as may well be the case with utterances such as 249. Such a sentence may be derived from a conceptual structure in which *Aux* includes the component [PASSIVE] and the role 'agent' is mentioned but not provided with a lexical exponent – no specific word. In these conditions the word-order-changing power of the passive transformation would be brought into action, but the agent, being lexically blank, would not pass into surface structure.

The other use for the passive – second in my exposition, but perhaps more important – is subtler. Consider the following sentences, and ask why the second is more 'natural'; a game such as tennis or golf is being discussed:

252. A professional beat Sám.
253. Sam was beaten by a proféssional.

Both sentences are to be read with the most prominent syllable in the normal position for the intonation-patterns of English utterances, marked above by the accents; but not with heavy 'contrastive' stress. 252 feels odd with this intonation, whereas 253 is natural, as is 254:

254. Sam beat a proféssional.

In 254 the agent is known to the speaker and audience, while the patient-*NP* presents new information. Typically, the agent of this type of construction goes on the left, the patient on the right, of the predicate. Now the final prominent syllable of a sentence, carrying the highest stress-pitch level, is the most 'informative' point of the sentence: so it is appropriate that the 'new' part of the meaning should occur there, the familiar part of the proposition being located at the relatively 'uninformative', because intonationally non-prominent, beginning of the utterance. So the conceptual content of 254, seen from the point of view of new and old information, neatly fits the typical intonation structure which goes with simple sentences. But when the agent is 'new' and the patient 'old', a mis-match between conceptual structure and intonation happens, leading to the unnatural 252. The resolution of this problem is either to employ the passive transformation, as is done in 253, or to alter the prominence by an especially high pitch level on the 'new' agent:

255.   A proféssional beat Sam.

Except in answer to certain kinds of insistent questions ('*Who* beat Sam?'), English speakers seem to prefer 253 to 255. The rule seems to be, then, that in an agent-process/action-patient sentence where the agent presents new information and the patient familiar information, the passive transformation is employed. As might be expected, the passive is found regularly when the patient-*NP* is a name, a personal pronoun, or is [+ DEFINITE] while the agent is [− DEFINITE]:

256.   Sally was approached by a complete stranger.
257.   He was found by a policeman.
258.   The car was stolen by some bank robbers.

(Try the effect of undoing the passive transformation with these examples.)

Since the passive transformation is motivated by semantic considerations, it fails to apply to certain kinds of proposition. 259 below has a complement, not a patient, as its left-hand *NP*, so it is ungrammatical – the passive must not be applied to the underlying structures of such sentences:

259.   *Three tons are weighed by this truck.

We come now to the final one of the four systems of choice which underlie *Aux*, the system of **mood** or **modality**. This very complicated, and as yet poorly understood, system expresses the speaker's attitude to, confidence in, or rhetorical orientation towards, the topic of discourse. For instance, the auxiliary *will*, now used to indicate future time, is descended from the Anglo-Saxon verb *willan*, which meant 'have the intention to': it attested to one's commitment to an action which was to be undertaken in the future. It expressed *attitude*, 'mood', rather than simple time. Compare modern English *may* in 260, which indicates possibility or uncertainty on the part of the speaker – a reduced degree of the confidence expressed by the old *will*, and not primarily a temporal meaning:

260.   I may cut the grass tomorrow.

May, will, must, need to, etc. all communicate 'marked' or positively specified choices of modality. They contrast with each other and with the unmarked or neutral choice – **indicative**, the mood of plain statement conveying no special stance or engagement on the part of the speaker. See, for example, 261 and 262 –

261.   The orchestra was disappointing.
262.   I'm writing a book.

– or any of the sentences 228–34 above. Notice that none of these sentences manifests any of the special words (*can, not, will*, etc.) associated with the classic 'marked' modals, or any of the rearrangements of morphemes, changes in word-order, found in questions and commands (which are also 'moods'). In its semantic neutrality as well as in its syntactic plainness, indicative mood has a formal status parallel to that of momentary aspect – though of course the two are in no way dependent on one another.

Indicative contrasts on the one hand with **negative**, and on the other with **affirmative**. Negative and indicative provide a dichotomous opposition of modality very similar to the lexical opposition in pairs of 'complementary' lexical items (see p. 66 above). *X is dry* is inconsistent with *X is wet*; and *X is not wet* is of course also inconsistent with *X is wet*, spoken of the same *X*. Evidently, negative and indicative are mutually exclusive moods – they cannot inflect the same proposition simultaneously. However, any proposition may be negated, and here the similarity with complementaries ends, for not every lexical item has a contrastively matched complementary term.

Having said that any proposition can be negated, there might seem to be little else to observe about negative mood. This apparent simplicity is illusory, however. The expression of negation embraces a varied miscellany of forms, not only the word *not* and the suffix *n't* – *He was not tall, He didn't run*. There are other negating words such as *never, no, none* which are inserted in positions in a sentence different from that occupied by *not* and which convey different shades of meaning; there are negative particles such as *un-* and *non-* which are governed by rather complicated rules; there are implicitly negative terms such as *scarcely, hardly, rather*. Finally, there are interesting differences in the **scope** of negation. A negative element in a sentence may apply to the whole underlying proposition, or it may relate only to one constituent. Some of the possibilities can be detected in the following – classic – ambiguous sentence:

263.　Brutus didn't kill a tyrant.

This may mean (a) 'It is not the case that Brutus killed a tyrant' – the truth of the whole proposition denied; or (b) 'It wasn't Brutus who killed a tyrant' – here it is asserted that a tyrant was killed, but Brutus's agency denied; or (c) 'Brutus didn't *kill* a tyrant' – he did something to a tyrant, but didn't kill him; or (d) 'It wasn't a tyrant that Brutus killed' – Brutus killed someone, but not a tyrant. Meanings (b)–(d), in which parts only of the proposition are denied, can be brought out by placing a disambiguating stress on the appropriate syllable:

264.　(b)　Brútus didn't kill a tyrant.
　　　　(c)　Brutus didn't kíll a tyrant.
　　　　(d)　Brutus didn't kill a týrant.

Extra prominence on crucial syllables is the signal of **affirmative** mood. To affirm, rather than simply indicate, a whole proposition, the auxiliary, if there is one, is made particularly prominent, or if there isn't, an auxiliary verb is supplied to carry the affirmative stress:

265.　The orchestra wás disappointing.
266.　I ám writing a book.

(Cf. 261–2 above.) Affirmative may also be combined with negative mood:

267.　Brutus dídn't kill a tyrant.

And as with negation, different sub-parts of a proposition may be affirmed:

268.　(a)　Brútus killed a tyrant.
　　　　(b)　Brutus kílled a tyrant.
　　　　(c)　Brutus killed a týrant.

Questions (**interrogative** mood), just like denials and emphatic assertions, have variable scope, sometimes querying a whole proposition (269 (a)) and sometimes only a part (269 (b)–(d)):

269.　(a)　Did Brutus kill a tyrant?
　　　　(b)　Did Brútus kill a tyrant?
　　　　(c)　Did Brutus kíll a tyrant?
　　　　(d)　Did Brutus kill a týrant?

There are also special forms spelt with *wh-* for querying subjects and objects:

270. Who killed Caesar?
271. Which tyrant did Brutus kill?

Although no definitive rules have yet been drawn up for the description of the three moods 'affirmative', 'negative' and 'interrogative', their meanings are fairly clear and their syntactic manifestations very systematic, so there is probably no insuperable barrier to their formal analysis. This is true of the **imperative** mood (command) also: action and process-action predicates may be inflected via *Aux* for imperative, with the consequence that a second-person agent is supplied and then deleted (the 'understood *you*'):

272. Shut the door!
273. Wash yourself!

Other modal systems, however – particularly those which are realized in the special modal auxiliaries *may, should, must*, etc. – can at the moment be described only most impressionistically. I will mention just two which are fairly clearly recognizable. One might be called **possibility** or **certainty**. This provides a scale (probably) of degrees of certainty communicated by the speaker; the following indicate various degrees of confidence in the truth of the statement:

274. He may have done it.
275. He must have done it.
276. He might do it.
277. He will do it.

Another system, which might be called **obligation** or **necessity**, obviously has some semantic affinity with imperative:

278. I ought to go home.
279. I must go and visit her.
280. I should have worn my seat belt.
281. I need to have a tooth filled.

One of the problems in the way of formalizing our description of these modal meanings is that some of the modal words belong to more than one system, producing frequent ambiguities:

282. He must do it. (certainty/obligation)
283. He may do it. (possibility/permission)

I shall conclude this necessarily long exposition of the important formative *Aux* with some illustrations, and then finally return to

121

the representation of our sample sentence 180 (last seen on p. 105 above). In the most general notation, *Aux* can be represented as a cluster of abstract features thus:

284.
$$\begin{bmatrix} \text{TENSE} \\ \text{ASPECT} \\ \text{MOOD} \\ \text{VOICE} \end{bmatrix}$$

In particular sentences, *Aux* appears in the deep structure as a set of selections from each of the four systems named in 284, as I indicated informally in discussing 220–2 (p. 113 above). Here are some examples, with notation but without discussion:

285. Was he being noisy?

$$NP + \begin{bmatrix} + \text{PAST} \\ \text{PROGRESSIVE} \\ \text{INTERROGATIVE} \\ \text{ACTIVE} \end{bmatrix} + \text{Adj}$$

286. The door was opened by Eric.

$$NP + \begin{bmatrix} + \text{PAST} \\ \text{MOMENTARY} \\ \text{INDICATIVE} \\ \text{PASSIVE} \end{bmatrix} + V + NP$$

287. Wás she leaving?

$$NP + \begin{bmatrix} + \text{PAST} \\ \text{PROG} \\ \text{INT} \\ \text{AFF} \\ \text{ACT} \end{bmatrix} + V$$

(*Note*: two simultaneous choices under mood.)

288. Whales are mammals.

$$NP + \begin{bmatrix} - \text{PAST} \\ \text{GENERIC} \\ \text{IND} \\ \text{ACT} \end{bmatrix} + NP$$

Our sentence 180 can now receive a complete deep structure representation:

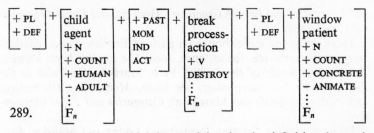

289.

This symbolization – which is not claimed to be definitive, but only as complete and delicate as possible within the limitations of the provisional grammatical model employed in the present book – gives a lot of information, and information of various kinds. First and foremost, it is intended to show semantic structure. But the display of semantic structure is arranged in such a way that a well-formed syntactic construction can be derived from such formulas as 289 and, in their more fully specified versions, 285–8. A tree-diagram associated with the linear representation above allows us to reconstruct the constituent structure of the sentence. And the components given within square brackets do not only designate the presence of values of semantic features; they also serve as 'cues' to the syntactic transformations which are responsible for bringing about surface structure arrangements of words, phrases and morphemes. For example, the presence of [PASSIVE] in 286 sets in motion the re-ordering processes which bring about the switching of the agent and patient-*NP*s, the insertion of *by*, etc.; the component [INTERROGATIVE] in 287 is responsible for transposing the order of the agent *NP* and the auxiliary. Such processes are the subject-matter of the next chapter.

Further reading for chapters 5–7

Voluminous materials on syntax are available. Some classic older grammars which will provide a wealth of information are those of Curme, Kruisinga, Poutsma, Zandvoort listed in the Bibliography below; and of all the grammars of this kind, Jespersen's *Modern English Grammar* is perhaps the most enlightening. Some more recent books are Francis, *Structure of American English*, Fries, *The Structure of English*, Long, *The Sentence and its Parts*, Nida, *Synopsis of English Syntax*, Quirk *et al.*, *A Grammar of Contemporary English*, Sledd, *Short Introduction to English Grammar*, Stageberg, *Introductory English Grammar*, Strang, *Modern English Structure*. A recent historical grammar is Traugott, *A History of English Syntax*.

Some standard, or once-standard, linguistics textbooks which may profitably be consulted are those of Gleason (both the *Introduction* and *Linguistics and English Grammar*), Hockett, and Lyons (*Theoretical Linguistics*).

There are many useful books on parts of English syntax, particularly on the verb: see, for instance, Joos, *The English Verb*, Palmer, *A Linguistic Study of the English Verb*, Svartvik, *On Voice in the English Verb*. On morphology see Nida, *Morphology* (theoretical and methodological) and Marchand, *Categories and Types* (descriptive).

Primary reading for transformational syntax is Chomsky, *Syntactic Structures* and *Aspects*, Katz and Postal, *Integrated Theory*, Lees, *English Nominalizations*, Rosenbaum, *English Predicate Complement Constructions*, Lakoff, *Irregularity in Syntax*, Bach and Harms, *Universals*, Chafe, *Meaning and the Structure of Language*. The changing interests and emphases of generative grammarians are admirably charted by Lyons in his little book, *Chomsky*, and in his chapter 'Generative syntax' in *New Horizons*. TG textbooks, written at various stages in the changing history of the discipline, by Bach, Fowler, Jacobs and Rosenbaum, Koutsoudas, Langendoen (both *Study of Syntax* and *Essentials*) and Thomas may be consulted, but none of these secondary materials should be substituted for the primary texts.

A valuable detailed English grammar from a transformational point of view is Stockwell *et al.*, *The Major Syntactic Structures of English*.

The richest materials are probably to be found in the linguistics journals: *Archivum Linguisticum, Foundations of Language, Journal of Linguistics, Language, Lingua, Linguistics, Transactions of the Philological Society, Word*.

Finally, there are three most important collections of articles, some original and some reprinted, edited by Fodor and Katz (*The Structure of Language*), Reibel and Schane (*Modern Studies in English*) and Jacobs and Rosenbaum (*Readings in English Transformational Grammar*). I strongly urge students of syntax to dip into these collections.

six

Transformations

Broadly considered, the previous three chapters were concerned with the underlying structure and meaning of sentences, while this one and the two following deal with more superficial aspects of structure; more precisely, with the mechanisms by which abstract meanings are set out in linear sequence and provided with a phonetic representation. For 'more superficial' we could say 'more concrete': as we progress into this sequence of chapters we will encounter representations of sentences which look more and more recognizable as bearing some similarity to flesh-and-blood sentences.

A note on the convention of 'progression' which governs the structure of chapters 5 and 6. The controlling structure is that of **derivation**. What I am doing is attaching progressively more concrete descriptions or representations to my example sentences. I do not claim to model any sequential process which might be involved in the construction of a sentence by an actual speaker. There is no evidence that speakers in real linguistic performance go through a sequence of operations like the ones I am carrying out to take myself and my reader from deep to surface structure. Derivation is a convention for describing in an orderly fashion the structure of a sentence, not its production.

The notation 289, with which we ended the previous chapter, exemplifies a most crucial stage in the derivation of a sentence. 289 claims to symbolize first all the components of the meaning of the sentence it represents; it also seeks to symbolize these components of meaning in such a way that the processes necessary for syntactic ordering can take place. Now 289 has two properties which make it amenable to syntactic development. First of all, we know the constituent-structure rules which helped to form it (see p. 109 above)

125

and so the hierarchical phrase-structure of 289 is known implicitly; this might be represented as the tree 290:

290.

Second, many of the components shown in 289 have automatic implications for syntactic structure. For instance, from the presence of [ACTIVE] in the *Aux* we know that the linear order of constituents shown in 289 must be broadly preserved: that *the children* is the superficial subject and therefore stays on the left of the sentence, as it is shown in 289, while *the window* stays on the right, etc. However, if *Aux* in 289 had shown the element [PASSIVE], this would have served as an instruction for major transformational reordering, with *the children* being moved to the right of the sentence and *the window* to the left (cf. 291 below). Thus the surface structure arrangement is implied in the choice of elements occurring in the deep structure. As another example of the power of the abstract 289 to determine superficial structure, notice that the componential representation of the left-hand *NP* determines that it must emerge as the actual phrase *the children*; similarly, the right-hand *NP* must be realized as *the window*. The actual phrases do not occur in 289, but enough information is supplied for us to predict them in every detail.

The word 'must', used in the previous paragraph, was not used loosely. I would like to argue that notations of the style 289 (with 290 implicitly attached) ought to be expressed in such a way that surface structures can be derived *automatically* from them: this is the true sense of the notion 'deep structure', if we extend the logic of Chomsky's, and Katz and Postal's, argument on this point. Deep structure is more than cognitive content, for it contains all information necessary to the automatic formation of a full syntactic structure. Since the same cognitive content may be expressed in different ways (cf. 180/291), deep structure must contain signals of expression as well as of content; yet of course it does display conceptual content, and remains a good deal more abstract than surface structure. In the case of my representation 289, I do not guarantee that it is the ideal way of expressing all this information, but it is offered as an example of the kind of notation that is necessary if we do aim to make deep structure show both conceptual content and the germ of syntactic form.

In the total process of grammatical analysis, objects of the kind shown compositely by 289–90 (corresponding roughly to **underlying phrase-markers** in a conventional Chomskyan grammar) form the input to the **transformational** component of the grammar. My brief mention of transformations, or transformational rules, so far has suggested various characterizations for them (see pp. 31–3 above). Put most abstractly, transformations form the bridge between deep structure and surface structure, necessary mediators between conceptual content and the concrete shape of utterances. They 'transform' elements of meaning into linear formats. Looked at from another point of view, transformations allow the linguist to show the relationships between sentences – for instance, the series of manoeuvres entailed by the passive transformation allows us to show step-by-step how 180 (*The children broke the window*) is related to its cognitive equivalent –

291. The window was broken by the children

– or 6 to its synonym 13 (p. 31 above). To put it more mundanely still, transformations change constituent structure, reordering 289/290 to generate the real surface structure 180. Altering constituent-structure is not the only function of transformational rules, but since it is the most dramatic operation they perform, it will best serve this elementary discussion.

Changes to constituent structure fall into three categories – **permutation, deletion** and **amalgamation**. Permutation is rearrangement of the order of constituents, as for example the switching of the positions of agent and patient *NP*s in passives, or the moving of the particle of some two-constituent verbs to the right of the object:

292. I put down the book.
293. I put the book down.

At the semantic level, *put down* is one single meaning (unlike *ran + down* in *He ran down the road*) and therefore appears in deep structure as one segment, one cluster of semantic components, just like any single-word verb such as *hit, defend*. Later in the derivation, two elements must be separated out from the one deep-structure segment, producing a string of this form:

294.   NP + Aux + V + Part + NP.

This skeletal notation in fact conceals two deep structures: one contains an instruction that the particle-shift transformation should apply, the other does not. In the former case the following process occurs:

295. NP + Aux + V + Part + NP $\Rightarrow$ NP + Aux + V + NP + Part.

The transformational rule (recognizable by the distinctive double arrow '$\Rightarrow$') takes the string 294 as its input and renders it as the string on the right of the arrow. (Note that '$\Rightarrow$' means 'becomes' or 'is changed into' whereas '$\rightarrow$' means 'consists of'.) The rule does not apply just to one symbol, as rewriting rules do, but to the whole of a string, or line in a derivation. The effect of this rule is to move the particle – which presents 'new' information – into the position of maximum informativeness, the final, pitch-prominent, syllable in the utterance. The rule may apply to any string with the constituent structure of 294 (cf. *put up, take off*, etc.) with one exception: where the object is a pronoun, the rule *must* be applied:

296. He put it down.
297. *He put down it.

This is presumably because a pronoun always presents familiar information, and in 297 is therefore pointlessly placed in the position of maximum information. To accommodate this exception, the rule 295 obviously has to be expressed in a rather more complicated way than it appears above.

Deletion is self-explanatory: transformations of this type *remove* constituents. There are many sentences where, for the sake of the meaning, some item is posited in deep structure which does not appear on the surface. The imperative construction is, as mentioned before, an excellent example. Structuralism of the American brand, concerned only with surface structure, was unable to accept the '*you* understood' of traditional grammar; but transformational grammar, with its distinction of deep and surface structure, makes this explanation very reasonable. If it is asked how the presence of an implicit second-person pronoun is justified, when it never occurs on the surface, the evidence comes from such sentences as the following:

298. Wash yourselves!
299. *Wash themselves!

A reflexive pronoun (*myself, himself*, etc.) can occur in a sentence only if there is an agent which has the same referent as that pronoun:

300. John injured himself.
301. You betrayed yourself.

If agent and patient are not congruent, ungrammaticalness results from reflexivization:

302. *John betrayed themselves.

From these observations we can argue that there is an implicit agent in 298 (otherwise reflexivization could not occur) and that this can only be a second person pronoun (since all reflexive imperatives other than those with *yourself/-selves* are ungrammatical).

Amalgamation transformations combine underlying phrase-markers to form complex sentences, or add segments to underlying strings. The passive transformation involves both amalgamation (the addition of *by*) and permutation; so, as we shall see, does one version of the question transformation. The following example displays the effects of both amalgamation and deletion:

303. I washed the dishes and then went out.

This is obviously derived from two underlying propositions: *I washed the dishes* and *I went out afterwards* or something of the sort. The amalgamation places these statements in an appropriate order, inserts *and* and renders the temporal adverb *afterwards* as *then*. Semantically, each predicate (*wash* and *go*) is attended by the agent *I*: there is no reason to think that *I* does not occur twice in deep structure. But in the finished sentence, it is redundant to identify the agent twice, so the second occurrence is deleted.

I shall fill the remainder of this chapter with further examples of transformational structure. My examples will be limited to the **local** transformations which are responsible for the realization of *Det* and *Aux*, principally *Aux*. These transformations are peculiarly important because some selection from them is involved in the derivation of each and every sentence. We start with a transformation which is very typical of the processes to be examined; it is generally called **affix-shift**. Affix-shift is necessary to ensure that the inflexions on nouns and verbs occur in the correct places in surface structure. Inflexional morphemes, in English, commonly occur both before and after the word they relate to:

304. *was going*
305. *the* cigarette*s*.

In the previous chapter I argued that such inflexions are manifestations of single, unitary, complexes of meaning, and so their underlying meanings were derived from single segments – the square-bracketed clusters of components reflecting the single symbols *Det* and *Aux*. These segments are positioned *before* the noun and the verb respectively in abstract representations such as 289, making some reordering essential to get the inflexions to *follow* the word in surface structure while preserving that part of the inflexional complex which remains preceding it. We may take a very simple example to show how this repositioning transformation works:

306.   He cleaned his shoes.

Aux here is [+ PAST, MOMENTARY, INDICATIVE, ACTIVE] so 306 shows as 307 at one level of representation:

307.   NP + $\begin{bmatrix} + \text{PAST} \\ \text{MOM} \\ \text{IND} \\ \text{ACT} \end{bmatrix}$ + V + NP.

Of the four components of *Aux*, only [+ PAST] is to have any impact on surface structure, so the remaining three components can be ignored – in fact they can be dropped from the derivation:

308.   NP + [+ PAST] + V + NP.

The 'impact' which the component [+ PAST] has (remember, deep structure components can 'trigger' transformations) is to bring about its own transposition with the *V* symbol, in accordance with the following transformational rule:

309.   X + Af + V + Y $\Rightarrow$ X + V + Af + Y.

This rule means 'any sequence of an affix followed by a verb must be reversed'. *X* and *Y* here are **cover symbols**: they do not stand for any constituent in particular (contrast the specific *V* which always represents 'verb') but for any constituent whatsoever. Here, *X* and *Y* symbolize the two *NP*s of 308, but they may stand for anything or nothing. Using these cover symbols allows us to formulate the rule so that it applies as generally as possible. It would not be advisable to state the affix-shift rules as 310 below – with only 306 and similar sentences in mind – because it has to apply also to sentences of the type 311, where there is no second *NP*; in symbolizing 311, the *Y* of 309 stands for 'nothing':

310.   *NP + Af + V + NP $\Rightarrow$ NP + V + Af + NP.
311.   The audience laughed.

The effect of 309 on 308, or, equivalently, on the underlying structure of 311, is to place the component [+ PAST] in the correct position so that it can later be realized as the morpheme *-ed*; and when the sentence becomes subject to phonological rules, this will be changed into the appropriate phonological shape /d/ for *cleaned*, or /t/ for *laughed*, or /əd/ or /ɪd/ for, say, *started*.

A similar transformational process controls the realization of determiners. Let us assume the phrase *the desks* as a target. Using the cover symbols again to show that the rest of the sentence is immaterial to the realization of *NP*s, we can display the relevant underlying structure as follows:

312. $X + \begin{bmatrix} + \text{PL} \\ + \text{DEF} \end{bmatrix} + desk + Y.$

(The lexical item *desk* is given here for legibility and as a typographical convenience. In a proper derivation *desk* would appear as a fully specified cluster of components, as the *N*s in 289 were.) The first move is to apply a highly particularized rule to 312, turning the *Det* in question into the morphemes which express it in surface structure:

313. $X + \begin{bmatrix} + \text{PL} \\ + \text{DEF} \end{bmatrix} + N + Y \Rightarrow X + (the + \text{-}s) + N + Y.$

Notice how the rule develops the article *the* and the plural inflexion *-s* simultaneously from *Det*, thus acknowledging the essential relationship which they have by virtue of their common origin in *Det*. Note also that *the* is not a simple substitute for [+ DEF], nor *-s* for [+ PL]: the two morphemes reflect a *complex* meaning in *Det*, not *two separate* meanings both based in *Det*. Next, the output string of 313 is subjected to a very much more general T-rule, very much like 309 in its form, which determines the relative positions of elements:

314. $X + Af + N + Y \Rightarrow X + N + Af + Y.$

The output of this rule is the string *the + desk + -s*, which becomes the input to the phonological section of the grammar and is eventually phonetically represented as *the desks*.

Often there is, superficially, no affix: with *the desks* compare *the boy*. To meet such cases, we introduce the symbol $\emptyset$ 'zero' into the derivation:

315. $X + \begin{bmatrix} - \text{PL} \\ + \text{DEF} \end{bmatrix} + desk + Y.$

316. $X + (the + \emptyset) + desk + Y$ (by a particular rule analogous to 313).

317. $X + the + desk + \emptyset + Y$ (by rule 314).

$\emptyset$ can be used twice, as in the derivation of the subject-*NP* of *John writes*:

318. $X + \begin{bmatrix} - \text{PL} \\ - \text{UNIV} \end{bmatrix} + John + Y.$

131

319. $X + (\emptyset + \emptyset) + John + Y$ (by a rule analogous to 313).
320. $X + \emptyset + John\ \emptyset + Y$ (by rule 314).

More complicated *NP*s are realized by a slightly more complicated process, but one which follows just the same principles. Suppose we have a phrase containing a **numeral**: *the three bags*. Numerals are either **cardinal** or **ordinal**, a choice which can be shown in the componential specification of *Det*; and if 'cardinal' is chosen, the phrase *the three bags* will appear as 321:

321. $X + \begin{bmatrix} + \text{PL} \\ + \text{DEF} \\ + \text{CARDINAL} \end{bmatrix} + bag + Y.$

The next stage separates out [CARDINAL]:

322. $X + \begin{bmatrix} + \text{PL} \\ + \text{DEF} \end{bmatrix} + [\text{CARDINAL}] + bag + Y.$

(A T-rule between 321 and 322 creates the necessary extra segment for *three*; similar rules are employed in the development of *Aux* – see, for example, 329 and 334 below.)

323. $X + (the + -s) + [\text{CARDINAL}] + bag + Y$ (by a rule analogous to 313).
324. $X + the + [\text{CARDINAL}] + -s + bag + Y$ (by a permutation rule).
325. $X + the + [\text{CARDINAL}] + bag + -s + Y$ (by 314).

Now the segment [CARDINAL] is replaced by a cardinal number other than *one*:

326. *the + three + bag + -s.*

This is the input to the phonology and will become *the three bags* in due course, the suffix *-s* being 'spelt' phonetically as the voiced /z/ as opposed to the /s/ appropriate to *desks*.

We now return to *Aux*, to examine some more complicated permutation sequences, and particularly to look at the insertion of extra words to carry the considerable amount of inflexional information which is associated with *Aux*. We have seen that in the simplest case, where only tense needs a special morpheme in surface structure (e.g. 306), the tense affix is transposed with the verb by rule 309. The next simplest situation occurs when there is a 'marked' selection from the mood system (on 'markedness' in relation to mood, see p. 119 above); for example:

327. I might go.

The relevant part of this sentence may be represented as follows; note that the transformationally ineffectual choices under aspect (*momentary*) and voice (*active*) have been ignored:

328. $\begin{bmatrix} + \text{PAST} \\ \text{POSSIBILITY} \end{bmatrix} + \text{V}.$

'Possibility' is indicated by a special modal auxiliary, so an extra segment has to be created (cf. 322 above):

329. [+ PAST] + [POSSIBILITY] + V.

The mood is now realized as *may*:

330. [+ PAST] + *may* + V.

It now becomes clear that there is justification for the creation of the extra modal segment to the right rather than the left of [+ PAST]: this positioning prevents the affix-shift rule applying to the sequence [+ PAST] . . . V, since they are not adjacent in the string. Why do we need this particular failure of affix-shift? A glance at the target sentence 327 will answer this question: in predicate-phrases containing a modal auxiliary, it is the auxiliary which is inflected, not the main verb – we do not encounter **I may went*. The correct inflexion of 327, and of other similar examples, is achieved by applying the affix-shift rule to yield the line

331. *may* + [+ PAST] + V

which can be turned into 327. Note that the success of these processes requires some modification of the affix-shifting rule. It must (a) be allowed to apply to auxiliaries as well as to main verbs; (b) be prevented from applying twice to the same affix (or, as we shall see, to the same verb, otherwise a pile-up of inflexions will occur: **walkeding*, **painteden*, etc.).

Suppose that we had an *Aux* containing [+ PAST, PROGRESSIVE, INDICATIVE, ACTIVE], as in

332. He was eating his breakfast.

[INDICATIVE] and [ACTIVE] have no effect on the surface structure, so are discounted. The part of the sentence in which we are interested is, then,

333. $\begin{bmatrix} + \text{PAST} \\ \text{PROG} \end{bmatrix} + \text{V}.$

Again, the extra segment is created to the right of the tense element:

334. [+ PAST] + [PROG] + V.

This string is further concretized as

335.　[+ PAST] + -*ing* + V

which contains an *Af* + *V* sequence, so the normal transposition takes place:

336.　[+ PAST] + V + -*ing*.

Because of the restrictions we have placed on the affix-shifting transformation, [+ PAST] is unaffixable: it must not be suffixed on *V*, since the place is taken by -*ing*. To cope with this difficulty, the pseudo-verb *be* is inserted to the right of [+ PAST]:

337.　[+ PAST] + *be* + V + -*ing*.

[+ PAST] is now subject to affix-shift, and finally the resulting sequence *be* + [+ PAST] becomes *was*. If the target sentence contains perfect rather than progressive aspect (*He had eaten his breakfast*) an exactly parallel series of transformations is worked through, except that -*en* is introduced where 335 inserts -*ing*, and *have* appears, in the line corresponding to 337, instead of *be*.

If we make *Aux* more complicated, we merely lengthen the derivation; we do not change the principles upon which it is constructed. To illustrate this, I will write out the pertinent section of the derivation for 338 – in which perfect and progressive aspects have been selected simultaneously – without commentary. The reader is advised to work through this carefully and to attempt more complicated derivations still on his own (e.g. *would have been eating his breakfast*).

338.　He had been eating his breakfast.

339.
$$
\begin{bmatrix} +\text{ PAST} \\ \text{PERFECT} \\ \text{PROGRESSIVE} \\ \text{INDICATIVE} \\ \text{ACTIVE} \end{bmatrix} + \text{V.}
$$

$$
\begin{bmatrix} +\text{ PAST} \\ \text{PERF} \\ \text{PROG} \end{bmatrix} + \text{V}
$$

$$
\begin{bmatrix} +\text{ PAST} \\ \text{PERF} \end{bmatrix} + [\text{PROG}] + \text{V}
$$

$$
\begin{bmatrix} +\text{ PAST} \\ \text{PERF} \end{bmatrix} + \text{-}ing + \text{V}
$$

$$\begin{bmatrix} + \text{PAST} \\ \text{PERF} \end{bmatrix} + \text{V} + \textit{-ing}$$

$$\begin{bmatrix} + \text{PAST} \\ \text{PERF} \end{bmatrix} + be + \text{V} + \textit{-ing}$$

[+ PAST] + [PERF] + *be* + V + *-ing*
[+ PAST] + *-en* + *be* + V + *-ing*
[+ PAST] + *be* + *-en* + V + *-ing*
[+ PAST] + *have* + *be* + *-en* + V + *-ing*
have + [+ PAST] + *be* + *-en* + V + *-ing*.

Finally, a surface structure is formed by combining the first and second segments as *had*, the third and fourth as *been*, and the fifth and sixth as *eating*.

'Pseudo-verbs' like *be, have* and *do* are introduced whenever the affix-shifting transformation fails to apply. So far, the conditions which have caused these words to be brought into play have been unavailability of the verb through prior inflexion (336–7) and separation of *Aux* from *V* by some inflectable intervening segment (330–1). Other instances of separation of *Aux* and *V* will be encountered below when we look at negatives and questions. A third situation in which affix-shift fails is where there is no verb at all to receive the tense suffix:

340. Mr Smith is cautious.
341. Long John Silver was a pirate.
342. The ink is on the table.

In such cases *be* is provided to take the inflexion which cannot be affixed normally – the predicate is an adjective (340) or an *NP* (341) or a preposition (342), not a verb. The required rule must be:

343. $X + \text{Aux} + \begin{Bmatrix} \text{Adj} \\ \text{NP} \\ \text{Prep} \end{Bmatrix} + Y \Rightarrow X + \text{Aux} + be + \begin{Bmatrix} \text{Adj} \\ \text{NP} \\ \text{Prep} \end{Bmatrix} + Y.$

(By the notational convention introduced on p. 108 above, the braces { } symbolize 'either . . . or' – but of course the *same* symbol must be selected on each side of the arrow; 343 is merely a condensation of three parallel rules, and must not be used to transform adjectives into prepositions as a by-product!) If the deep structure of 340 (simplified) is

344. NP + [– PAST] + Adj

rule 343 will turn it into 345:

345. NP + [– PAST] + *be* + Adj.

135

The usual processes of affix-shift and morphological combination can now render the *Aux* as *was*. It can easily be seen that 341 and 342 are realized in just the same way. As a matter of interest, some slightly more complex meanings of *Aux* may require *be* to be inserted more than once: *Mr Smith is being cautious* and the like.

I now turn to the transformations which are responsible for the concretizing of **negative, interrogative** and **affirmative** moods. We have already noticed some similarities between them: how the whole proposition or one of its parts may be qualified, so that for every particular affirmation, say, there is an exactly corresponding denial and question:

346.   It was the Queen that Eric saw.
347.   It wasn't the Queen that Eric saw.
348.   Was it the Queen that Eric saw?

A further relationship between these three moods is that they all employ the pseudo-verb *do* in their expression (not on all occasions; but *do* is used by all three of them on every occasion when a pseudo-verb is required). This morphological parallelism I take to reinforce the semantic common ground. In negatives, where the entire proposition is negated, *Aux* is separated from the verb by the negative particle:

349. $NP + [+ \text{PAST}] + n't + V$

n't (or *not*) is not an affix; it is the surface structure realization of the deep structure component [NEG], moved out to the right of *Aux* in the usual fashion, but unlike elements such as *-ing* and *-ed*, it is not moved any farther to the right to serve as a suffix on the verb; **walkn't* is ungrammatical. If *Aux* yields a modal auxiliary, the negative morpheme is either assimilated to that or juxtaposed with it as a separate word: *won't, will not*. The same happens if an auxiliary verb has had to be introduced to support tense under certain aspectual conditions, or if the predicate is an adjective or a noun phrase:

350.   He hasn't been working.
351.   The dancers aren't slim.

But under other conditions, *do* is introduced to the left of the negative particle, carries the tense element and may have the negative assimilated to it:

352.   He didn't (did not) open the window.

The fact that *didn't* carries both the tense affix and the negative particle is further confirmation that *n't* is not an affix: stems may take only one affix.

136

Now consider 353:

353. Did he open the window?

This is a 'yes/no' question, i.e. it asks for assent to or disconfirmation in respect of the whole proposition: replies such as *John did* are inappropriate (so long as *he* is not strongly emphasized: *Did hé open the window?* is a different form of question). Yes/no questions are formed by a permutation rule which has the effect of moving *Aux* to the left of the subject-*NP*:

354. [+ PAST] + *he* + *open* + *the* + *window*.

Now *Aux* is not adjacent to the verb any more, so *do* is placed between [+ PAST] and *he*, affix-shift occurs, and the surface structure 353 may be formed. Just as is the case with negation, the insertion of *do* is unnecessary under certain modal or aspectual circumstances, for the auxiliary verb is moved to the left with the tense element and carries the tense inflexion:

355. Could he open the window?
356. Had he opened the window?

The construction just discussed is not, of course, the only kind of question, nor is it the only way of managing yes/no questions: a rising intonation and no change in word-order from the indicative may be encountered. This is a realization which often suggests the expression of surprise; the question is almost rhetorical:

357. You haven't been here before?

Apart from yes/no questions, there is a whole range of interrogatives which presuppose the validity of part of a proposition and restrict their query to some other part. In 358 below, for instance, it is assumed that the window has been opened, and only the agency is questioned:

358. Who has opened the window?

Compare 353, in which (unless *he* is accentuated) the speaker does not commit himself to any belief in the openness or otherwise of the window. It seems that any part of a semantic structure which is expressed by a separate syntactic constituent may be queried; for instance, patient:

359. Who did the doctor visit?

Adverbial functions:

360. How are cakes made?
361. Why should he get all the credit?

Qualifiers of nouns, rather than whole *NP*s:

362.   Which boy opened the door?

Predicates only, excluding the rest of the proposition:

363.   Did he stéal this book?

The predicate is picked out by increased phonetic prominence, usually referred to as 'contrastive stress': 'did he *steal* it, or by contrast did he *buy* it or acquire it in some *other* way?'

We have already mentioned that affirmative mood is manifested in increased prominence. Where some sub-part of a statement is affirmed, the main syllable of that constituent is rendered prominent by a high pitch level:

364.   Márk stole the book.

Among other possibilities, the predicate alone can be affirmed, just as it can be queried; compare 363 and 365:

365.   He stóle the book.

There is a definite, if fine, semantic distinction between 365 and 366 below:

366.   He díd steal the book.

365 means 'I assert that he stole the book (rather than doing something else to it)'; 366 means 'I assert that the proposition *He stole the book* is true (rather than that something else happened)'. It appears, then, that the pseudo-verb *do* is positively semantically justified: it is evident that the affirmative stress could fall on the *V*, as it does in 363, 365, but that this syntactic device is already claimed by another meaning; so whole-proposition affirmation must be achieved by some other form of expression. The auxiliary *do* is particularly convenient for this purpose, since, being semantically empty, it stands quite outside the details of the affirmable semantic content of a sentence, represented by its lexical items. So the prominence of *do* signals the fact that none of the individual semantic constituents of the sentence is being affirmed, but that the whole proposition is being emphatically asserted.

This chapter has been intended merely to give a hint of the complexities of transformational structure – not as an exhaustive survey of the transformations involved in arranging the linear structure of even the simplest English sentences. In general, transformations function to render abstract semantic elements as actual words and morphemes, and to arrange these concrete formatives in their proper places in sentence-structure. We have seen that transformational rules perform several different types of formal operation: changing the order of words, deleting or adding words and morphemes, amalgamating sequences of words, assigning prominence to significant syllables. The fact is that it is transformations which are responsible for every aspect of syntactic order which can be observed on the surface of sentences. A second general observation on transformational structure is this; each part of syntactic structure has been formed by a lengthy *sequence* of transformations. When we speak of 'the passive transformation', 'the imperative transformation' and so forth, we are really using a shorthand form of expression to refer to a whole cycle of transformations, each individual one carrying out a distinct task, all arranged in a strictly ordered series, and all combining to provide a surface structure according to the prescription of the deep structure. For example, the 'passive transformation' entails at least seven different operations: (1) creation of a separate passive segment; (2) switching the subject and object *NP*s; (3) inserting *by* before the right-most *NP*; (4) replacing the passive segment by *-en*; (5) reversing the order of *-en* and *V*; (6) inserting *be* to the right of the tense component; (7) transposing tense and *be*. And the full surface structure demands further operations still, which are not part of the passive process itself – for instance, making sure that the new subject (the patient, now on the left of the sentence) agrees with the verb in number and (if relevant) person. Thus the passage from deep to surface structure is a many-phased operation involving a complex series of often radically distinct structural modifications. Finally, this chapter has discussed only *syntactic* transformations: those which, triggered by relevant 'cues' in the deep structure, realize the meanings of sentences as conventionally ordered sequences of words and morphemes, i.e. as surface structures. The level 'surface structure' is not to be equated with the most concrete level of all, 'utterance' – surface structure is just the output of the *syntactic* processing described in this and the following chapter. After the level of surface structure has been reached, still more rules must be applied to complete the derivation of a sentence: the phonological rules illustrated at the end of chapter 8. These rules also may be stated in a transformational format.

Note on the derivation of passives. I stated that part of the passive operation consisted in the insertion of *by* before the right-most *NP* (the *NP* which represents the agent in the revised order). This explanation is compatible with the traditional account, but more recently it has been suggested that *by* has a different origin. If, as I have granted in chapter 4, every *NP* has a certain role or case in syntagmatic semantic structure, prepositions can be seen as external manifestations of these cases, in a language like English. It is possible that segments for the prepositions are introduced in deep structure when the cases are introduced: *by* for agent, *with* for instrument, etc. It follows that prepositions are not inserted by transformations, but rather *deleted* in certain circumstances. Thus *by* is inherently present and does not need to be supplied for the passive; on the other hand, it would have to be deleted in the formation of active sentences.

Further Reading: see pp. 123–4 above.

seven

Complex sentences

At this point we might remind ourselves of some elementary definitions which are central to syntactic theory. I called chapter 5 'Simple sentences', and chapter 7 brings in the contrast of 'Complex sentences'. **Simple** and **complex** are not crudely evaluative words, but technical terms which mark a fundamental distinction between types of sentences. A simple sentence is one which is based on a single underlying phrase-marker, or, in traditional terms on just one **clause**. In turn, the clause is the realization of a semantic structure derived from a single predicate. My decision to begin the discussion of syntax with what might be called simple sentences was not arbitrary, nor was it a decision based on syntactic considerations alone: convenience of syntactic exposition coincided with a semantic criterion. The clause might be thought of as an abstract intermediary step between semantic structure and syntactic surface structure, a representation of the syntax associated with primitive semantic units, a stage in the derivation designed to provide a base on which transformations may operate. Now we already know that the route between meaning and surface structure is a long and complicated one and that it is charted as a sequence of transformations which may make radical alterations to constituent-structure. We would therefore expect the clarity of separation of clauses in deep structure, hence the separateness of single-predicate semantic units, to become obscured under transformation. If we compare, say, *John lost his watch* with the longer sentence *John lost his watch and Paul lost his wallet*, there is no difficulty deciding that the first is a simple sentence and the second is complex, by our criteria. But the distinction is not always immediately determinable from the appearance of sentences. In particular, many ostensibly simple sentences turn out, upon closer examination, to be

141

the expression of two predicates and therefore a transformational rendering of more than one clause: *John lost his watch and Paul his wallet* has had one of its predicates deleted, and if we simply counted verbs we would not realize that this is a complex sentence – intuitively it is complex, of course. Less obviously complex as far as our intuitions are concerned are sentences like *The fleeing criminal tripped over* (which has two predicates) and *A tall man entered* (which also has two predicates). Finally, closer inspection might show that I have cheated with the example *John lost his watch*, which, to all appearances simple, might be said to conceal two predicates, the second being hidden beneath the surface of *his*, a predicate indicating possession. In this chapter such subtle and problematic cases will be considered only after more easily segmentable types of complex sentence have been discussed.

Simple sentences are, as it happens, relatively rare in most styles of English. Texts constructed with a preponderance of simple sentences are stylistically tedious: complex sentences introduce flexibility and variety into linguistic performance by increasing enormously the range of sentence-*types* available, and also are responsible for the theoretical potential of an indefinite number of individual sentences (sentence-*tokens*). Several types of complex sentence-structure allow extension without limit by the addition of extra clauses (see examples 1–3 in the first chapter, p. 13). The rules for combining clauses are **recursive,** which means that they may be re-applied over and over again: the output from a rule can serve as the input to a subsequent reapplication of the same rule. For example, a conjoining transformation brings together the two clauses in 367 as 368:

367. Stephen was running.
     Charles was running.

368. Stephen and Charles were running.

The same rule can be applied again to join together 368 and 369 as 370:

369. The dog was running.
370. Stephen, Charles and the dog were running.

There is obviously nothing to prevent further applications of the rule, incorporating additional clauses in 370 and in its expanded versions, with as many re-applications as the topic of discourse demands. Furthermore, there is nothing to bar a cycle of applications of *different* recursive rules, yielding a more interesting kind of open-ended sentence with various types of clause joined together in a variety of ways:

142

371. Stephen, in the lead, Charles second, and the dog bringing up the rear, were running.

371 can, of course, be further extended. Note that its potential 'indefinite length' is a completely theoretical property: in real linguistic behaviour there is obviously no sentence of infinite length, and indeed only sentences of moderate length are tolerated, because very long utterances place too great a strain on memory and attentiveness. The difficulty of 'decoding' is compounded by certain ways of combining clauses; 370 and 371, presenting items of information in a straightforward sequence, are easy enough, but 372, in which clauses are embedded within other clauses of the same type, is much harder to understand, particularly in spoken form:

372. The plants the gardener the Council employed tended died.

This is perfectly grammatical: the ordering of clauses, the deletion of relative pronouns, are completely in accordance with the syntactic arrangements allowed by the rules of English. The unacceptability of this sentence, and similarly that of any inordinately long utterance, is to be explained non-linguistically, by reference to psychological properties of the human speaker which are distinct from his linguistic capabilities. If we say that 372 is 'too complicated', we are invoking a norm of complexity which is quite external to the grammatical characterization of 372 as a complex sentence.

However, in this chapter we are not concerned with monsters – even if well-proportioned monsters – like 372 or some excessive expansion of, say, 371. We are concerned with the range of ordinary complex sentences which present no distracting psychological problems. Here is a list which illustrates something of the range of types to be accounted for:

373. John came but Bill didn't.
374. I went out and had a meal.
375. John or Bill will oblige.
376. That he has escaped is regrettable.
377. It is regrettable that he has escaped.
378. To give in would be a mistake.
379. They would like Peter to go.
380. The man who bought the car gave a false address.
381. An enormous dog chased us.
382. He walked on the pavement.
383. Cooking is boring.
384. The defeat of the English team appalled the selectors.
385. The collapse of the English team appalled the selectors.
386. He lost his watch.

(For another list with relevant discussion, see chapter 5, examples 163–70, p. 104 above.) I have arranged this list so that the most obviously complex sentences occur at the beginning, with examples that the reader may regard with greatest suspicion (as candidates for the label 'complex sentence') at the bottom. But it should not be thought that there is a formal linguistic scale evidenced here, moving from transparency to density of structure. The arrangement is merely for convenience of exposition.

In fact, a single distinction between two types is of overriding importance. Two clauses may be put together in such a way that they retain equivalent status (373–5), in which case they are said to be **co-ordinated** or **conjoined**. Alternatively, one clause may be **subordinated** to another or, as TG terminology has it, **embedded** within another. 376–86 all contain embedded clauses, some particularly clear instances being *that he has escaped* in 376, 377, *to give in* in 378, *who bought the car* in 380; the remaining sentences have embedded elements whose status as clauses has been obscured by further transformational processing, principally deletion. The two kinds of amalgamation – conjoining and embedding – can be shown diagrammatically; 387 below represents 373, 388 represents 380 (in simplified form: the word *false* also indicates the presence of an embedded clause, as we shall see). In 387 and 388 an economical notational convention is employed whereby a plain triangle replaces a fully articulated tree when it is not necessary to show the internal structure of a clause in detail.

387.

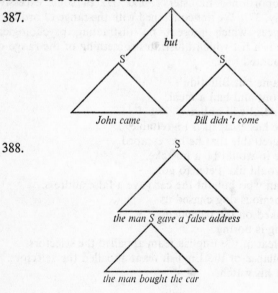

388.

387 shows that the two constituent clauses are of equivalent status: each is an independent clause, as important as its companion – neither of them is semantically dominant. But in 388 the **main** or **matrix** clause is clearly of superior semantic status to the **subordinate** or **embedded** clause. The primary statement is about a man giving a false address; the embedded clause *who bought the car* serves to identify the referent of the agent noun in the main clause: it therefore performs a subsidiary propositional function in the sentence as a whole.

Let us look more closely at conjoined constructions. A 'purer' example than any one of the sentences 373–5 is 389, in which two propositions which have no lexical content in common are linked together without either of them receiving any transformational modification:

389.   She washes the clothes and I do the shopping.

The two constituents of 389 have an implicit contextual relationship – one assumes that this is a description of the division of labour in a co-operative household. But usually the nature of the relationship, the *point* of the conjoining, emerges from the language itself and is reflected in deletion – as for instance in 374 (*I went out and had a meal*). 'Going out' and 'having a meal' sound like parts of some single event, hence the conjoining, with the essential link signalled by the deletion of the second 'I', a transformation which makes it clear that the predicates share a single agent. 389, though 'pure', is not 'typical' – 'pure' conjoining, in this sense of full and non-overlapping lexical specification of both clauses, is rarely encountered because it is a recipe for pointlessness:

390.   This is a Picasso and my daughter likes strawberries.

This is not ungrammatical; just unmotivated – there is no communicative factor which would give good cause for a conjunction of this kind to be constructed.

As a normal rule, then, conjoined clauses have some element or elements in common, and this repeated part is deleted in the process of combining them into one complex sentence. The repeated part may be any type of constituent. In 370, 373 and 375 the same predicate-phrase is shared by a number of agents, and so is mentioned only once in the complex product. Note that a repeated predicate-phrase in deep structure *may* be expressed more than once in surface structure; with 375 (*John or Bill will oblige*) compare the synonymous 391:

391.   John will oblige or Bill will oblige.

Usually, though, all instances of a repeated predicate-phrase except one are deleted: 375 is much more likely than 391. An exception is where deletion would suggest *joint* performance by the agents of some action where the deep structure has the agents acting separately. 392 below implies the interpretation 'arrived together', so 393 is preferred if 'arrived separately' is the intended meaning:

392. John and Mary arrived.
393. John arrived and Mary arrived.

(On the distinction between co-operating and separate agents, see above, p. 76; below, pp. 147–9.)

The principle of deletion of the repeated predicate-phrase applies whatever word-class is the exponent of the predicate:

394. 'Captain' and 'Sergeant' are military ranks. (*NP* predicate)
395. John, Mary and Peter are successful. (*Adj* predicate)
396. The coffee and sugar are in the cupboard. (*PrepP* predicate)

It may happen that just one part of a predicate-phrase is repeated, in which case the repeated part is deleted and the variant phrases spelt out in full:

397. We build cars and motorcycles.
398. We build and repair motorcycles.

With conjoined clauses sharing a common predicate but differing in subject, we normally delete one occurrence of the predicate (*John or Bill will oblige*), but sentences which preserve both predicates are quite acceptable (*John will oblige or Bill will oblige*). But when conjoined clauses share the same subject and differ in predicate, deletion of one occurrence of the subject is virtually mandatory. 399 below is usual; 400 is at best strange and at worst ungrammatical:

399. Max can read and write.
400. ?*Max can read and Max can write.

400 is acceptable if we assume either (a) that the two Max's refer to the same individual and that there is some exceptional contextual reason for spelling out his achievements distinctly; or (b) that the two Max's are different. But it is extremely difficult, if not impossible, to speak 400 in such a way as to indicate that meaning (b) is intended. These alternatives are much more likely:

400 (a) Max can read and he can also write.
400 (b) Max Smith can read and Max Jones can write.

When the subject is *I*, alternative 374 (*I went out and had a meal*) is much preferable to 401 below:

146

401.   ?* I went out and I had a meal.

Non-deletion of the second *I* suggests a (b)-type interpretation, which makes the sentence absurd: whereas it is possible that two different Max's should be mentioned in the same sentence, two I's which are not co-referential obviously cannot be accommodated within a single sentence, for one sentence must be the utterance of one speaker. 401 is acceptable only under special stylistic conditions, e.g. if the speaker wants deliberately to emphasize the separateness of his actions.

We now return to the distinction between conjunction involving 'joint' nouns and conjunction where nouns designate discrete objects or persons. We have just seen that 392 is ambiguous as between arrival together and arrival separately. This is a common ambiguity in conjoined sentences, a result of the compression which follows the reduction of conjoined clauses with shared constituents. Some more examples are as follows: I have appended paraphrases to bring out the rival meanings.

402.   Sticks and stones may break my bones.
    (a) Sticks may break my bones and stones may break my bones.
    (b) The combination of sticks and stones may break my bones.

403.   Peter and Jane are married.
    (a) Peter is a married man and Jane is a married woman.
    (b) They are married to each other.

404.   Professor Smith and Professor Jones write college textbooks.
    (a) Both of these professors are writers of academic texts.
    (b) The two of them together are co-authors of texts.

The (a) interpretation for each of these examples assumes a derivation by what is often called **sentence conjunction** – in our terms, **clause conjunction**, that is to say, the amalgamation of two separate clauses in the manner described in the last few pages. The deep structure contains two underlying phrase-markers, two predicates, as diagrammed in 387 (p. 144 above). The (b) interpretation, however, presupposes that 402–4 are *simple* sentences. Each is based on just one predicate attended by a subject noun phrase whose *Det* contains the component [COMBINED]. The type is called **phrase conjunction**, and its underlying structure is diagrammed in 405.

405.

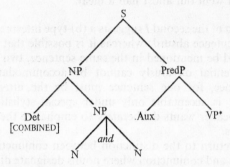

*or any other constituent of *PredP*, as permitted by rule 205 of chapter 5.

Phrasal conjunction may of course occur in constituents other than the subject – e.g. in the object, as in 406, on a (b)-type interpretation:

406.   I like ice cream and cake.

Deep structures such as 405 are carried through to surface arrangements which contain the constituent *N and N*; the ambiguity of examples like 402–4, 406, arises because *N and N* is also found in surface structures which are underlain by conjoined *clauses* with the repeated parts deleted and the remainder, the non-repeated constituents, amalgamated. In the deep structure appropriate to (a)-type interpretations, there is no constituent of the form 407.

407.

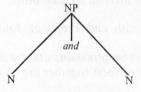

This appears in surface structure only as a product of an amalgamation transformation.

Before we leave this subject, we may note that some predicates require a subject *NP* marked [COMBINED]: *collide, meet, mix* (in one sense), *kiss* (in one sense), *resemble* (*each other*), *agree, combine*, etc. The subject may be a single *N*, as in the examples in 408 below –

408.   The lines met.
       They met.

– or it may contain two *N*s, in which case a phrase conjunction interpretation is demanded and a clause conjunction reading precluded.

409. The car and the bus collided
     (not derived from conjoining of the clauses *the car collided* and *the bus collided*).
410. Oil and water do not mix
     (not derived from *oil does not mix* plus *water does not mix*).

This property of a few predicates is of course part of their semantic description and must be included in that description as a selection restriction controlling the character of any nouns associated with such predicates. This is a good example of the power of the semantic structure of verbs to determine semantic and syntactic structure elsewhere in the sentence.

We now move from conjoining to **embedding** processes. The basic difference between the two modes of combining clauses is that the first preserves the equivalent status of the two joined clauses whereas the second, the process we are about to discuss, 'subordinates' one clause to another: the traditional term is strikingly appropriate. For a convenient visual contrast between these two modes of clause-linkage, see diagrams 387 and 388 above (p. 144). In the interests of space I must restrict my discussion to just one broad category of embedding, **nominalization**. All the remaining examples in our list on p. 143, that is to say 376–86, contain instances of nominalization, with the exception of 382, *He walked on the pavement*, which I included in order to dramatize the fact that simple-looking sentences are not always simple in our technical sense of the term. We have already encountered some evidence that at least some prepositions are realizations of deep-structure predicates (cf. example 140, *The baby crawled under the table*, and discussion p. 91; 121–3 and discussion p. 87). Probably the word *on* is to be considered a predicate in *He walked on the pavement*, in which case 382 is complex, since it contains also the undeniable predicate *walked*.

To return to nominalization, this is a process by which a whole clause, with certain structural modification, is assimilated to a noun phrase in another clause (the matrix of the composite whole), either taking the place of the complete *NP*, as *that he has escaped* in 376, or forming just one part of it, as *who bought the car* in the subject-*NP the man who bought the car* in 380. Nominalization, in all its various forms, is the most fertile process for the construction of complex sentences in English: a very large proportion of the nominal expressions in our language are derived from predicates. And as we shall see, this statement holds for a good part of the noun lexicon also.

149

To start with we will consider the derivation of sentences such as 376 (*That he has escaped is regrettable*) and 377 (*It is regrettable that he has escaped*), beginning by distinguishing the type of nominal found there from the one illustrated in 380 (*The man who bought the car gave a false address*). The first type (376, 377) is a **noun phrase complement**, the second (380) a **relative clause**. We may understand the distinction by examining a pair of very similar-looking sentences, one of which is based on one of these two constructions, the other on the second one:

411.   The idea that he was a linguist surprised us.
412.   The idea that he presented surprised us.

That these sentences have different structural descriptions is suggested by some transformational modifications which work in one case but not in the other:

413.   (a) It surprised us that he was a linguist.
       (b) *It surprised us that he presented.

414.   (a) That he was a linguist was the idea which surprised us.
       (b) *That he presented was the idea which surprised us.

415.   (a) We were surprised that he was a linguist.
       (b) *We were surprised that he presented.

416.   (a) His being a linguist surprised us.
       (b) *His presenting surprised us.

417.   (a) *The idea which he was a linguist surprised us.
       (b) The idea which he presented surprised us.

The last of these contrasts points to a distinction between two separate *that*s in 411 and 412: *that* in 412 is a relative pronoun, a substitute for the *NP the idea* which exists in the deep structure of 412's relative clause – *he presented the idea*. It can therefore be replaced by the alternative relative pronoun, *which*, in 417 (b). Since *that* in 411 is not a relative pronoun, it cannot enjoy that replacement. There is a related substantial distinction between the *NP*s *the idea* in the two sentences. In 412 *idea* is a significant lexical item, the patient of *presented*, and *that* replaces *the idea* in the relative clause when it is embedded: 412 is about an idea. 411 is not about an idea, but about the fact of being a linguist (or not being a linguist!): there is no question of *idea* being a fully self-sufficient lexical item. In 411 it is simply a formula for introducing the **factive nominal** 'that he was a linguist'. *Fact, notion, statement* etc. would substitute for *idea* in 411 and hardly change the meaning: all that is required is a 'completable' noun which has its meaning fully written out by the embedded clause which follows, hence the term 'noun phrase complement'. *That he was a linguist* in 411 is a complement to *the idea* in much the same way as *160 pounds* is a complement to the predicate in *I weighed 160 pounds* (cf. p. 91 above); the complement serves to complete the semantic content of the intrinsically imprecise item which it follows. The difference from relative clauses is that no important semantic content is given by the head noun (*idea*, *fact*, etc.), only by the nominal complement; whereas relative clauses do *not* supply lexical material which is lacking in the head noun, but *add* lexical information to that given by the head noun. In 412 and similar constructions the head noun is semantically complete; the relative clause has the deictic function of pinpointing – by giving new information – the referent of the noun – which supplies its own complete *sense*.

If clauses such as *that he was a linguist* in 411 are 'complements', it follows that they must always attend a 'completable' noun phrase. *The idea* in 411 fulfils this requirement, but the presence of a completable *NP* is not at all obvious in our other examples (376–9, 383, to give the whole set). Take 376–7:

376. That he has escaped is regrettable.
377. It is regrettable that he has escaped.

These are synonymous, and can also be paraphrased by 418:

418. The fact that he has escaped is regrettable.

But 419 and 420 are both unacceptable:

419. *It that he has escaped is regrettable.
420. *The fact is regrettable that he has escaped.

418 suggests that the underlying structure is as follows:

421. NP – that he has escaped – is regrettable.

The *NP* of the matrix clause may either be filled lexically with a noun and an article, the noun chosen from the limited set *fact, idea,* etc., or it may have the word *it* as its exponent. If a full *NP* occupies this place, the sentence may be realized in its full form, e.g. as 411, 418 or equivalent. But if the *NP* of the matrix is expounded by the word *it*, the sentence must not be furnished with a surface structure which preserves the order of 421 – as the ungrammatical 419 testifies. 376 and 377 show that two courses are open in these circumstances. Either the underlying *it* may be removed by the aptly named **it-deletion** transformation; or the whole of the embedded nominalized clause may be moved to the right of the matrix, preserving the *it*, by an **extraposition** transformation. It is the existence of sentences such as 377, together with consideration of symmetry with 418 and its kind, which justifies the proposal of an *it* in the deep structure of 376. The two sentences 376 and 377 are synonymous, their deep structures differing only in that 376 contains a cue for the it-deletion transformation whereas 377 has a deep structure marked for extraposition. It-deletion and extraposition (similarly particle-shift) are excellent examples of purely 'stylistic' transformations – rules which vary surface structure without changing meaning.

A final observation on the above system of rules is that extraposition is not permitted if the subject-*NP* of the matrix is expounded by a regular *NP* – see the ungrammatical 420.

The above analysis of 376 – a deep structure in which the matrix clause has *it* as its subject – might well be extended to 378, 379, 383, and perhaps 384, 385, though I will look at them from a different angle. That all these sentences contain nominalized clauses is proved by the **cleft sentence** test, in which the underlying *it* is converted to *what* and the suspected noun clause is moved to the right of the sentence:

378. To give in would be a mistake.
422. What would be a mistake would be to give in.
379. They would like Peter to go.
423. What they would like is for Peter to go.
383. Cooking is boring.
424. What is boring is cooking.
384/5. The defeat/collapse of the English team appalled the selectors.
425. What appalled the selectors was the defeat/collapse of the English team.

If all these are noun clauses or noun complements, their morphological diversity is impressive. In fact, this variety reduces to four basic types. Noun phrase complements may be realized as *that*-clauses, like the first group we discussed; or as *-ing* forms, often called **gerundives**, as 383; as **infinitive** forms, i.e. using the base version of the verb preceded by *to* or *for . . . to* (383, 424); or as noun-like words followed by *of* and a second noun (384, 385). The first examination of these types within a transformational framework was by R. B. Lees, and the reader is referred to his book, cited on p. 124 above, for a wealth of examples and an attempt at classification. Lees indicates that different types of nominal perform different kinds of semantic function; but these are not correlated exactly with the distinct morphological types, and there is variation from dialect to dialect. *That*-clauses are generally **factive** nominals, as is plain from their tendency to combine with *the fact . . ., the opinion . . .*, etc. Nominals in *-ing* are usually **action** nominals, as 383 is, but on the other hand they are often ambiguous; there is for example the much-discussed sentence:

426.   His driving terrifies me.

which means either 'The fact that he drives' or 'The way that he drives'. Finally, noun-like words of the kind illustrated in 384, 385 retain the semantic function of the predicates from which they derive. *Defeat* is a process-action of which *the English team* is the patient and the agent is unspecified. A typical morphology for expressing an agent as well would be *India's defeat of the English team. Collapse* is a process, and the *NP* following the *of* is again patient. With some other predicate, *the English team* might well be agent: *the victory of the English team.* And, of course, role-ambiguity of a predictable kind is encountered: *the conquest of the English team.* The fact that we can so easily begin to discuss such nouns, and their relationships with other nouns in complex *NP*s, from the perspective which is natural to predicates surely confirms the proposal that these are nominalized verbs which carry into their derived forms all the semantic structure associated with full clauses.

There remains 386, a most innocent-looking sentence which I have suggested is complex by virtue of nominalization: *He lost his watch.* The so called 'genitive case' of pronouns and nouns – *his, the team's, John's* – expresses a variety of roles. In 426 it ties *he* to *driving* with the role 'agent'; in *his defeat, he* is patient; in *his delight* it is experiencer; and in *his watch, he* is beneficiary. *His watch* differs from the other examples in that each of the others is followed by a nominalized predicate, whereas the predicate in *his watch* is not explicit; and *watch* is the patient for this unexpressed predicate. So *his driving* reflects a clause *he drives*, while *his watch* answers to an underlying structure *he + Aux + have + a watch.* The proposed verb *have* in the deep structure – not the same as the pseudo-verb *have* which performs auxiliary functions – is necessary to convey the idea of 'possession' which is undoubtedly present in the meaning of 386.

In the *his* of 386 we meet perhaps the ultimate in the compression of a nominalized clause: even the predicate is lost. By comparison, the reduction in sentences like 381 (*An enormous dog chased us*), where only one word remains but that is the predicate, seems much less severe. Nominalization, with reduction, is in fact the origin of prenominal adjectives such as *enormous* in 381; predicative adjectives, as in *the dog was enormous*, are of course introduced directly in the deep structure, before transformations operate. We shall see that prenominal adjectives are derived by way of predicative adjectives in relative clauses, and it is with relative clauses that we continue this discussion of nominalization. Our sample sentence in the list on p. 143 was 380, which contains one relative clause and one prenominal adjective, i.e. it is a complex sentence with three clauses in all:

380.   The man who bought the car gave a false address.

The clause structure of this sentence is diagrammed in 388 on p. 144 above (ignoring *false*, which of course marks the presence of a reduced clause). Readers will know already that the relative is derived from a full sentence-like structure which has been inserted to the right of the *NP* which it modifies:

427.   The man – the man bought the car – gave a false address.

We will look at the transformational organization of relative clauses in a moment: the replacement of the repeated *NP* by a relative pronoun and various other modifications to surface structure which may occur. Before we do so, it will assist our understanding of the *meaning* of relatives to compare them with a superficially very similar, but semantically quite different, type of construction. With 380 compare 428:

428.   The man, who bought the car, gave a false address.

The commas, and their phonetic counterpart in intonation, make all the difference. 428 has a particularly identified man as its topic and offers two perhaps completely unconnected statements about him. The distinctness of the two major predicates (*buy* and *give*) shows up in the following paraphrase:

429.   The man bought the car and gave a false address.

Notice that both 428 and 429 assume that we know who *the man* is: the sentences themselves give no help with his identification. But the subordinate clause in 380 actually serves to specify the identity of the subject of the matrix: from the universe of possible referents of the *NP the man*, the relative clause pinpoints one – the man who bought the car. Because the relative clause in 380 has this special function, 429 is not an accurate paraphrase of 380. It appears that 380 and 428 have the same lexical content, but that the propositions which make them up are put together in very different ways. In fact, 429 suggests that 428 has more in common with conjoined constructions than it does with relative clauses; two distinct propositions are linked together, and they are either linked by *and* or by inserting one – it doesn't matter which – within the other, between commas.

The embedded clause in 380 identifies, specifies, delimits, restricts, the reference of the *NP* to which it is attached; in acknowledgment of this function, it is called a **restrictive** relative. Its apparent counterpart in 428 might be called **non-restrictive**, as it has no similar delimiting function in relation to the *NP* which it adjoins. This terminology has its usefulness, for it speaks directly of the semantic distinction which is the crux of the contrast. But it is a little bit misleading, as it suggests that these are two versions – restrictive and non-restrictive – of essentially the same kind of construction; this is not the true situation, however: the two structures are quite distinct, and there is some advantage in employing totally different names. I shall use the term **relative** to refer only to the type represented in 380; the subordinate clause in 428 and similar structures will be called **appositive**. The opposition relative/appositive applies to the semantic contrast between the two types; their surface structures remain very similar, down to sharing various transpositions and shortenings in the process of embedding.

The first stage of relative clause embedding has already been shown, in the representation 427: the clause to be embedded is positioned to the right of an *NP* in the matrix. This *NP* must be identical to one *NP* in the embedded clause; that is a prerequisite to relativization. It may be the subject of the matrix, as in 380, or the object, as in 430:

430.   The man gave an address – the address was false.

Similarly, the shared *NP* may be the subject of the subordinate clause – again, 380 illustrates this type – or it may be the object, as in 412, where the unmodified form of the relative clause is *he presented the idea*. Another possibility is shown in 431, where the *NP* which the two clauses have in common is the agent of a passive construction:

431.   The doctor by whom I was examined was very reassuring.

In cases like 412 (*The idea that he presented surprised us*) and 431, the repeated *NP* is moved so that it is directly juxtaposed with its twin in the matrix:

432.   The idea – the idea he presented – surprised us.
433.   The doctor – by the doctor I was examined – was very reassuring.

When the crucial *NP* is at the front of the subordinate clause, its *Det* is replaced by a *wh*-pronoun form:

434.   The man – *wh*-man bought the car – gave a false address.
435.   The idea – *wh*-idea he presented – surprised us.

436. The doctor – by *wh*-doctor I was examined – was very reassuring.

The *wh*- form is finally realized as an appropriate word *who(m)/that* or *which/that*, and the second occurrence of the repeated *NP* is removed. The realization rule which performs this final operation must take account of the fact that, if the relativized *NP* contains the component [+ HUMAN] (e.g. *man, doctor*), *wh*- must be rendered as *who* or *that* if it is the subject of the subordinate clause, and *who* or (conservatively) *whom*, or *that*, if it is the object; but that if the relativized *NP* contains [− HUMAN] (e.g. *idea*) it must appear as *which* or *that*, regardless of whether it is subject or object.

Various modifications to this subordinate clause structure are allowed, which affect both relatives and appositives. The chief of these is **relative pronoun deletion**, which is permissible in some constructions but not in others:

437. The idea [*which*] he presented surprised us.
438. The girl [*who was*] sitting on the beach remained quite impassive.
439. The boy [*who was*] noticed by the talent scout was an extremely gifted player.

But not:

440. *The man [*who*] bought the car gave a false address.
441. *The car [*which had*] crashed was being towed away.
442. *The doctor by [*whom*] I was examined was very reassuring.

437 shows that *wh*- may be deleted when the relativized *NP* is the object of the verb in the subordinate clause; 440, that this may not happen if it is the subject. 438 demonstrates that deletion may take place if the clause is in progressive aspect, but 441 shows that it is impermissible with the perfect. *Wh*- and the auxiliary may disappear if the noun which *wh*- has replaced is the patient in a passive construction, as 439 makes clear; but 442 shows that this is not allowed if it is the agent which has been replaced by a relative pronoun. However, 443, in which the word *by* has been retained in its original position after the verb, is well-formed:

443. The doctor I was examined by was very reassuring.

This paraphrases 431, and despite its structural oddity is increasingly preferred to 431, especially with the demise of *whom* outside very formal and conservative styles of discourse.

Another situation in which deletion of relative pronoun and auxiliary is prohibited is when the predicate of the subordinate clause is an adjective:

444. *The girl [*who was*] impassive sat on the beach.
445. *A dog [*which was*] enormous chased us.

But such deletion does in fact happen, though only as an *intermediate* stage in derivations. If, as in 444, 445, the relative pronoun and the auxiliary are followed by an adjective, their deletion makes compulsory a further transformational operation before a well-formed surface structure is achieved: this is the **adjective-preposing** transformation, which gives superficial structures such as 446, 381 – and which is responsible for the complex *NP* on the right of 380:

446. The impassive girl sat on the beach.
381. An enormous dog chased us.
380. The man who bought the car gave *a false address*.

The adjective has been positioned before the noun to avoid the ungrammaticalness of, for example, 444, 445. This final process is unnecessary for most adjectives in French, since with some exceptions they follow the head noun of a complex endocentric *NP*. The French equivalents of 444, 445 would be well formed. Thus French is, at one point, simpler than English at the transformational level of structure: one fewer transformational rule is required to derive a comparable structure.

Prenominal adjectives are, then, derived from relative clauses. This solution, this way of generating phrases like *a false address*, may seem unnecessarily complicated and laboured to a non-linguist. Why not extend rule 198 of chapter 5 (p. 107) so that it contains the option

447. $NP \rightarrow Det + Adj + N$

thus allowing prenominal adjectives to be generated in the deep structure? Why go through the labour of deriving a relative clause and of passing through an ungrammatical stage like 444, 445? The justifications for proposing the relatively tortuous derivation by which we proceeded to the surface structures 380, 381, and 446 typify the general motives for TG itself, and are therefore worth setting out plainly.

Although the transformational derivation of prenominal adjectives entails a long and indirect route to surface structure, the alternative of allowing them into underlying structures by way of the phrase-structure part of the grammar carries its own mechanical disadvantages:

448. An old, black, tattered suitcase was found.

A constituent-structure rule for the subject *NP* of 448 would be 449:

449.   NP → Det + Adj + Adj + Adj + N.

As it stands, 448 contains only three preposed adjectives, so the above rule is adequate; but a phrase of this type can be lengthened without apparent limit, so more rules must be proposed:

450.   NP → Det + $\begin{cases} \text{Adj} + \text{N} \\ \text{Adj} + \text{Adj} + \text{N} \\ \text{Adj} + \text{Adj} + \text{Adj} + \text{N} \\ \text{Adj} + \text{Adj} + \text{Adj} + \text{Adj} + \text{N} \\ \text{Adj} + \text{Adj} + \text{Adj} + \text{Adj} + \text{Adj} + \text{N} \\ \text{etc.} \end{cases}$

Evidently, on this analysis we would need as many rewriting rules as there are adjectives before the noun – in fact, an indefinite number. By comparison with the transformational analysis, 450 is obviously extremely wasteful: the transformational account requires only one rule (more exactly, one sequence of rules, but that does not affect the present argument) which is reapplicable, recursive. A single rule can derive an indefinite number of adjectival phrases. There is an important *psycholinguistic* reason for preferring the transformational analysis to the open-ended series of phrase-structure rules in 450. A grammar with mentalistic pretensions – one which claims to represent speakers' internalized knowledge of their language – must be finite: it must contain a determinate number of rules. A human being is a finite organism: therefore it is impossible that such an organism could acquire any knowledge which had to be represented in a non-finite set of rules. If we intend a grammar to tell us something about linguistic competence, we must not let the grammar enshrine a psychologically falsifiable principle.

Having decided on a transformational explanation of the origin of prenominal adjectives, we have several options on how to frame the required transformations. The chosen solution, remember, is one which places an appropriate clause to the right of a noun which is to receive the adjective –

451.   Det + N – Det + N′ + Aux + Adj – PredP

(where N = N′) – relativizes the *NP* in the subordinate clause, deletes the *wh-* form and the *Aux* –

452.   Det + N – Adj – PredP

– and finally transposes the *N* of the main clause with the embedded adjective:

453.   Det + Adj + N + PredP.

453 would serve as an underlying structure for, for example, 381 *An enormous dog chased us* or any other of thousands of similar sentences. Notice that the structure of 453 is such that it can be subjected to exactly the same process as the matrix of 451 was: another subordinate clause can be placed to the right of the noun *dog*, ultimately giving *An enormous fierce dog . . .*; in turn this can be the input to the same transformational sequence – *An enormous fierce old dog . . .* and so on indefinitely. Our chosen solution thus fulfils the requirement of recursiveness, which as we saw could not be achieved acceptably using phrase-structure rules.

A competing transformational rule, apparently much neater, would be as follows:

454.   N $\Rightarrow$ Adj + N.

A string of symbols such as 455 could be instantly converted into 456 by the application of rule 454:

455.   Det + N + Aux + PredP.
456.   Det + Adj + N + Aux + PredP.

454 is of course recursive, since the *N* stands in 456 available for the preposing of another adjective by the same device as was used to put the first one in. The defect of 454 is that it is totally uninformative about the origin and status of adjectives. It seems to assume that an adjective appears out of the blue, may be simply lifted out of the lexicon as an isolated word which can be just dropped into a string such as 455. It ignores the fact that adjectives appear in sentences as the predicates of complete structures. An adjective cannot be introduced into a sentence except as the semantic nucleus (predicate) of its own clause; it must be supplied with its own patient noun (or other role) – it cannot usurp a noun which belongs to another predicate, as happens in 456. These necessities are fulfilled when an adjective is embedded in a matrix as part of a relative clause: *The girl who was impassive sat on the beach.* This is, of course, the *only* way of introducing embedded adjectives in matrix clauses, so it is the way which we must adopt. I would not want to present this method as a regrettable inevitability, however; it is semantically very well justified. Sentences with prenominal adjectives are synonymous with sentences which have the same adjectives as the predicates of relative clauses:

457.   The girl who was impassive sat on the beach.
458.   The impassive girl sat on the beach.

I can think of no more natural way of displaying the relationship of these sentences than by having them both pass through a series of shared derivational stages. From one semantic structure we can move to a surface structure 457, or we can go a stage further, deleting the relative pronoun and *Aux* and placing the adjective before the noun. In effect, 458 presupposes 457 as a more 'primitive' version of a single semantic structure. The two sentences share all but the final stages of their transformational 'histories', and provide an excellent example of the way transformations may be said to 'relate sentences to each other' (cf. p. 32).

Further reading: see pp. 123–4 above.

eight

Sounds

Language behaviour is like an iceberg. The observable tip – sounds, written marks, movements of the vocal organs – testifies to the presence of a mass of inner processes to which we have no direct access. There are neurological events put together in sequences of almost unimaginable complexity, controlling the muscular movements which set in motion the organs of speech. These neurological processes are in turn initiated by activities in the central nervous system of which linguists are largely ignorant; the speaker has the intention of communicating a message, and he 'encodes' it as an utterance in a particular language – how does he accomplish this? The preceding five chapters have attempted to give a *non-physical* account of the linguistic knowledge which must be assumed to lie behind the encoding – and, *mutatis mutandis*, decoding – process. A physical description of the below-the-surface bulk of the linguistic iceberg is at present unachievable, and may be ultimately unattainable anyway, since the brains of healthy human beings are not open to any but the shallowest techniques of neurophysiological investigation. The impossibility of a physical description of the inner processes of speech is, however, not a crippling limitation on linguistics, since linguistics is not a physical science: the abstractions which express grammatical structure are the natural concepts and terms of linguistics, and not an apologetic substitute for some 'real' terminology.

But *sounds*, their qualities and their origins, are inescapably physical, and in studying the sounds of speech linguistics is for once concerned with concrete entities. The first part of this chapter, an introduction to **phonetics**, is necessarily preoccupied with physical description. Because phonetics is non-abstract, it has often been denied a position within the linguistic sciences, and, strictly speaking, in this respect it does have a quite distinct status from general and descriptive linguistics. Later in this chapter, however, we shall see that in order to appreciate how sounds function in the communication of meanings – rather than just as noise – we must approach them from an abstract, structural, point of view.

Sounds may be studied under three different perspectives. We may concern ourselves with their causation, with their reception or with their own inherent quality; to these three focuses correspond **articulatory, auditory** and **acoustic phonetics** respectively. Articulatory phonetics (sometimes called **motor phonetics**) and auditory phonetics are really branches of physiology specially directed to linguistic interests (psychology of perception also has relevance to auditory phonetics); similarly, acoustic phonetics is a speech-oriented sub-division of physics. Auditory phonetics is the least well developed of these three styles of phonetics, and the common feeling of phoneticians is that it is unlikely to supplant the articulatory and acoustic approaches, which between them have amassed a very considerable amount of information on the sounds of speech. The study of vocal articulation is of great antiquity, but it only achieved objectivity and precision in the latter part of the nineteenth century. The work of such pioneers as Alexander Ellis (1814–90) and Henry Sweet (1845–1912) issued in a 'classic' English tradition of exact articulatory description, brilliantly represented in the many books of Daniel Jones (1881–1967), particularly his *Outline of English Phonetics*, which remained the standard textbook from its first appearance in 1918 down to 1962, when Jones's pupil, A. C. Gimson, published his *Introduction to the Pronunciation of English*, keeping up with changes in pronunciation and in the technique of experimental phonetics but remaining essentially within the Jones tradition.

Articulatory phoneticians proposed that differences between speech sounds are caused by differences in the disposition of the vocal organs during vocalization – variations in the shape of the mouth, in the relative positions of the tongue and the lips, in the movements of the inner parts of the larynx, and so on. Ingenious techniques for observing the internal workings of the speech mechanism were contrived, but the details of the hypothesis had to remain unsubstantiated until facilities for precise **acoustic** observation were available: until a non-impressionistic description of sound-waves could be correlated with the physiological account of vocal production. These capabilities came with the development of electronic devices for acoustic analysis in the 1940s, analytic instruments which have become increasingly refined and powerful ever since. The basic tool in phonetic research, and the instrument which precipitated radical progress in the field, is the **sound spectrograph,** a machine which was originally conceived as an aid to speech therapy for deaf patients by providing a visual display of the acoustic make-up of speech. The patient was to improve his pronunciation by visually adjusting the spectrographic picture of his own speech to models of correct speech displayed in the same way. The potentialities of the equipment for phonetic research were quickly realized, and an adaptation was designed and marketed specifically for this purpose. The spectrograph can analyse the acoustic composition of any utterance up to 2.4 seconds long. By exposing a tape-recorded signal to a set of filters, the spectrograph can record the intensity (loudness) of any part of the utterance at each of a number of predetermined frequencies and at definite moments of time. It is thus possible to tell what frequencies are especially prominent in a particular vowel, what points of an utterance are characterized by silence, where the utterance is made up of **noise** (in the technical sense of energy randomly and densely spread over a range of frequencies, producing an unmusical sound) and so on. Since the resulting **spectrogram** shows time, pitch and loudness, with loudness displayed relative to pitch, it gives an informative break-down of speech sounds. The principal limitation of the spectrograph is that it cannot deal with extended speech, but this deficiency can be made good by the use of supplementary instruments. Even a quite basic phonetics laboratory can yield a great deal of information about the acoustic composition of sounds, adding a further dimension to the physical observations of articulatory phonetics. Instrumental analysis is a particularly valuable supplement to the direct study of articulation in situations where the movements of the vocal organs are fluid and difficult to pin down to precise locations within the speech tract: vowel articulations, for instance, do not put the tongue in contact with any definite place within the mouth, and are much more precisely described in terms of their acoustic composition than in terms of tongue position, which is necessarily difficult to specify clearly. On the other hand, there is much convenience in articulatory description where tongue position can be specified clearly, e.g. where the tongue touches a definite part of the roof of the mouth in some consonant articulations. Thus the technical precision of acoustic/instrumental analysis may be seen as a supplement to articulatory description rather than as a technique which will supplant it.

The outline of the process of speech is well established: much of it is open to direct observation, and other parts are a matter of simple inference. The sentence a speaker is to utter is somehow translated into an exceedingly complex set of simultaneous and sequential impulses in the central nervous system. These constitute instructions to the muscles which control the movements of the speech organs. The muscles are activated to perform an exact pattern of contractions and relaxations, each movement taking place with a precise force and at a set time in relation to other movements of the same and of other muscles; the tolerances for the timing and strength of these operations must be very fine indeed. Consequential movements of tissues in the regions of the upper abdomen, chest, throat, mouth and face lead to the emission of a controlled stream of air from the lungs, through the windpipe, larynx, and oral cavities, reaching the outer air by way of the lips and/or nostrils. At certain critical points in its passage outwards the air-stream is obstructed by the 'moveable vocal organs' (the tongue being the principal among these) which are all the time assuming a changing series of positions relative to each other and to areas of immobile tissue (e.g. the palate). These obstructions interfere with the escaping air-stream in such a way that non-random changes in air pressure occur. The result is of course a sound-wave – a pattern of disturbances in the air spreading outwards from the lips and nose. The pressure-wave for speech is both regular and complicated. It presents itself as a pattern of stimulation on the eardrums of the speaker and of any hearer who happens to be within range. The speaker experiences aural feedback from his own sound-wave, and also feedback in the form of vibrations conducted to the ears along the bones of the face. Feedback is essential to enable him to monitor his speech as he produces it: his ears present information about his acoustic performance to his brain, which is thereby enabled to adjust the commands sent to the vocal organs, thus ensuring a nearer approximation to the requisite acoustic product. The hearer's ear-drums are stimulated by the varying pattern of energy imparted to them by the pressure-wave, and by the normal auditory process a pattern of neural stimulation is transmitted to the brain. How the brain 'recovers' the abstract formal structure of a sentence from this physical information is not known. The regions of obscurity in this chain of activity are, then, the transitions from intention and grammatical competence to neurological energy and (at the hearer's end) from perceived utterance to comprehension. We do not know how speakers come to select a certain sentence and encode it as an appropriate set of commands to the vocal organs; nor do we know how hearers come to ascribe appropriate semantic interpretations – total abstractions – to utterances on the evidence of perception of physical sound-waves.

Speech is a feat of very considerable 'oral dexterity'. Even a poor approximation to the community's norm for the pronunciation of a sentence requires extremely precise temporal co-ordination of about 100 muscles to ensure that the rate of breathing is appropriate, the tensioning of the structures of the larynx correct, the tongue in the relevant position at a particular point of time, etc. The hearer, for his part, though he has no such physical programme to carry out, is responsible for a delicate perceptual task. Sound-waves are 'broadcast' rather than 'directional' (unlike light-waves). Because we have binaural hearing, we can locate a source of sound roughly, and thus concentrate our attention on it. But because we cannot choose not to hear noises from irrelevant sources, we are presented with a sound-wave containing not only linguistic information but in addition more or less noise not issuing from the speaker on whom we attempt to focus: voices from other conversations, traffic noise, music, noise from machinery, and so on. Notwithstanding this potential interference, speakers are well able to hold conversations against a mess of background noise (e.g. a busy restaurant), even if this noise is of great intensity – as in a heavy engineering factory, for instance. The irrelevant noise is physically present at our ear-drums, but we manage to isolate the speech-wave under the most adverse conditions. Our task is not made easier by the fact that speakers often do not produce very clear acoustic signals; yet we rarely fail to comprehend.

Apparently we cope with these problems by relying to a considerable extent on our expectations of structure: we impose a simplifying linguistic pattern on the complex acoustic signal – a linguistic *Gestalt* operation which lets us 'hear' as a result of understanding (rather than hearing an exact signal and *then* attaching an interpretation to it).

Let us now follow the production-line for speech from its deep-seated source to the peripheral orifices from which it issues. All communication through a physical channel requires a source of energy to activate the chosen medium. In the case of speech, the source is lung air escaping outwards through the glottis, lips and nostrils. (At least, this method is almost universal; some sounds in some languages, e.g. clicks, are made on an indrawn breath, but continuous speech while breathing in is unnatural and strainful.) In the ordinary state of affairs, breathing out is a virtually silent operation. But if the vocal cords are closed lightly during the exhalation phase of quiet breathing – breathing when the body is, for example, sitting at rest – a very soft, medium-pitched hum may be heard. This hum could be said to constitute the rudiments of speech, although speech requires a great deal more activity and energy than is involved in making this sound. However, the basis is there: a sound has been made by obstructing, interfering with, the outgoing stream of air by manipulating an organ higher than the lungs. The energy supplied by exhalation is applied to acoustic production by letting it work against the resistance of one of the vocal organs.

Breathing serves to renew the oxygen content of the blood, and so cleanse it by filling the lungs with air and then emptying them of carbon dioxide. The lungs are filled by inducing a state of negative pressure within them, and emptied by creating pressure within greater than that of the outer air. The lungs are elastic, but they are not equipped with any intrinsic musculature, and so the necessary pressure changes must be brought about by forces acting on the lungs from outside. These forces are supplied by the diaphragm, and the rib-cage, which exert pressure on the pleurae, the air-tight sacs which enclose the lungs. The diaphragm is a large, dome-shaped membrane below the rib-cage, fixed to the breast-bone at the front, the lumbar vertebrae at the rear and the cartilages of the six lower ribs at each side. The inspiration phase of the breathing cycle begins with the lowering and flattening of the diaphragm. As the diaphragm is pulled downwards it exerts sideways force on the lower ribs, pushing the rib-cage outwards. The rib-cage is thus expanded, the pressure it applies to the pleurae by its natural weight is reduced and air is automatically drawn into the lungs. The speed and scale of this operation can be increased by using the intrinsic muscles of the rib-cage – the intercostal muscles – to further expand that structure: this is what we do when we 'take a deep breath', as for example after intensive physical action which leaves the blood short of oxygen. In quiet breathing we do not usually expand the rib-cage beyond the degree attained as a consequence of the sideways push of the diaphragm. When the lungs are filled, the diaphragm gradually relaxes from its flattened, tense position to its convex resting shape. The rib-cage is thus allowed to fall back, and its weight presses on the pleurae and increases pressure in the lungs: air, by this time foul with carbon dioxide, is emitted from the lungs as the pressure within them exceeds that of the outer air. Finally, there is a short pause or moment of equilibrium before the inspiration–expiration cycle begins anew.

Air passes from the lungs to the oral and nasal cavities by way of the trachea or windpipe. The trachea itself plays no active part in speech, but its top-most cartilaginous ring (the cricoid cartilage) supports the laryngeal mechanism employed in speech. A complex structure of muscle and cartilage, the larynx need not be described in detail here. Its major component is a pair of lip-like muscles, the **vocal cords** or **vocal bands**, which lie horizontally within the Adam's apple, hinged at the front and capable of being closed, held open (as in quiet breathing) or vibrated by the outgoing airstream. When the vocal cords are pulled apart, a triangular opening, known

166

as the **glottis,** appears between them. The open (a) and closed (b) glottis positions are shown in the schematic diagram 459.

459.

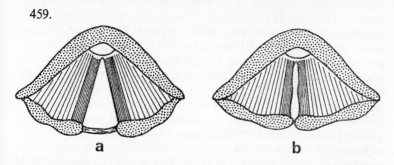

a   b

The glottis, evidently, operates as a valve, and in that function performs several distinct tasks. It may be closed to prevent foreign bodies entering the lungs: it is shut during swallowing to prevent inhalation of food. It closes to assist certain movements of the upper arms and abdomen requiring considerable muscular effort, e.g. lifting heavy weights, excretion, childbirth. In these cases closing the glottis seals a resistant cushion of air within the lungs, helping to stabilize the muscular effort involved. Notice that it is impossible to talk or to breathe out continuously while lifting a heavy object above shoulder level. Now presumably the phonetic uses of the glottis are genetically late superimpositions upon these biologically more basic necessities. Secondary functions or not, however, the exact quality of vocal uses in modern man makes it clear that the internal construction of the larynx has evolved to meet the needs of very precisely controlled vocalization. (Compare the remarks on p. 3 above concerning the different structures of man and the apes.) Several distinct positions are adopted in normal speech, switching extremely rapidly one to another as the needs of linguistic structure dictate. The glottis may be tightly closed, causing a build-up of pressure beneath it, and then sharply released: the result is the glottal stop [ʔ] as heard in Cockney, Norfolk and in some Scottish speech substituting for a voiceless plosive ([bɒʔl, kɒʔn] *bottle, cotton*), and, less usually noticed, employed to reinforce initial vowels where a firm 'attack' is needed:

460.   [ʔ] Í'm not going in, even if yóu are.

The sound is not unlike a sharp, quiet cough. Second, the glottis may be held open so that air can pass through smoothly without disturbance, giving no vibration at the level of the larynx: this is the situation for all the 'voiceless' sounds: [p], [t], [k], [s], etc. Here the vocal cords are only negatively functional. Finally, in the production of 'voiced' sounds – the vowels, plus consonants such as [b], [d], [g], [z] – the vocal cords may be held together, but not so tightly as for [ʔ]. What happens as a consequence of this closure is not well described in some of the elementary textbooks on phonetics – vague words like 'vibration' or 'held loosely together' do not help. We may contrast the closure for [ʔ]: this is so tight that the pressure beneath the vocal cords increases to a high level. The firmness of closure is such that the increased air pressure cannot cause separation of the vocal cords except when they are deliberately released. By this device a quite substantial increase in lung air pressure is achieved and a perceptible 'explosion' is caused. But in the case of the non-plosive glottal closure for 'voice', pressure is not allowed to build up to this extent, and there is not just one single explosive parting of the vocal cords. When we say that in this type of articulation the vocal cords are closed 'loosely', we mean that they are held together by relatively light, but definite, constant muscular tension. The relaxation of the diaphragm and consequent contraction of the rib-cage during the exhalation phase of breathing causes lung air pressure to increase against the resistance offered by the closed vocal cords. When pressure in the lungs exceeds that of the outer air, the glottis bursts open and the pressure of the lung air is relieved, restoring equilibrium with the outer air pressure. Because the muscular force exerted on the cords is held steady (rather than suddenly removed, as for [ʔ]), the glottis closes again automatically. The diaphragm continues relaxing, air pressure builds up again, the cords burst open and then close. Provided the muscular forces acting on the cords are maintained, this opening and shutting routine can continue for as long as the supply of lung air holds up: the cycle is repeated over and over with great rapidity (a hundred or more times a second), and, if the balance of muscular forces holding together the vocal cords and controlling the relaxation of the diaphragm is kept constant, the rate of opening and closing of the glottis becomes **periodic**, that is, the moments of opening are equally spaced out in time. Whenever the vocal cords break open, a puff of air escapes from the trachea through the glottis into the pharynx above: thus the relatively stable air in the pharynx is 'bombarded' periodically from below. Just as happens with wind instruments, regular disturbance of air in an enclosed space produces a musical note. The air immediately above the glottis is set in motion: particles of air are displaced to a minute extent, push adjacent particles out of position, and then move backwards again into the rarefied space formed by their own displacement (the movement is like that of the weight on the end of a pendulum). A chain activity is initiated, alternate compressions and rarefactions, displacements and returns, rapidly spreading

168

through the air within the throat and mouth, then into the outer air, where these periodic disturbances eventually stimulate the ear-drums of speaker and listener. The perceived **pitch** of the note which is produced in this way is directly related to the number of compression-rarefaction cycles per unit time: this is known as the **frequency** of the note, measured in cycles per second (cps). The greater the number of cycles per second, the higher the perceived note; by the same token, what we perceive as low notes are produced by relatively fewer compression-rarefaction cycles per second. Now the absolute length and mass of the vocal bands contribute to the overall pitch-range of the voice. Adult males have heavier and longer cords than women and children (about 23 mm as against 18 mm) and therefore the cords vibrate at a lower natural frequency, in the same way that the long thick wires associated with the low notes on a piano do. Men's voices sound at about an octave lower than women's. This difference is linguistically irrelevant – males and females communicate not-withstanding, and thus it is demonstrated that *absolute* pitch is of no importance in language. *Relative* pitch within the natural register of the voice is significant, however. For instance, a rise in pitch at the end of an utterance can make all the difference to its meaning: try 461 both ways in succession:

461.   He went home

With a falling pitch on *home* this is a flat statement; substitute a rising pitch, and it becomes a surprised or disbelieving question. In a different way, 460 (*I'm not going in, even if you are*) illustrates the influence of pitch on meaning: the syllables *I'm* and *you* are of higher pitch than the rest of the sentence, to point up the semantic contrast being offered between the two words. This kind of frequency variation, variation within the biologically determined range of the individual speaker, is managed by a fine adjustment in the balance of muscular forces – the balance between, on the one hand, the tension with which the vocal cords are held together, and on the other, the building air pressure beneath them, which is increased by the contraction of the rib-cage. An increase of pressure within the lungs, while the tension of the closed vocal cords is held constant, must cause the cords to burst open more swiftly; if this new balance of forces is maintained, the rate of opening and closing will continue raised, thus giving a note of continuously higher frequency than the one which was produced by the original balance of power. Lower notes are produced by relaxing the cords and simultaneously reducing the force of exhalation to a proportionately even lower level: so the cords open and close at longer intervals, and with minimal expenditure of energy. (The different levels of intensity between high and low frequencies give important support to the above description. High notes sound loud, while very low notes must be played or sung softly: those who play wind instruments will readily recognize this technical contrast.)

Frequency is only one of four acoustic properties of speech sounds in respect of which variation occurs. The others are **duration**, **amplitude** and **complexity**. Duration needs no special discussion: it is simply the length of a sound, the time occupied by it in relation to the length of other sounds and other lengths of the same sound. Only some sounds can be prolonged – vowels and continuous consonants such as [s] and [m]; obviously plosive consonants such as [p], [t] cannot have long versions, for their essence is an instantaneous burst of noise. Variation in **amplitude** relates to the amount of energy which goes into a sound, and is perceived as variation of loudness. If frequency relates to the number of disturbances in air pressure per unit time, amplitude relates to the *size* of the disturbance: the extent to which each air particle is displaced from its point of rest. Clearly, the distance an air particle is displaced depends on the force which is imparted to it. In crude terms, the amplitude of speech depends on the 'size of the puffs of air' which pass through the glottis: the volume of air which escapes at each opening of the vocal cords. This in turn depends on the intensity of the muscular force imparted to the escaping air, the amount of 'thrust' available at the brief instant when the cords are pushed apart. In the case of voiceless sounds (sounds during which the glottis is open), the relation between amplitude and rate of air flow (volume escaping per unit time) can be easily studied. Try saying a prolonged [ʃ] ('sh . . .'), first very quietly and then loudly, in each case holding your hand in front of your lips and prolonging the sound until the lung air is exhausted. It will be noticed that the louder sound (a) causes a palpable impression of air flow against the palm, and (b) uses up the available breath very much more quickly.

'Amplitude', like 'frequency', is an *acoustic* term; 'loudness' and 'pitch' are their *perceptual* counterparts. I emphasize the distinction between acoustic and perceptual labels because a clear separation of these two levels is necessary. There is no one-to-one correlation between auditory impression and acoustic stimulus, as the case of 'loudness' well illustrates. When we feel that a syllable is louder than its neighbours (e.g. the two accented syllables in 460), relative amplitude is rarely the sole cause of such an impression. These syllables may indeed have marked amplitude as a consequence of high muscular force being employed in pronouncing them, but usually other factors contribute to the impression of loudness, and indeed other factors may *replace* amplitude as a cue to loudness. A *long* sound appears loud in the context of a sequence of short ones, even if it is not of pronounced amplitude; a *high frequency* is felt to be louder than a low frequency. In the case of 460 the two 'loudest' syllables certainly appear so as a result of a combination of all three acoustic causes – length and raised frequency as well as amplitude. Linguists generally recognize the complexity of the acoustic causation, in cases like this, by employing the term **prominent**, which is neutral as between the three types of stimuli and acknowledges that all three co-operate. (In fact, pitch-level is the most powerful determinant of prominence, but not to the exclusion of the other two factors.)

Finally we come to acoustic **complexity**, the fourth parameter of the sound-wave. The least complex acoustic phenomenon is the pure tone, a sound-wave resulting from one single disturbance-cycle, particles vibrating at one and only one rate during any period of time. Pure tones may be generated electronically, but they cannot be produced by any physical instrument, musical or vocal. When a physical body produces a musical note, not only that part of it which is actively concerned in production (the vocal cords, the reed of an oboe, the strings of a violin) vibrates; in addition there are sympathetic vibrations from other parts of the instrument. These secondary vibrations give musical instruments their distinctive timbres: a violin sounds different from a viola playing the same note because the gross physical characteristics of the two instruments (and hence their potentialities for secondary vibration) differ. Now the larynx, because it is an extremely complicated physical structure, is very rich in possibilities for secondary vibrations. The opening and shutting cycle which the vocal cords perform during 'voice' is accompanied by numerous subsidiary muscular movements and consequential disturbances of the air-stream, in addition to those oscillations which are induced in sympathy with the primary impulses from the glottis. So the wave which issues from the larynx carries a complex sound. The wave consists of a fundamental frequency within the range natural to the sex/age of the speaker, plus a set of **overtones**, frequencies much higher than the fundamental, resulting from secondary vibrations. The most important of these overtones are the **harmonics**, overtones which are simple multiples of the fundamental frequency: as we shall see, these harmonics are of vital importance to the differentiation of vowels.

In summary, the breath stream issuing from the trachea may be subjected to any one of three acoustic manipulations at the level of the larynx: it may be checked and then exploded glottally; it may be set in vibration by adjustment of a lightly closed glottis, resulting in a perceptible fundamental frequency and a set of overtones; it may pass through the larynx unobstructed, acoustically largely inactive.

(Note, however, that this inactivity is potentially significant when the alternative is vocal tone: compare the initial consonants [f] and [v] in *fine* and *vine* – in the first the vocal cords are inactive, in the second they are in vibration, and in other respects the sounds are identical. The passivity of the vocal cords (or its acoustic consequence) is made significant by the contrast with the active state.)

So far I have considered only the physiological conditions associated with speech which occur at the level of the larynx or below. We have seen that 'below-the-surface' activities are responsible for certain basic contrasts, but it should be clear that the majority of distinctions between speech-sounds are effected elsewhere in the vocal mechanism. We should now turn our attention to the vocal areas above the larynx, to the articulatory activities which produce finer acoustic differentiations.

The acoustic properties associated with the upper vocal tract are quite various, but they can all be subsumed under the general qualities of **resonance** and (in a technical sense) **noise**. Because the sound-wave bearing the fundamental frequency of the voice has to pass from the larynx to the outer air through a number of resonating – 'amplifying' – chambers in the throat and mouth, all voiced sounds are resonant; some are, in addition, perceptibly 'noisy'. All voiceless sounds contain acoustic noise – they could not be heard otherwise. Resonance is produced by the passive co-operation of the oral and nasal cavities. An enclosed or semi-enclosed body of air can be made to vibrate sympathetically if a complex tone is sounded adjacent to it. The frequency of the vibration so induced is dependent on the volume of air contained by the resonator. Now if a complex tone, sounded near a resonator, contains as one of its overtones the natural frequency of the adjacent resonator, this frequency is amplified, and so the timbre of the original note is changed: it now contains one harmonic, or set of harmonics, particularly heightened. The vocal tract above the larynx contains three potential resonators: (a) the area between the larynx and the back of the tongue (the **pharynx**); (b) the area above the tongue extending outward to the lips; (c) the nasal cavities. These three cavities, together with details of other parts of the vocal tract above the larynx, are shown in the cross-section in 462 (p. 173).

It can be seen that the nasal resonator (c), when in use, adds considerably to the volume of the upper vocal tract. Any tone which is exposed to it must clearly have its frequency spectrum much modified. Exposure is achieved by lowering the velum and uvula (as shown in 462); for non-nasal sounds they are lifted to rest against the back wall of the pharynx, isolating the nose from the mouth. When the velum is lowered, either the whole of the air stream can be allowed to escape through the nose, or the air can be directed out of the

462.

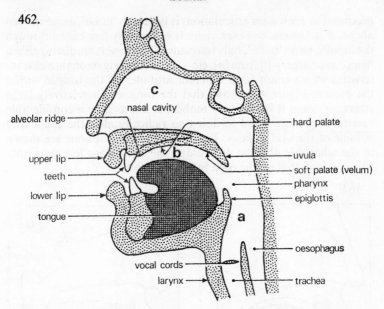

mouth and nose simultaneously. In the latter case the result is a
nasalized vowel, containing not only the resonances which give the
quality of a particular vowel, but at the same time an overlay of
nasal resonance. Nasal vowels are familiar in French: in the phrase
un bon vin blanc each word ends with a nasal vowel, despite the
spelling, which shows consonants. A typical English mispronunci-
ation of this phrase adds a nasal consonant – [n], or [ŋ] as in *sing* –
on the end of each word, and keeps the vowels un-nasalized, as they
would be in English. Nasal consonants are produced with air issuing
from the nose only, the mouth being stopped at some point. For
[m] the lips are closed; for [n], the tip of the tongue is pressed against
the hard ridge behind the teeth; for [ŋ] the body of the tongue
pushes against the back of the palate. The effect of these three different
closures is to adjust the total volume of the oral and nasal cavities
together: so the resonating chamber for [m] is larger than that for
[n] and much larger than that for [ŋ], hence the differences in the
quality of the three sounds.

The shutting-off of the mouth in the articulation of [m, n, ŋ]
illustrates the criterion for consonants as against vowels: obstruction of the air-stream within the mouth. Here the obstruction is
complete, but in other cases it may be only partial: [s, f] etc. It is the
degree, the manner and the position of the obstruction which give
individual consonants their distinctive qualities, and the sound

produced in consonant articulations is generally 'noise', as mentioned above. For vowels, however, there is completely free egress through the mouth, so no 'noise', only resonance. The vowels are distinguished from one another – [i] from [u], etc. – by contrasting resonance characteristics which result from different attitudes of the tongue within the mouth. Figure 462 shows that the tongue is a relatively large structure; since it is also very mobile, it can assume a considerable variety of postures, and in doing so radically alter the shape and volume of the oral cavities. Two very different positions are shown in the schematic diagram 463 below: the one on the left represents [i] (as in *sea*), that on the right [ɑ] (as in *farm*):

463.

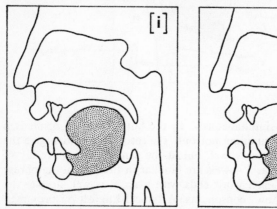
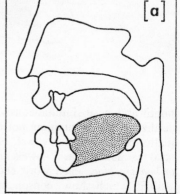

The relative positions of the highest point of the tongue are of great interest (for the sake of clarity I have drawn them with slightly exaggerated 'peaks'). For [i] this peak is high in the mouth and well towards the front, while [ɑ] has a low back position. We may regard the highest point of the tongue as marking the watershed between two resonance chambers of variable relative volumes. In the articulation which gives rise to [i], the front cavity – (a) in 462 – is minute in relation to the enlarged space (b) extending from the vocal cords to the rear of the tongue-peak. In [ɑ] the pharyngeal part is nothing like as large, and the front cavity is correspondingly larger than it is for [i]. It is the *balance* between the two cavities separated by the peak of the tongue which determines the quality of each vowel: a particular pairing in the sizes of these two resonance chambers leads to a particular vowel sound. Each of the two chambers picks up and amplifies a given frequency, the frequency of course depending on the size of the chamber. It is these two amplified harmonics, the ones which answer to the natural frequencies of the chambers established by a particular tongue position, which we respond to when we recognize a given vowel. The spectrograph shows that vowel sounds do indeed contain two very prominent harmonics which vary systematically according to the vowel being produced. Each vowel – [i], [u], [æ] as in *cat*, [ɔ] as in *caught*, etc. – has its own distinctive pair of enhanced supplementary frequencies above the fundamental: emphasized harmonics picked out by the varying resonance chambers shaped by the tongue. Vowels display, through their marked resonance bands, a kind of acoustic precision: their recognition depends on the hearer picking up particular frequencies generated by the disposition of the two oral cavities.

Noise, the acoustic property of most consonants, is a much less simple sound-wave. It is a 'mess' of frequencies randomly spread over a broad spectrum, with no particular frequencies predominating. Of course, the band of frequencies which are active may be more or less wide and, as a mass, relatively high or low: the noise made by a match against a matchbox is a disordered mixture of rather high frequencies, whereas the noise made by the wheels of a train is composed of mainly low frequencies. In each case there is a spread of frequencies, with no 'internal structure', within a quite broad band: the range is determined by the physical characteristics (mass, rigidity, etc.) of the vibrating 'instrument'. Naturally, the noises which are a part of normal human speech are of high (but perceptually indeterminate) overall frequency. The classic noise sounds of speech are the **fricative** consonants, which are aptly said to be characterized by 'audible friction': for example, [s] and [z], where the tongue is placed close to the roof of the mouth, leaving only a very small gap through which the stream of breath can escape. After flowing through a free and relatively wide channel, the air-stream is forced to pass through an extremely constricted space. The abrupt change of pressure which is suffered by the issuing air inevitably causes turbulence at the point of near-obstruction. This is experienced as 'hiss', a clear instance of high-frequency noise. This noise is the prime constituent of [s]; its counterpart [z] comprises voice, oral resonance, and noise. Other fricatives are formed by creating narrow constrictions in other parts of the oral cavity. The **labiodental** fricatives [f] and [v] are produced by forcing air between the lower lip and the upper front teeth: the **dentals** [θ] and [ð] (as in *thigh* and *thy*) involve a close constriction between the tip of the tongue and the top teeth; [ʃ] and [ʒ], as in *shoot* and *beige* respectively, utilize a point of articulation at the front of the palate – the air-stream, voiceless for [ʃ], voiced for [ʒ], is forced through a narrow opening between the front of the tongue and the roof of the mouth. Fricatives articulated further back on the palate are found in some languages, e.g. German.

The fricatives establish that at least three variables enter into the description of consonants: the kind of obstruction of the air-stream which is involved – e.g. narrow constriction for fricatives; the place at which the obstruction occurs, or to put it another way, the parts of the vocal mechanism which are concerned – e.g. lip and teeth for [f] versus tongue and teeth for [θ]; and presence or absence of voice – [v] versus [f]. A contrasting *manner* of articulation (kind of obstruction) is illustrated by the **plosive** or **stop** consonants. The outgoing breath is checked completely, pressure builds up behind the closure, which is then suddenly released, the release leading to a short burst of noise. Stops show up on the spectrogram as periods of silence followed by a brief scatter of frequencies through the whole spectrum. This noise may be accompanied by a fundamental glottal tone, as with [b], or not, as with [p]. Plosive consonants typically exist in voiced–voiceless pairs: [b] and [p] formed by closure of the two lips (**bilabial**), [d] and [t] in which the air-stream is checked by the tongue pressing against the teeth-ridge (**alveolar**), [g] and [k] with the body of the tongue pressed against the palate (**palatal**). The **glottal** stop [ʔ] requires tight closure of the vocal cords, and of course cannot be voiced.

The description of vocal movements and of associated sounds begun in the last few pages obviously does no more than introduce in the most superficial way the potentialities of the human phonetic apparatus. Its acoustic powers are quite evident if we consider only the range of voice qualities exhibited by our friends' speech, the variety of dialect accents we encounter, not to mention the vast repertoire of special sound effects which are achieved by ventrilo-quists, professional bird-imitators and the like. This unrivalled variety of potential sounds is made possible by the great complexity and plasticity of the organs of speech. The fixed pieces of the speech mechanism – teeth, palate, walls of the resonance chambers – are of diverse shape, texture and physical structure; the movable parts are extremely mobile. Since the movable organs are not restricted to a fixed set of predetermined positions, but can adopt an indefinite number of attitudes within their natural physical limits, and since the same freedom is available to the shape of the whole vocal tract by movements of the lower jaw and the cheeks, an infinite number of different sounds can be produced ('infinite' in the sense of 'speedometer' infinity – cf. p. 9 above; I do not mean, of course, that there are no sounds which cannot be produced). Note that I said 'different sounds' – not 'separate sounds'. Another important fact about the raw sound of speech is that utterance is a seamless, continuous, flow. We are in the habit of discussing articulation as if it consisted of a series of quite distinct postures assumed by the vocal organs one after the other. In fact, X-ray cinematography reveals that the movable organs are in continuous motion during speech, a fluid, unbroken chain. There are no 'separate sounds' in continuous speech.

In a moment I will discuss how the *structural linguist* handles two apparent paradoxes: the infinite variety of speech sounds and at the same time the fact that listeners feel their language to be made up of a finite set of repetitions of 'the same sound'; and the acoustic continuity of speech contrasted with our feeling that utterances consist of a succession of discrete phonetic units. First, however, we must dwell a little longer on the problems of the *phonetician* faced with such acoustic and articulatory complexity. The pure phonetician, who unlike the linguist is unconcerned with meaning, studies the gross physical properties of speech, the acoustic signal and its articulatory determinants. He has nowadays a battery of instrumental aids to analysis, chief among them the sound spectrograph (see above, p. 163). Experienced phoneticians can 'read' spectrograms, reconstruct the sound from the pictorial display. But for ordinary purposes of representing utterances graphically, spectrograms offer too much information. For centuries, phoneticians have worked with various styles of written notations for speech – phonetic alphabets. Modern systems of phonetic transcription derive from the alphabet of the International Phonetic Association (founded in 1886). This is based on the ordinary Roman alphabet, supplemented by special characters to symbolize distinctions which cannot be shown by the normal range of letters, plus diacritics – marks above or below letters – for finer distinctions still. A list of phonetic characters is given on p. 267 below, and here is a short passage of transcription:

464.

mɒdən sɪstəmz əv fənetɪk trænskrɪpʃən dɪraɪv frəm ði ælfəbet əv
ði ɪntənæʃnəl fənetɪk əsəʊsieɪʃən faʊndɪd ɪn eɪtin eɪti sɪks ðɪs
ɪz beɪst ɒn ði ɒdənri rəʊmən ælfəbet sʌpləmentɪd baɪ speʃəl
kærəktəz tə sɪmbəlaɪz dɪstɪŋkʃənz wɪtʃ kænət bi ʃəʊn baɪ ðə
nɒməl reɪndʒ əv letəz plʌs daɪəkrɪtɪks mɑks əbʌv ə bɪləʊ letəz
fə faɪnə dɪstɪŋkʃənz stɪl ə lɪst əv fənetɪk kærəktəz ɪz gɪvən ɒn
peɪdʒ . . . bɪləʊ ənd hɪər ɪz ə ʃɒt pæsɪdʒ əv trænskrɪpʃən

The transcription shows – with some finer details omitted – my pronunciation of the passage in fast but careful speech. It notices explicitly several features that are obscured by normal orthography: for instance, that the word *ordinary* has only three syllables in this style of speech, not four as the conventional spelling suggests; that some letters have widely different pronunciations depending on context (*o* represents [ɒ, ə, əʊ, ɑ]) and conversely some sounds have a range of spellings – [ɪ] is spelt *i, e, a*; that some single letters symbolize sequences of sounds – *x* is [ks] – and some sequences of letters spell single sounds – *wh* is [w]. In general, the phonetic inconsistency and inexplicitness of English spelling are shown up.

The transcription has the advantage of readability, but is actually rather uneconomical and uninformative from the point of view of phonetic *analysis* (as opposed to *notation*). We can understand how this is so if we enquire into just what it is that a phonetic character represents. Obviously a phonetic symbol is an abbreviation for a complex of acoustic/articulatory properties – we have seen that each 'distinct sound' is the product of a combination of many simultaneous motor activities, and is itself a highly complicated configuration of acoustic events. [k] as in *kin*, for example, is a plosive consonant, voiceless, checked by the tongue pressing against the front of the palate, released with an audible rush of air, articulated with considerable muscular tension. Now the terms of this kind of description recur in the analysis of other sounds – [t] in *tin*, for instance, has the same analysis as [k] except that the position of closure is different, the tongue being placed in contact with the tooth-ridge rather than the palate. The position is different again for the [k] in *can*, but it is more like the [k] in *kin* than the [t] in *tin*: the tongue and the middle part of the palate are brought together. We can simplify and systematize the phonetic description by regarding each sound as a set of **components**, exactly parallel to semantic components (see chapter 3 above). As proposed by Roman Jakobson and Morris Halle, acoustic/articulatory variables can be reduced to a small number of parameters or phonetic **features** with multiple **values**. The number of features is smaller than the number of sounds, so there is a gain in economy (just as with componential analysis in semantics, which is, historically, modelled on Jakobson's phonetic componential analysis).

The three sounds discussed informally above – [t] and two varieties of [k] – may now be given more ordered analyses as bundles of phonetic components (see 465 opposite).

For comparison, [d] in *do* is [+ VOICE, − ASPIRATE, − TENSE, etc.], [t] in *stone* is [− ASPIRATE, etc.], [g] in *gift* is [+ VOICE, − ASPIRATE, − TENSE, etc.], [k] in *cool* (as opposed to the [k] in *kin* or the [k] in *can*) is [3 PALATAL, etc.]. It can readily be seen that any individual sound can be represented, using these conventions, as a collection of components assembled by selection from an overall phonetic structure expressible in terms of features. Furthermore, phonetic feature-

465.

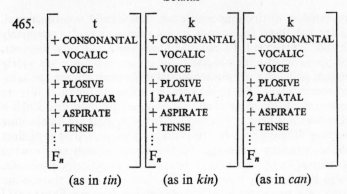

t	k	k
+ CONSONANTAL	+ CONSONANTAL	+ CONSONANTAL
− VOCALIC	− VOCALIC	− VOCALIC
− VOICE	− VOICE	− VOICE
+ PLOSIVE	+ PLOSIVE	+ PLOSIVE
+ ALVEOLAR	1 PALATAL	2 PALATAL
+ ASPIRATE	+ ASPIRATE	+ ASPIRATE
+ TENSE	+ TENSE	+ TENSE
⋮	⋮	⋮
F_n	F_n	F_n
(as in *tin*)	(as in *kin*)	(as in *can*)

charts can be drawn which are exactly parallel to the semantic diagram on p. 60 above.

I assume that, because the human vocal apparatus has determinate physiological characteristics, the number of *features* available for phonetic description must be finite. But presumably the phonetician is at liberty to propose as many *values* of features – hence, distinct *components* – as the delicacy of his description and the nature of his materials demand. The various [k] and [g] sounds in English require three values of the [PALATAL] feature; closer examination might make it necessary to invoke more than three values; a different language might require less. The variety of tongue-positions in vowel articulations is very considerable, indeed unpredictable in advance of describing a language; this variety is accommodated by referring to as many points as are needed, on just two scales – a **high-low** dimension and a **front-back** dimension. That is to say, the universal facts of phonetic structure provide two features for tongue-position, and the existence of particular sounds leads us to propose whatever values of these features are called for to account for observed cases. **Lip-rounding** yields another illustration: the pursing of the lips which occurs in some vowel pronunciations leads us to propose an appropriate feature, but what range of values we attach to this depends on the details of our particular observations. We may express the feature as [± ROUNDED] if we wish to note merely that, say, English front vowels are unrounded and English back vowels rounded; but if we want to go into more detail, noticing that the lips are more tightly pursed for [u] (as in *boot*) than for [ɔ] (as in *bought*), we can assign numerical values to [ROUNDED] – e.g. [0, 1, 2 ROUNDED].

The phonetician needs to postulate multiple values of phonetic features because he is concerned to observe and record minute distinctions of sound and of articulation. He deals with sound *as sound*, without regard to meaning; it is inevitable, then, that the phonetician is interested in distinctions which are semantically non-functional. Consider the three [k] sounds in *kin, can* and *cool,* respectively [1, 2 and 3 PALATAL]. In physical terms these are very different, as the phonetician must observe – the points of closure are widely separated, and there are consequential differences among the associated sound-waves. But to the speaker of English the three [k]s are all instances of 'the same sound': a phonetically untrained English speaker does not hear any distinction between what are, in absolute terms, very different sounds. [tɪn] and [kɪn] are perceived as distinct words, contrasting meanings, so the phonetic contrast between [+ ALVEOLAR] and [+ PALATAL] is not merely phonetically detectable, but also linguistically significant. On the other hand, there is no semantic use to be made of the distinction between [2 PALATAL] and [3 PALATAL]: no pair of words distinguished only by these two values of [PALATAL] can be perceived by English speakers as having different meanings. Let us add another example of a distinction which is noticed by the phonetician but is semantically immaterial: the contrast between the two values of the feature [± ASPIRATE] (which relates to the presence or absence of an audible hiss of air on the release of plosives). Plosives are released with aspiration when they are voiceless and in initial position in a word: [pʰɪn], [kʰɪn], etc. Voiceless plosives preceded by [s] are not aspirated, nor are voiced plosives: [spɪn], [bɪn]. (Cf. the representation of [t] in 465 and the notes on *stone* and *gift* just above it.) You can check for the presence of aspiration by pronouncing words such as these with the palm of the hand close to the lips, or with a lighted match: [pʰɪn] should blow the match out, but not [bɪn]. People are usually unaware of this substantial phonetic difference until it is pointed out to them: they need to be trained to perceive it. Why do people (with normal hearing) fail to notice such major differences of sound? The answer seems to be that the failure occurs because there is no linguistic gain in noticing such differences; only if there were *semantically* contrasted pairs [pʰɪn] and [pɪn] would it be useful for English speakers to recognize the phonetic distinction between [pʰ] and [p]. As the structure of English stands, there is every advantage in regarding [pʰ] and [p] as 'the same sound', in learning not to hear the irrelevant distinction.

We have, then, two versions of the concept 'sound'. The phonetician, unconcerned with meaning, observes the integrity and individuality of absolute phonetic phenomena, making distinctions which may be as delicate as his purposes decree or his instruments permit. If we take into account linguistic structure, however, we notice only those sound-distinctions which are functionally – ultimately, semantically – important in a particular language. This distinction of aim is better expressed by positing two levels of 'sound-structure': the **phonetic** level, the level of the raw sound of utterances; and the **phonemic** or **phonological** level, in which 'sounds' are seen as patterned according to the structural characteristics of an individual language. The term **sound** is best used literally, i.e. for items which have their existence at the phonetic level. Thus [p] and [pʰ] are different sounds; the English speaker uses them as variants of the same phonological unit, which we should not call a 'sound', but rather a **phoneme**, to use a traditional term. (In transcription, sounds are conventionally enclosed within square brackets, a practice which I have followed so far, whereas phonemic transcriptions are enclosed within slashes //: e.g. [pʰɪn] versus /pɪn/. In the latter, the phonemically irrelevant feature of aspiration is ignored.)

It is clear that, at the phonological level, considerations of the structures of individual languages determine what our analysis shows – more or less in disregard of the actually occurring phonetic data of utterances. Let us look again at some of our examples with this observation in mind. As we saw, at least three positions of palatal articulation – three values of one feature – are needed in the phonetic description of the various [k] sounds in English: *keep, calm, cool*. However, this is not a distinctive feature in English, so there is only one /k/ phoneme. In Arabic, however, the contrast between [1/2 PALATAL] and [3 PALATAL] *is* distinctive, so two phonemes must be proposed (and an Arabic speaker is likely to hear the initial sounds of English *cat* and *caught*, or French *car* and *coup*, as different phonemes – he interprets the phonetic structure of a foreign language in terms of the phonological structure of his own tongue). Lip-rounding is not a distinctive feature in English: front vowels are unrounded (see *hit, hat*), back vowels more or less rounded (*hoot, haughty*); there are no rounded front vowels or unrounded back vowels, so the contrast between rounding and unrounding never occurs with the same tongue-position, and the feature [ROUNDED] need not be mentioned at the level of phonological representation. In French, however, there are rounded, as well as unrounded, front vowels, so the feature is distinctive – phonemic: *père* versus *peur*, *vie* versus *vu*. Aspiration is non-distinctive in English: [p] and [pʰ] belong to the same phoneme /p/ (are **allophones** of the same phoneme); but in Greek and Hindi contrasting phonemes /p/ and /pʰ/, /t/ and /tʰ/, etc. are found. English has two main allophones of the /l/ phoneme, very different phonetically: 'clear [l]', which has a front vowel colouring about it, and 'dark [ɫ]', which has a back vowel resonance. The two allophones are found in the word *little*; or, the clear variety in *leap*, the dark in *peal*. These two sounds are contrasting phonemes in some languages, e.g. Polish *laska* 'stick' verus *łaska* 'favour'.

181

Innumerable other examples could be produced of the very different ways in which different languages select their linguistically distinctive features from the available set of phonetic contrasts.

Let us now try to fit the phoneme/allophone relationship into the transformational model of grammar. It will be useful here to recall the central notion of a *derivation*. A derivation is a step-by-step process which the linguist goes through in order to explain how, by the rules of a particular language, an intended message is associated with a concrete signal which 'expresses' it. For a simple sentence, the operation begins with a semantic nucleus, a predicate; the predicate has a set of roles associated with it, and the predicate and the roles acquire particular lexical items as their exponents. At this stage the lexical content is completely abstract, a collection of bundles of semantic components. Non-lexical elements of the meaning of the proposition are present too: modal, quantificatory, deictic, temporal, etc. This whole complex of meanings is the input to the syntactic portion of the grammar, and by an intricate sequence of transformational operations a surface structure is formed: that is to say, the abstract meanings are endowed with a linear organiz- ation so that they can be turned into a regular succession of mor- phemes and words. Obviously, the last stages of a derivation control the 'spelling' of surface structures, the provision of a graphic or phonetic shape for the abstract meanings.

In the last sentence I used the plural 'stages', because surface structures are not turned into utterances all at one go: there is a series of transformations for linking the separate phonological and phonetic levels referred to above. At the first phonological stage of a derivation, each semantic cluster is replaced by a cluster of phonetic components, together with instructions for the position- ing of word-boundaries, stress, pitch contours, etc., as required by the syntax. The output of the syntactic transformations (see chapter 6) is rendered as a sequence of sets of phonetic components, *but only those components which are essential to distinguishing the meanings present at the beginning of the derivation*. For instance, the lexical item *pin* is given only a skeletal phonological notation, expressed as a distinctive-feature matrix (see 466 opposite).

'Etc.' at the foot of this diagram indicates that English utilizes more distinctive features, but that none of them is relevant to the phonological spelling of this word. Omitted features include, for instance, [PALATAL], [FRICATIVE].

466 gives much less information than a phonetic representation would. A phonetic analysis of the vowel [I] in this context – to give one example of phonetic information omitted here – would not contain an 'o' on the [NASAL] line, but a '−' or a '+', depending on

466.

	p	I	n
CONSONANTAL	+	−	+
VOCALIC	−	+	−
VOICE	−	+	o
PLOSIVE	+	o	−
BILABIAL	+	o	−
ALVEOLAR	−	o	+
NASAL	−	o	+
HIGH	o	+	o
LOW	o	−	o
FRONT	o	+	o
BACK	o	−	o
TENSE	+	−	−
etc.			

whether the velum was lowered or not during an actual pronunciation of [I]. Vowels are usually [− NASAL] in English, but [+ NASAL] *might* occur before a [+NASAL] consonant, as here. Irrespective of the actual phonetic state of affairs, 'o' is marked in 466 because nasality is not *distinctive* for English vowels, and 466 shows only distinctive features. Because of this restriction to distinctive features, 'o' also appears on the [VOICE] line under /n/, and on first inspection this 'o' may seem to be a perverse decision, since all nasal consonants in English are [+ VOICE]. Why not put a '+' in the box? The answer is that we do not mark /n/ [+ VOICE] for the very reason that all [n]s *are* voiced, in English (likewise [m]s and [ŋ]s): we make the phonological representation as simple as possible, and supply the component [+ VOICE], which of course must occur in the *phonetic* analysis, by a general phonological rule of English:

467. $\begin{bmatrix} + \text{CONSONANTAL} \\ - \text{VOCALIC} \\ + \text{NASAL} \end{bmatrix} \Rightarrow \begin{bmatrix} + \text{CONSONANTAL} \\ - \text{VOCALIC} \\ + \text{NASAL} \\ + \text{VOICE} \end{bmatrix}$

(The left-hand segment in this transformational rule exists on the phonological level; that on the right is a phonetic segment.) The rule says that 'all nasal consonants are voiced (in the language to which the rule applies)'.

The transition between the phonological and phonetic representations of *pin* involves at least one more general phonological rule for which our discussion should already have prepared us. **Aspiration** is not mentioned in 466, since, as we have seen, it is not a distinctive feature in English: it cannot appear in the phonological notation for any English morpheme, in any diagram of the type 466. (But aspiration was noticed in 465, p. 179, because 465 diagrammed phonetic, not phonological, structure.) At the phonetic level, plosives are aspirated or unaspirated non-randomly – whether or not aspiration occurs depends on the phonetic context. The appropriate value of the feature [± ASPIRATE] is supplied in accordance with three rules which apply between the phonological and phonetic levels:

468. $\begin{bmatrix} + \text{PLOSIVE} \\ + \text{VOICE} \end{bmatrix} \Rightarrow \begin{bmatrix} + \text{PLOSIVE} \\ + \text{VOICE} \\ - \text{ASPIRATE} \end{bmatrix}$

'Voiced plosives are unaspirated'; see *bin, do, gap.*

469. $\begin{bmatrix} + \text{PLOSIVE} \\ - \text{VOICE} \end{bmatrix} \Rightarrow \begin{bmatrix} + \text{PLOSIVE} \\ - \text{VOICE} \\ + \text{ASPIRATE} \end{bmatrix} / \# \underline{\quad} V$

'Voiceless plosives are aspirated when they occur between a word boundary (#) and a vowel (V)'; see *pin, to, cat.* (The slash '/' in this type of rule means 'in the context specified by the following sequence of symbols'. 469, and 470 below, are 'context-sensitive' rules.)

470. $[+ \text{PLOSIVE}] \Rightarrow \begin{bmatrix} + \text{PLOSIVE} \\ - \text{ASPIRATE} \end{bmatrix} / C \underline{\quad} X$

'Plosives are unaspirated when they occur between a consonant (C) and anything else (X)'; see *stop, skit, speck; strip, screw, sprat.*

Rules 469 and 470 make it clear that allophonic differences such as that between [p] and [pʰ] relate solely to necessities of the sound-structure of the particular language, and have nothing to do with meaning. The phonetic contexts stated on the right of the / control the application of the rule: there is no deep structure determinant. Exactly the same kind of phonological rule accounts for other allophonic differences mentioned in this chapter: the variation between [l] and [ɫ] is governed by phonetic context, as is that between the three varieties of /k/ – the value [1 PALATAL] occurs before front vowels (*kin*), [2 PALATAL] before a vowel with a slightly back tongue position (*cup*) and [3 PALATAL] before a fully back vowel (*cool*). Context-sensitive rules can easily be devised which ensure that the correct value appears in the final, completely specified, phonetic representation of an utterance.

To summarize my observations on phonology and phonetics, it seems to be necessary and useful to recognize them as two quite distinct levels of linguistic structure. The phonetic level is described by means of as many features, and values of features, as are necessary to differentiate particular utterances as absolute acoustic phenomena. Many features have no semantic implications whatsoever; however, these same features may exhibit regularity of distribution in the language concerned, patterning according to purely phonetic circumstances. Where phonetic features are completely predictable in this fashion, they may be supplied, in a derivation, by phonological rules (such as the complementary rules 469–70) which are specific to one particular language. These rules serve both to characterize the phonetic structure of the language in question and to simplify phonological representations. A phonological representation should show only those features which serve to distinguish meanings, or, to put it another way, only such information as a speaker needs to possess if he is to distinguish different words and sentences in his language. We have already seen that surprisingly little information needs to be given at the phonological level: e.g. a speaker who knows the word *man* does not need to 'store' the facts that /m/ and /n/ are voiced, or that /æ/ is unrounded, non-nasal, at least he does not have to store these facts separately for the individual word concerned; he can rely on the general rules of English that all nasal consonants are voiced, no front vowels are rounded and no vowels are (distinctively) nasalized. Further simplifications can be achieved as a result of the *syntagmatic* regularities in the sound structures of languages: there are restrictions on what *sequences* of phonemes may occur. For instance, if a syllable begins with /b/ or /p/, any consonant which follows must be /l/, /r/ or /j/ (*black, brick, beauty, please, pray, puma* but not **bwack, *pnack*, etc.), so it is unnecessary, in the phonological representations of words like *brick*, to mark any features in the second consonant which may deliberately exclude /w/, /n/ etc. – this is done automatically by the rules for syntagmatic structure. Similarly, /k/ and /g/ may only be followed by /l/, /r/, /j/ and /w/; /t/ and /d/ may be followed only by /r/, /j/ and /w/, and so on. (In all cases, syllable-initial position is referred to: of course, further possibilities are found at the ends of syllables (cf. *cats*) and across syllable boundaries (cf. *napkin*).)

To end this chapter I will offer one more example of the effect of rules in simplifying phonological representations. On p. 183 above I sketched the representation of the word *pin* (diagram 466), illustrating the fact that many features do not have to be mentioned at this level of analysis. If the word concerned is *spin*, an even more radical economy is possible. The fact is that any sequence of the type 471 *must be* realized as 472:

471. $\#$ + C + Bilabial plosive + X
472. $\#$ + /s/ + /p/ + X

('$\#$' represents word-boundary, 'C' represents consonant, 'X' represents any segment or segments); e.g. 471 may be *spa*, *spin*, *spat*, etc. To express it more formally (and ignoring $\#$ and X), the phonological representation 473 is all that is needed to derive the phonetic display 474:

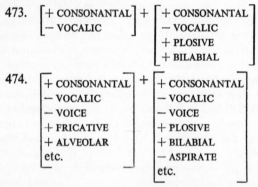

473. $\begin{bmatrix} + \text{CONSONANTAL} \\ - \text{VOCALIC} \end{bmatrix}$ + $\begin{bmatrix} + \text{CONSONANTAL} \\ - \text{VOCALIC} \\ + \text{PLOSIVE} \\ + \text{BILABIAL} \end{bmatrix}$

474. $\begin{bmatrix} + \text{CONSONANTAL} \\ - \text{VOCALIC} \\ - \text{VOICE} \\ + \text{FRICATIVE} \\ + \text{ALVEOLAR} \\ \text{etc.} \end{bmatrix}$ + $\begin{bmatrix} + \text{CONSONANTAL} \\ - \text{VOCALIC} \\ - \text{VOICE} \\ + \text{PLOSIVE} \\ + \text{BILABIAL} \\ - \text{ASPIRATE} \\ \text{etc.} \end{bmatrix}$

Several rules are responsible for automatically filling in the phonetic components of 474. We have met one of them already – 470, which stipulates that a plosive must be unaspirated when it occurs after another consonant in the same syllable. Another rule determines that the right-hand consonant is voiceless: it is a fact of English that no voiced plosive occurs in the context $\# + C + \_ + X$. So the right-hand phoneme in 473 must be /p/, phonetically [pʰ]. We now turn to the left-hand segment in 473, about which all we know is that it is a consonant in word-initial position, followed by /p/. As it happens, this is all we do need to know, for the only consonant which (in English) can fit in the slot is /s/. In a full derivation the passage from 473 to 474 would entail a sequence of rule-applications: the component [+ FRICATIVE] would be added (there are no English words **mpin*, **kpin*, etc.); [+ ALVEOLAR], because palatal fricatives are excluded from the position in question – except in loan-words from German and Yiddish (*spiel*, etc.) but these are so

186

few that they are best listed as exceptions to a general rule which prohibits the sequence /#ʃp-/; finally, [– VOICE] is added to the left-hand segment because /p/ is voiceless and sequences of consonants usually take the same value of the feature [± VOICE].

Phonological rules of the kind which have been presented, or informally summarized, here are an innovation in phonological/phonetic theory, a mode of representation designed under the impetus of generative-transformational grammar. They are transformational rules, of course, so they are peculiarly suitable for use in unified derivational descriptions of the kind employed in TG; when the system is perfected – in particular, when agreement has been reached on the status of the semantic component of a grammar – it will be possible to assign complete structural descriptions to sentences, passing from the meaning to the signal in one coherent sequence of applications of rules all of the same format but functioning at different 'levels' of structure: transformational rules for filling out semantic specifications, for creating linear syntactic (surface) structures, and finally for expanding the skeletal phonological 'spellings' of the morphemes in those syntagms as fully detailed phonetic entities. At this moment we are concerned with the status and consequences of phonological transformations only. Their *status* is in fact quite clear: the phonological rules of a language between them describe what is distinctive about the sound-structure of that particular language (just as the syntactic transformations specify the idiosyncrasies of word-order in a language, the body of syntactic information which a child born into a particular speech-community has to acquire). Their *consequences* are both methodological and psychological. The methodological gain has already been hinted at – simplifying the description; and the psychological gain is implicit, for we remember that a grammar (with the subscript $_2$) is designed to be a description of the linguistic knowledge (grammar$_1$) which speakers tacitly possess. Recall the case of *spin* once more. From the linguist's point of view, phonological rules permit a most economical representation of this word. From the psycholinguist's viewpoint, this methodological economy is passed on to the speaker: phonological rules are well motivated because they let us impute to the language-user the simplest and most convenient mode of storing information about the phonemic shape of morphemes – a minimal phonemic 'spelling' which is nevertheless serviceable because the full phonetic realization can be achieved by reference to a set of extremely powerful general conventions such as those I have schematized in the illustrative rules above. If we think about the task a child is faced with as he learns the language of his community, we are likely to come to the conclusion that this simplification of 'spelling' is a most valuable help in the learning of the complex knowledge which constitutes language.

Further reading

Important and informative manuals of general phonetics are Heffner, *General Phonetics* and Pike, *Phonetics*; see also Abercrombie, *Elements of General Phonetics*, and Malmberg, *Phonetics*. For those who prefer to learn their phonetics in relation to the sound pattern of English, Daniel Jones's *Outline of English Phonetics* is indispensable; a more modern account, within the same tradition, is Gimson's *Introduction to the Pronunciation of English*.

Peter Ladefoged's *Elements of Acoustic Phonetics* is the beginner's book in that field; see also his *Three Areas of Experimental Phonetics* and the same author's more recent discussion of phonetics in linguistics, *Preliminaries to Linguistic Phonetics*. Potter, Kopp and Green, *Visible Speech*, is a lavishly illustrated early description of the sound spectrograph and its capabilities; see also Pulgram, *Introduction to the Spectrography of Speech*.

Pre-generative phonological theory is well represented in Pike, *Phonemics* and Trager and Smith, *Outline of English Structure*. The standard American structuralist introductions to linguistics – Gleason, Hill, Hockett – all give reliable accounts of modern views of the phoneme.

But the classic works in phonological theory are Sapir, 'Sound patterns in language', Trubetzkoy, *Principles of Phonological Description*, Jakobson and Halle, *Fundamentals of Language* and Jakobson, Fant and Halle, *Preliminaries to Speech Analysis*. Some idea of the fluidity of phonological theory in the last decade may be gained by comparing Halle, *The Sound Pattern of Russian* (1959) with Chomsky and Halle, *The Sound Pattern of English* (1968). The ideas of the latter book are extended in Halle and Keyser, *English Stress*. Elementary accounts of generative phonology are only just beginning to appear. Langacker's section on phonology in *Language and its Structure* may be consulted; Bach's *Introduction to Phonological Theory* is not as straightforward as it might be; perhaps the best introductory work is Schane's *Generative Phonology*.

Bach's book also indicates a rather confusing aspect of current phonological theory: disagreement and variation of practice in naming the distinctive features. Since there is such disagreement, I have compromised by employing very traditional articulatory labels; this way out at least has the advantage of securing continuity with the discussion of articulatory processes earlier in the chapter (and with the discussions of the older standard phoneticians).

nine

Learning language

In the last seven chapters I have attempted to give a flavour of the descriptive statements which linguists make about the structure of language at the semantic, syntactic and phonological levels. Remembering the systematic ambiguity of the word 'grammar' itself, symbolized earlier in the shorthand references of 'grammar$_1$' and 'grammar$_2$', the reader should have borne in mind throughout that sequence of chapters that the subject-matter of the grammarian's description is, however obscured by the quasi-algebraic rules, ultimately *psychological* fact. We say that a speaker 'knows' a language: by this we mean that he possesses, has internalized and shares with his national-language peers a vast and intricately structured capacity for human verbal communication. In the individual, this knowledge or capacity is of such a kind that it approximates – in some fundamental respects which may not be obvious on the surface – the linguistic competence of every other normal individual on earth. But while all languages are fundamentally of the same design, they differ spectacularly in detail. The linguistic competence of a speaker matches quite precisely that of a sub-set of individuals who 'speak the same language' (English or Norwegian or Tzeltal) but seems to be sharply divergent from that of most other sub-sets. English diverges from Norwegian – or even from Dutch, to cite our closest linguistic relative – to such an extent that communication is impossible. The theory of language is called upon to explain these different kinds of similarity and dissimilarity, and the explanation appeals to the notion of transformation to account for these facts. Languages are transformationally distinct, communicatively non-overlapping, though built on the same universal foundation. The theory of transformations is a hypothesis seeking to explain how languages may be very different on the surface yet

189

profoundly similar underneath – just as a non-racist human biology may aim to show that diversely pigmented and featured peoples are all equivalently structured tokens of the type *homo sapiens* (or *homo loquens!*) beneath the skin.

Like all scientific theories, the linguistic hypothesis expressed in a grammar$_2$ has to make certain concessions in the cause of abstract statement. The laws of Newtonian mechanics, to give a parallel, are not totally detailed accounts of actual rocks rolling down slopes or of jagged objects falling through a smoke-polluted atmosphere. The rules of gravity are expressed in terms which idealize, or abstract from, physical situations: they must discount 'interfering' factors such as friction, ballistic instability and so on. So also, linguistic theory, in its separation of linguistic competence from the much more complicated behavioural reality of linguistic performance (see chapter 2, pp. 38–9, and the beginning of chapter 10) is an 'idealizing' science. The grammar-writer is forced to imagine his subject as fixed in an instant of time, stable, coherent, free from interference (no distractions, errors, etc.). Such a fiction is wholly necessary if grammar is to be studied, but the scholar who commits himself to the fiction must realize just what it is he is conceding, what he has to ignore. The next three chapters are intended to provide a glimpse of language varieties and language in use, against the background of a general homogeneity of linguistic form. This chapter looks at the incipient and formative stages of language acquisition in the infant; chapter 10 examines the rich stylistic diversity within single languages as they mould themselves to the communicative purposes of their idiosyncratic societies; and the final chapter looks more closely at the uses or functions to which language may be applied, and its values and implications for the individual.

The processes by which children come to understand, and to speak, the language of the community into which they are born are both mysterious and controversial. Although I do not wish to give undeserved prominence to the controversy – for it seems to me to be a potential inhibitor of unbiased research – I will notice it at the outset. Most of the further reading listed at the end of this chapter takes a firm stand on one side of the issues or the other, so students can hardly fail to be aware of raging discords in the theory of first language acquisition.

The facts are that human infants are born without any overt sign of possessing language; that within a few months they acquire, by 'babbling', a considerable repertoire of vocal sounds, some language-like and some not; that they show evidence of understanding some of their parents' utterances before their first birthday; that around

190

the age of twelve months they begin to produce one-word 'sentences' with clearly intended, decipherable, semantic content; that from this time on their language advances steadily towards the norm of adult speech; that most children, during their second and third years, progress linguistically with great speed; and that the *order* of acquisition of the elements of language is much the same for all normal children, in whatever community, even though the *rate* of progress may differ somewhat – quite a lot of children go through the various stages more slowly than I have indicated above.

The controversy concerns the *origin* of the child's linguistic competence, the *causes* of his acquisition of this knowledge. Does the child come to be a language-user because he has an intrinsic pre-disposition, as a member of a certain species, to develop in that way? Or can his learning of language be attributed to experience, practice, imitation, etc., without appeal to a pre-existing innate faculty? These alternatives locate the controversy at the heart of the 'innate ideas' dispute, which dominated European philosophy in the seventeenth and eighteenth centuries and has provided the basic framework for most epistemological speculation ever since. Not only language is involved – the questions may be posed of any capability manifested by any organism – but language is central to the dispute, since it has been so often invoked as a species-specific and even species-defining attribute of man. The innatist answers 'yes' to the first question: man talks because he is designed to talk, has at birth an inborn 'idea' of linguistic communication. The empiricist comes down strongly for the second explanation: man talks because he happens to be born into a community of talkers, picks up the 'non-natural' code used around him because it is beneficial to his social integration and his survival to conform and to possess this learned skill. Now modern science, as it emerged from the nineteenth century and consolidated itself in the twentieth, professes militantly empiricist ('positivist', 'behaviourist', 'experimental', 'mechanist') ideals. (Whether the great scientific insights of this century actually derived from experimental practices which conformed to these ideals is doubtful, but that is a question which need not concern us here.) Empiricism dominated linguistics as it did learning-theory in psychology. Bloomfield's account of language-learning and language function (see *Language*, chapter 2) is straightforwardly empiricist and reflects the beginnings of a tradition of behavioural psychology which has culminated in the work of the notorious and influential B. F. Skinner, whose major work, *Verbal Behavior* (1957), performed the amazing *tour de force* of explaining human language by extrapolation from his laboratory studies of animal learning. Chomsky and his associates, in the late fifties and early sixties, revived the innatist tradition, vehemently attacking Skinner and his work. The attack was all the stronger because general ideological, social, political and (basically) aesthetic considerations were at stake, but these need not concern us; what is particularly relevant is that, since the new Chomskyan linguistics was the main stimulus to a wave of research into language-acquisition, the innatist/empiricist controversy assumed great – perhaps excessive – prominence in discussions of child language. Undoubtedly, Chomsky performed an invaluable service by reminding us that there are aspects of children's language which cannot be explained as 'imitations' of adult speech; but on the other hand, it cannot be denied that interaction with the family and with the social environment is the major influence on the exact form of language which the child achieves: after all, a child learns English, French or Russian depending on where he grows up, and that cannot be explained as a result of pre-programming. By exaggerating the innatist argument, Chomsky and his followers lost sight of that fact. But judging from studies and theoretical papers which have been published in the last two or three years, researchers are now keen to redress the balance. A moderate position is emerging which, while granting primary importance to man's biological disposition to learn language, regards the actual process of first-language acquisition as a delicate co-operation of nature and nurture. In the following discussion I will mention some characteristics of children's language which seem to testify to an innate endowment independent of parental influence and others which are best explained as reflections of the linguistic models to which the children are exposed. These observations are not to be regarded as points for and against two mutually exclusive theories of language acquisition, to be totted up in order to decide which theory is correct; rather, they are parts of a single, complex, picture.

Very many parents – including linguists – keep records, in diary form or on tape, of their children's earliest utterances. Most people are conscious of the crucial early stages in children's linguistic development – babbling, comprehension, single words, short sentences – so even the most amateur diarists usually impose some sort of schedule or structure upon the materials they collect. But as the growing number of graduate students writing theses on child language can witness, there is a world of difference between informal notes and thorough, systematic study. It is worth dwelling on the difficulties of such research, for by doing so we can begin to become aware of the qualities of the phenomenon – child language – itself. For a start, there are practical problems in the collection of data. At the stage when their development is most interesting (when sentences two or three words long are being produced) young children are extremely talkative, mobile and inquisitive. Fortunately, the physical difficulty of keeping up with the child has been reduced by the availability of small but sophisticated cordless tape-recorders with sensitive multi-directional microphones. But these machines produce a super-abundance of material for analysis. Transcribing tape-recorded speech in large quantities is an unbelievably laborious and time-consuming activity, and the investigator is forced to work with small, but hopefully representative, samples. The best-documented studies published so far have been based on tape records, each several hours long, of all speech uttered by, or to, single children visited at home by an investigator every two, four or six weeks. Naturally the child's language cannot, in these circumstances, be presented as a smooth continuous development: it appears as a sequence of temporary grammars, each more complicated than its predecessor, growing closer to the adult norm by apparently discrete stages.

There are mechanical difficulties in the analysis of both tapes and transcripts. The child's phonological system is poorly realized phonetically and, for quite a long time, incomplete. For instance, many children develop the phonemic oppositions /t:k/ and /t:tʃ/ rather late in their emergent linguistic careers. Suppose a child demonstrates that he can distinguish semantically between *tap* and *cap*, *tin* and *chin* when other people address him, but in his own speech uses the consonant [t] as the first sound in all of these words: what does the investigator put down in his transcription? [t] throughout, in recognition of the subject's limited productive capability? or /t/, /k/ and /ts/, on the grounds that the child must know these oppositions 'receptively'? Of course, to be able to face this decision at all, the investigator must be able to hear exactly what the child says in the first place – which is often not an easy requirement to fulfil, since the child speaks indistinctly and the investigator's perception is markedly prejudiced by the expectations of his own adult phonology. (He may 'hear' /tʃɪn/ when the child says [tɪn] for *chin*.)

Assuming that we achieve an accurate record of what the child *says*, there is another level of difficulty, deciding what he *means*. By this I do not mean what lexical items he utters, but what semantic interpretation he wants the utterance of those lexical items to receive. Children's speech is severely truncated, by adult standards: there are one-word utterances, e.g. *Car*, and two- and three-word utterances without inflexional morphemes, auxiliaries, articles, etc. – *Put shoe, Mummy make lunch*, etc. Such utterances are obviously potentially ambiguous in the extreme: think of the number of alternative interpretations which *Mummy make lunch* may be given by supplying various morphemes. However, it is a fact that parents can more often than not understand their children's speech; that is, they can assign an appropriate meaning to a structure where more than one is possible. (Interestingly, young children usually misunderstand or fail to interpret each other's 'telegraphic' speech; their evident frustration on such occasions attests to the fact that they *do* intend quite precise meanings.) It seems that parents interpret their children's speech by responding to features of the context in which an utterance occurs, as well as to the utterance itself. Children's speech is almost invariably intimately integrated with immediate context. The most interesting of recent analyses have supplemented the transcription with a detailed and systematic account of ongoing context, physical and interpersonal. In this way some access is provided to the richer deep structure which undoubtedly underlies the sparse surface of infant speech.

Merely noting the order of words in utterances like *Mummy make lunch*, comparing it with that found in similar 'sentences' – in brief, distributional analysis – is inadequate as analysis of the intended structure of such pieces of discourse. This inadequacy typifies a general problem in the study of child language: without careful analysis of contextual hints of meaning, as above, our data is restricted to the bleak facts of utterance. Studying adult language, we can consult an informant about his 'intuitions' of linguistic structure – 'which is more acceptable, this sentence or this one?'; but two-year-olds are not amenable to this sort of questioning, as the psychologist Roger Brown discovered: one of his child subjects was asked 'Which is right, "two shoes" or "two shoe"?', and the boy replied 'Pop goes the weasel!' Nor can we administer psycholinguistic *tests* to young children with any confidence, at least if the tests demand (as most must) the subjects' active co-operation. Infants are not conscientiously attentive for long enough periods to allow controlled experiments to be carried out, nor can one ever be certain that the instructions have been properly understood. The burden is, then, squarely on the observational care and sensitivity of the investigator: he must employ all his ingenuity to extract the linguistic competence of his subjects, when virtually all he has to go on is their performance, their production of sentences. In this respect he is much disadvantaged by comparison with scholars researching adult grammars.

As I have said, much of the nature of child language – and particularly the processes by which it is acquired – is mysterious. Ideally, we would like to have detailed analyses of the child's phonological, syntactic and semantic development over several years, beginning well before the first birthday. In actuality, almost nothing is known about semantics, and most of the information on phonological development is anecdotal – a brilliant hypothesis by

Roman Jakobson concerning the phonetic progress from babbling to the possession of a phonemic system, first published in 1941, remains largely untested. But we do know quite a lot about the growth of syntax, thanks largely to a set of longitudinal studies carried out by Roger Brown and others. It is this research which provides the basis for my account of the development of syntax.

Most of the material below is drawn from the actual utterances of children, i.e. the most manifest part of their linguistic performance. Wherever possible, we should try to take account of what children *mean* as well as what they *say*, as I mentioned above: the utterances by themselves are not a full guide to children's linguistic competence (children mean more than they say). This observation seems to be true in another sense, too: in the sense that children's *understanding* of language is commonly in advance of their linguistic *production*. Comprehension precedes production (i.e. babies understand some utterances before they produce any) and exceeds production (children at every stage seem to understand more complicated utterances than they can yet produce). Parents report this phenomenon so consistently that it cannot reasonably be put down to the exaggeration of a proud mother. I recently observed a fifteen-month-old nephew whom I had not seen before (Timothy, an extremely lively and outgoing boy obviously encouraged to interact with adults and enjoying the interaction). He was said to possess a few words productively; I heard him utter none spontaneously during the four hours of my visit, though he imitated sounds on demand. He did, however, respond accurately to a large number of commands (to touch things, fetch things, etc.), and for me his ability to understand such structures was adequately demonstrated. One couldn't say that the capacity was scientifically proven, though. For the observation to have that status, it would have to be expressed in terms which would enable one to attempt to *dis*prove it, and that is not possible, for comprehension tests cannot be administered successfully to children below about three years of age. All informal observations suggest, however, that it is safe to assume that children understand more than they say, and this assumption is consistent with a rather more provable thesis, that children *mean* more than they say.

'Babbling' has been mentioned. Apparently all children babble; but we must make sure exactly what we mean by this term. Babbling is usually prolific in the middle and the second half of the first year. It is non-semantic, a purely playful and expressive toying with a very extensive range of vocal sounds. The baby will imitate arbitrary sounds addressed to it by adults, but its babbling bears no specific likeness to the phonemes of the language of the surrounding community. Indeed, sounds in the babbling phase are linguistically random. Sometimes it is said that in its babbling phase the baby 'tries out' the sounds of all the world's languages before discarding all but the set appropriate to his parents' tongue. This is a romantically attractive idea, but foreign to the facts, for babbling does not mutate smoothly into the phonology of English (or whatever other language is spoken around the child). Babbling stops abruptly, often at the eleventh or twelfth month, and there is discontinuity with 'native' speech sounds. Because, as we saw in the previous chapter, the significant sound structures of a language cannot be accounted for in purely concrete phonetic terms, a baby's phonemes cannot just emerge from a period of phonetic practice. He stops 'playing with sound' and, after a break, begins the more businesslike job of building the economy of his phonological system. His task at this point is to learn those sound-distinctions which are used by his language to effect differences of meaning. Fulfilling this task depends on knowledge of the meanings of words so that the child may recognize that different meanings are marked by contrasting phonetic qualities. Learning phonemic distinctions is thus primarily a cognitive rather than articulatory process, and it goes hand-in-hand with the acquisition of semantic knowledge: the child has proved, by his babbling, that he has the sounds *as sounds*, and he has now to acquire the abstract phonological system which defines the phonemes of his language and no other.

Naturally, the learning of phonemic distinctions – /p/ versus /æ/ versus /b/ versus /ɪ/, etc. – happens while the child is acquiring semantic distinctions – *pin* versus *pan* versus *bag* versus *big*, etc. When he begins to speak (round about the first birthday or a bit later, but, as Dr Spock never tires of pointing out, there is no 'normal' rate of development for babies), he produces just the sort of examples that the linguist offers to illustrate phonemic contrasts: syllabically simple words (*pat*, *mat*) often with reduplication of syllables (*dada*, *mama*). There is a period, sometimes several months long, of one-word utterances – a few recognizable names for common figures and objects in the child's environment: *mama*, *dada*, *doggie*, *car* and so on. The single-word utterances are mostly nouns in terms of adult syntax, but we must not attribute too much significance to this fact. The child has no syntax (no word-combinations) at this stage, so words like *milk*, *egg*, *cup* cannot belong to a determinate 'part of speech' *from the point of view of the child's own grammar*. (We will see, as this chapter progresses, how important it is, at every stage of the analysis of child language, to regard the grammar as independent and self-consistent at that stage; and particularly to avoid imposing the inappropriate categories of adult language upon it.)

Although it is not helpful to call these one-word utterances 'nouns' ('verbs', 'prepositions', etc., where such occur), they may well be regarded as 'sentences', since children seem to intend to communicate semantically complete messages by them. These communicative fragments have often been called **holophrastic** utterances or **holophrases**, by which is meant that each single-word fragment serves as a complete proposition. There are good grounds for thinking that the child who utters the single word *cup* is actually saying, according to circumstances, 'Give me the cup', 'This is a cup', 'Here is the cup', 'It's in the cup', etc. Certainly, parents who observe this sort of utterance in their children usually assign just such distinct, specific interpretations to them, and more often than not succeed in responding so as apparently to satisfy the desire expressed in the baby's holophrase. This interacting behaviour suggests that holophrastic speech is not (as babbling is) merely expressive, but that it has referential properties: that it relates to aspects of the situation in which it is uttered in some regular and significant way. This fact once granted, it is incumbent on the student of child language to explain how these utterances work. Some adaptation of the notion of deep structure seems appropriate: the baby appears to be saying more than is manifest on the surface. It would not be sensible, in my opinion, to regard holophrases as 'shortened' or 'elliptical' versions of full sentences: this view would credit the child with a most complicated set of deletion transformations for reducing a full proposition to just the one element which is within his productive capability. What is more likely is that children in the holophrastic phase are just beginning to employ the fundamental semantic relationships (see chapter 4), which are probably universal and hence innate, to organize their perceptions and the expression of their perceptions. An event is conceptualized as a configuration of objects and processes in semantic 'roles', only one role being picked out for expression. A child who says 'table' when asked 'Where's the cup?' demonstrates that he possesses the role *location* (i.e. if the cup actually is on the table). Detailed observations of similar in-context exchanges will no doubt enable this hypothesis to be tested, but the research has yet to be carried out. However, the knowledge of basic semantic relationships is fairly clear from the immediately following stage of children's development (two-word sentences), and it seems reasonable to project this knowledge backward in time, postulating that competence precedes performance.

The origin of syntax usually dates from between the eighteenth and twenty-fourth month, often between the eighteenth and twentieth. The single-word utterances remain, and the number of lexical items associated with them increases fairly rapidly. At the same time a new system of two-word sentences emerges. These are not formed by random juxtaposition in pairs, but the pairings are systematic, rule-governed. Detailed studies of such sentences have been carried out by Martin Braine, by Roger Brown and his colleagues, by Susan Ervin-Tripp and Wick Miller, and by Lois Bloom, and the materials cited below are mostly taken from their analyses (for references, see p. 211 below). All these scholars have pointed out that the children they have studied seem to possess two types of word: there are 'lexical' words, a mixture of nouns, verbs and adjectives, but mostly nouns: *sock, baby, girl, pretty, sleep, cookie, lunch,* etc.; and there are 'functional' words such as *do, off, up, allgone,* etc. The lexical or **open** class contains more members than the function class, and is indeed open-ended – the child puts most of his new words into that class. The class of function words is small, and its members occur in fixed positions in the child's syntactic constructions: for instance, *allgone* may, in one child, be restricted to appearing only at the beginning of the sentence, *up* at the end – *allgone baby* or *baby up* but not **baby allgone* or **up baby*. It is this stability of position of the function words – which are for this reason sometimes called **pivots** – which confirms the feeling that children in the two-word-utterance stage have syntax. Typical constructions are as follows; $O + P$ ('open' followed by 'pivot'):

475. *boot off, light off, pants off; do it, push it, close it; bunny do, daddy do, momma do.*

(These are from three different children studied by Martin Braine.) And some $P + O$ structures from one of the children studied by Lois Bloom:

476. *'nother noise, 'nother clown, 'nother toy; out toy; more noise, more apple.*

$P + P$ constructions, and occurrences of P words by themselves, are virtually unrecorded. These two types are of course aberrations from the point of view of the child's grammar, since the function of P words is to provide syntactic frames to accommodate 'lexical', O-class, words. However, O words form whole utterances by themselves:

477. *dirty, hole, turn, push, pull, toys, diaper, Mommy, shadow.*

The examples in 477 are all from Bloom's subject, Kathryn, at age twenty-one months. The syntax of Kathryn's predominantly two-word stage, in Bloom's analysis, is interesting because Kathryn shows a preference for $O + O$ combinations as against the $O + P$

and $P + O$ found in some other children. She uses Pivot/Open constructions, but she also produces a large repertoire of $O + O$ structures, and in the contexts described by Bloom these seem to display clear differentiations of semantic structure. There are possessives (*Mommy sock*), modifier + noun structures (*party hat, baby book* = book about babies), locatives (*sweater chair*), combinations of noun and predicative adjective (*Mommy busy*), agent-action constructions (*Mommy push*), etc. Kathryn certainly seems to be putting words together in constructions, not stringing them together randomly. This seems to be true of all children from a very early stage. One very important confirmation of this fact is that not all possible combinations of words in the child's vocabulary occur: Kathryn does not say *Sock Mommy* when she intends to communicate a possessive relationship; and, as I have pointed out, a child who says *allgone baby* does not say *baby allgone*: the combinations of 'open' class words show definite regularities, and the function or 'pivot' words have their own rigidly fixed positions.

Some general comments on the first phase of syntax may be made. First, the acquisition of a rudimentary syntax accelerates lexical development and overall talkativeness. Braine's subject, Gregory, produced 14, 24, 54, 89, 350, 1400 and 2500+ sentences of two words (counting distinct combinations) in the successive months after his first two-word combination appeared. It might be suggested that the availability of syntax provides the child with 'slots' into which he can fit, and thereby learn more readily, new vocabulary items. Second, although the 'Pivot-Open' constructions are ill-formed from an adult point of view, and the classes 'Pivot' and 'Open' contain a mixed assortment of word-types, nevertheless the 'Pivot/Open' dichotomy itself does correspond to a profound and powerful distinction in mature language. Most obviously in the surface structure of languages like English, French and German, words fall under two distinct types: **grammatical** words such as *will, the, of*; *de, en, suis*; *kann, er, wie*, etc.; and **lexical** words such as *fire, oxygen, map*, etc. (The distinction is often expressed as **function** words versus **content** words.) The set of 'grammatical' words is virtually closed, or at least, its membership changes very slowly indeed; but the 'lexical' inventory is open-ended, and losses and gains in that department – most noticeably, gains – provide the chief means by which man adjusts his capacity to refer to new experiences. In infant speech the P/O distinction seems to be the 'function/content' division in embryo. It is likely that the realization of this distinction, and in particular the possession of a definite 'O' class, enables the child to extend his vocabulary simply by formalizing the tacit concept of an 'extendable' part of the language.

The third general comment which needs to be made on children's early syntax is that the constructions appear to express fundamental semantic relationships in a regular, ordered, way. Researchers into child language have usually suspected that basic semantic relationships are expressed by children in their two-word and three-word 'sentences' (not to mention the holophrases) and indeed it is difficult to see why children should utter *constructions* at all if this were not the case. David McNeill and, more recently, Lois Bloom have paid attention to the question of the structural meanings of these elementary, truncated utterances, but no one has, as yet, attempted to describe the semantic structure of child language in terms of the 'case' or 'role' categories of Fillmore, Chafe, McCawley *et al.* reported in chapter 4. It seems fairly obvious that such a description could be achieved, given reliable information on the context of utterance (i.e. indirect insight into the child's communicative intentions). The $O + O$ constructions, in particular, seem to display systematic distinctions between types of semantic structure. Lois Bloom prints extensive materials of a very suggestive kind and, because she provides careful notes on the situation of utterance, these materials could probably be re-analysed in terms of a semantically based grammar (see chapter 3 of *Language Development*). For instance, she notes that the utterance *Mommy sock* occurred in two separate contexts: (i) as Kathryn picked up her mother's sock; (ii) as mother put the child's sock on her. The context (i) suggests a semantic structure *beneficiary-patient* (i.e. what I called the 'possessive' relationship above); (ii) *agent-patient* (with the predicate unexpressed in both cases). These two structures seem to underlie a large number of the two-word utterances of the child concerned (Kathryn). Reading the transcripts of Kathryn's utterances in Bloom's book, one gets a strong impression that the basic semantic relationships, which we suspected existed, only partly expressed, in the holophrastic phase, have at last come to the surface in the two-word stage.

In the six months or so after the child produces his first two-word utterance, his syntax grows rapidly in complexity. His sentences grow longer, and as they do so he learns hierarchical structure. Within the same period, and even much later, his morphological competence is very primitive. He uses word-order as the primary grammatical signal. Interestingly, this gap between syntactic and morphological competence in infants appears to hold not only for languages like English which, in the mature state, rely heavily on order as a signal of syntactic relation, but also for languages like Russian which are highly inflected and thus can afford a much less rigid word-order: the Russian-learning child begins with a quite rigid word-order which is relaxed only gradually as the child acquires the complicated morphology of the language. The sentences of young children lack noun and verb inflexions, auxiliaries, articles, prepositions:

478. there go one
      put truck window
      Adam make tower
      Eve lunch
      where ball go?
      hear tractor.

The absent formatives happen to be elements which are lightly stressed and often obscurely articulated in adult speech, and this phonetic fact may partly explain children's tardiness in learning them. Possibly of greater importance, however, is that a grammar of adult language proposes that such formatives are inserted transformationally. Their absence from the speech of young children suggests the general proposition that children's early competence contains only phrase-structure rules; they do not learn transformations until a fairly sophisticated constituent-structure grammar has been established. (This assumption about lack of transformations in the very early stages is borne out by the fact that children do not produce complex sentences until after they have mastered simple sentences.)

Note that deictic formatives are 'absent' rather than 'omitted' from child speech. Sentences of the type just illustrated are often called **telegraphic** since they lack just those formatives which adults omit from cables (and newspaper headlines) to save cost. Although the metaphor conveys well the character of child speech at this stage, the analogy is partly misleading: the adult composing a telegram possesses transformational rules for inserting deictic formatives, but chooses not to employ them; the child, however, simply does not possess these rules, so his speech is not, in this respect, a reduced or impoverished variety of adult utterances. Because his speech is, at the earliest stages, very much in the here and now, referring to features of the ongoing situation of discourse, lacking displacement almost entirely, he can rely on overtly present features of the situation to assist his interlocutors in their task of interpreting his incompletely formed utterances. The 'deixis', the 'orientational' properties of discourse, is supplied by the context. Presumably the infant does not actually notice that this is so and then capitalize on this discovery to save energy; presumably, because he has no notion of displaced speech, he naturally accepts the ongoing context – the presence of the cup on the table, and so on – as a natural part of the process of communication. It is the need for displacement which puts pressure on him to learn the transformations which will insert the 'orientational' morphemes of adult language. That part of his learning is too complicated, and too speculative, to go into here.

To illustrate the growth of transformations, let us rather look at questions and negatives, the transformational areas so far most fully investigated in studies of child language. Both types of construction require (a) special formatives (e.g. *why, not, n't,* the rising intonation of questions); (b) repositioning transformations (e.g. *You can come ⇒ Can you come?*); (c) special treatment of *Aux* (e.g. *We came ⇒ We didn't come*). There are, in addition, certain selectional restrictions managed by transformational manipulation of some very delicate syntactic features (e.g. *I saw* SOMEONE ⇒ *I didn't see* ANYONE). It appears that these operations present different degrees of difficulty to children (increasing order of difficulty roughly in the order of listing above); at least, they are learnt at distinct stages of the child's development. The child who has learnt positional stability in two- and three-word sentences, and is also in the process of increasing his vocabulary, predictably forms questions and negatives by adding special, simple, formatives to his primitive structures:

479.	Mommy eggnog?	No . . . wipe finger.
	See hole?	No a boy bed.
	Sit chair?	No singing song.
	What cowboy doing?	No money.
	Where milk go?	Not a teddy bear.
	Where horse go?	Wear mitten no.

(These examples, and the discussion below, are based on the study by Klima and Bellugi referred to on p. 211.) Yes/no questions are formed by adding a rising intonation to simple declaratives; others by special lexical items (*what, where, who*). Negatives are even simpler: *no* is preposed, or, less usually, *not*; in one example *no* comes at the end of the sentence. Note that these child sentences with preposed *no* are quite different from adult sentences like *No, it isn't time for lunch*: in the adult construction the initial *no* has its own separate intonation contour and serves to add emphasis to the primary negator *isn't*. The child's *no* is *within* his sentence and carries the full weight of negation: he has simply incorporated it in his phrase-structure rules. Sentences like *No a boy bed, no money, a boy bed* and *money,* for example, can be generated by constituent structure rules with an optional negative symbol. Once again, then, we have evidence that children begin their linguistic careers with a simple phrase-structure grammar, adding transformations only at a later stage.

Negation by simple addition of *no* continues for some time; but during the same phase a new method develops which produces sentences which are apparently identical to the 'targets' of adult speech:

480. I can't catch you.
      I can't see you.
      We can't talk.
      You can't dance.
      I don't sit on Cromer coffee.
      I don't want it.
      I don't like him.
      I don't know his name.

The child has learnt the negative auxiliaries *don't* and *can't*, and he has learnt to put them in the right place relative to the subjects of his sentences. But it would be a mistake to attribute to the child at this stage the same set of rules which generate these sentences in the adult grammar. He has not learnt the rules for the English auxiliary: this is proved by the non-appearance of sentences like

481. Can you catch me?
      Do you want it?
      You can dance.

Especially significant is the lack of sentences such as the first two of the three just listed. In Klima and Bellugi's material the question-system at this second stage is still non-transformational. If – as might be suggested by the appearance of *I can't catch you*, etc. – the child had learnt how to deal with auxiliaries at this time, we would certainly expect sentences like *I can catch you, Can you catch me?*; their absence leads one to believe that the child has merely learnt *can't* and *don't* as separate lexical items, together with a rule for positioning them in the sentence; that these words are not transforms of the non-negatives *can* and *do* (as they are in adult grammar). Thus *can't* and *don't* in child speech at this stage have an utterly different basis from *can't* and *don't* in adult speech.

The third stage shows considerable advance in both negatives and interrogatives. The primitive rule which produced *No . . . wipe finger* has disappeared, and there are some adult sentences like

482. No, I don't have a book.
      No, it isn't.

The range of auxiliaries has increased:

483. Paul can't have one.
I don't want cover on it.
You didn't eat supper with us.
I gave him some so he won't cry.
That was not me.
It's not cold.

And, since 'the modal auxiliaries now appear in declarative sentences and questions, as well as in negative sentences' (Klima and Bellugi), we can credit the child with a knowledge of the auxiliary system rather than of just two lexical items *can't* and *don't*. Thus, the child has begun to acquire transformational rules. But note that the child has not yet learnt the selectional restrictions involved in negation:

484. Because I don't want somebody to wake me up.
You don't want some supper.
I didn't see something.

Questions at stage 3 (which occurred at about twenty-six months for one of the children studied, forty-two for the other two) also display constructions which must be accounted for transformationally. Yes/no questions usually have the appropriate auxiliary, and the adult positioning of the auxiliary and the subject:

485. Does the kitty stand up?
Does lions walk?
Is Mommy talking to Robin's grandmother?
Did I saw that in my book?

Questions introduced by a special question-word, however, show much less assurance in the relative positioning of subject and auxiliary:

486. What he can ride in?
Sue, what you have in your mouth?
Why he don't know how to pretend?
Why kitty can't stand up?

And we see that the details of the inflexional system are still rather imperfectly realized; in fact, many children are still in the process of learning inflexional morphology in their early school years. My own nine-year-old is quite normal in persisting with *fighted, hurted, buyed*. Children learning Russian – a richly-inflected language in which the inflexions make a major contribution to sentence-meaning – do not achieve command of the requisite complexities of local transformation until several years after they manage basic linguistic competence.

Let us now try to evaluate and explain the achievement of children's language learning. We have seen that babies can understand before they speak; that their earliest utterances, even those just one word long, seem, in their interaction with communicative context, to display an awareness of some of the basic grammatical relationships – how else could they be meaningfully intended by the child and successfully interpreted by the parents? Then, as the second and third years of life pass, the child comes to express these relationships in a way which agrees more and more precisely with the linguistic models of his speech-community. This progress, this gradual approximation to the adult norm, is obvious even from the small selection of child utterances which I have reproduced in the last few pages; also evident are growth in complexity, increase in sentence-length, enrichment of vocabulary. Close examination shows that the language capacity of the pre-school child is quite considerable; that it is neither extremely limited nor extremely ungrammatical – as used to be thought, or might be thought from a superficial glance. However, we must guard against exaggerating the scale of the child's achievement. The first workers in the field of child language within the transformational-generative framework were so impressed with their early results – and with Chomsky's forceful application of the innatist hypothesis to language acquisition – that they were prepared to credit the six-year-old with a complete grasp of language. This judgment is manifestly an exaggeration. As I have said, the learning of morphology continues into the school years; vocabulary is obviously still limited; stylistic flexibility – fitting the form of the utterance to the occasion – still has to develop; so does fluency in the control of complex sentences; and, as Carol Chomsky has recently shown (for reference, see p. 211 below), there is still some *basic* syntactic learning to be undertaken. Knowing what we do about other areas of intellectual growth (e.g. the prolonged development of basic experiential concepts as described by Jean Piaget and others), we might suspect that the learning of language would not be complete by such an early age. But in any case the judgment begs the question of what might be reasonably said to be 'a complete grasp of language'. If all that is meant is ability to communicate about a variety of topics in simple sentences, then most young children possess this ability. On the other hand, some adults possess no more than this ability, while the linguistic capacity of others is much more richly developed. Most obviously, size and readiness of vocabulary vary considerably as between adults of different educational and social backgrounds, but vocabulary is not the only property of language that varies in this way: 'fluency' and 'articulateness' are variable, and all aspects of language enter into these capacities. Five- and six-year-olds may be very talkative, but they are not generally very fluent: they employ a limited range of sentence-types, often stringing together long sequences of simple sentences all of the same kind; and they tend to be stylistically monotonous. The fact that they have command of the semantic, syntactic and phonological bases of language, and can therefore communicate and understand readily, makes them linguistically competent in the strict sense of the term 'competent' (see chapter 2, pp. 37–8) but this is a somewhat narrow judgment.

However, the basic achievement is there, by the age of five or six, in most children, and we must seek to explain how it comes about.

One fact to begin with is that children do not need to be taught language. The 'idea' of language seems to be there from the beginning, and it takes only exposure to the speech of the family to bring the 'idea' to the surface, expressed in active and relentless steps towards acquiring competence in the linguistic code of the community. If a child is *not* exposed to a natural language in infancy he will not develop language, and furthermore if for this reason he has no language, it is well-nigh impossible to teach it to him later in life. (Roger Brown reports several cases of children isolated from society in his *Words and Things*, including the 'wild boy of Aveyron', Victor, the subject of François Truffaut's film, *L'enfant sauvage*.) Exposure to language is essential to 'trigger' the innate language-learning faculty, and apparently there is a critical time for this exposure – optimally, early in infancy, and certainly before puberty. Babies who are brought up in linguistically impoverished environments, for instance orphanages or the homes of deaf-and-dumb parents, do less well than babies born into normal families, but nevertheless *do* learn language; similarly, children in working-class households, which are typically less 'verbal' than middle-class families, less speech being addressed to the child, acquire language but acquire it in a relatively restricted form. These facts suggest that (a) exposure to speech is the minimal prerequisite; (b) teaching or coaching is not essential; but (c) a linguistically rich home is an advantage. In fact, most mothers (of those who have time to do so) talk to their babies and generally encourage them linguistically quite a lot. A very characteristic form of mother–child interaction involves the child taking the lead in conversation, usually 'commentary' on whatever is going on at the time (preparing a meal, changing a diaper, etc.), and the mother repeating the child's utterances, correcting or 'expanding' them by supplying words or morphemes which the child (in the 'telegraphic' stage) omits. If the child says 'Mummy make lunch' the mother will echo it with 'Yes, Mummy's making the lunch'; 'sock foot' will be expanded as 'Your sock's on your foot', and so on. One function of these parental expansions may be to check whether the meaning has been understood, or to reassure the child that meaning *has* been understood. Undoubtedly they contribute to the general linguistic richness which seems helpful to a child. Whether they fulfil a *specific* instructional purpose (e.g. whether they assist the child in passing out of the telegraphic stage) it has not yet been possible to prove. One experiment designed to test the influence of 'expansion' turned out indecisive. However, there can be no doubt that parental expansions are, if not immediately corrective for the child, a valuable part of the general atmosphere of linguistic encouragement which helps his progress along the path to adult verbal ability.

Note that in these repetition-with-expansion conversations parents do not seem to be trying deliberately to force the correct version on the child's attention. Indeed, attempts to coerce a child into correcting his mistakes are usually fruitless. The following dialogue, reported by McNeill, is an excellent illustration of this failure:

487.   Child: Nobody don't like me.
      Mother: No, say 'nobody like*s* me'.
      Child: Nobody don't like me.
      (eight repetitions of this dialogue)
      Mother: No, now listen carefully; say *'nobody likes me'*.
      Child: Oh! Nobody don't like*s* me.

The child is apparently so dominated by the dictates of the rules of his own grammar that he either cannot notice, or cannot reproduce, structures not generated by those rules, at least, not without an enormous amount of effort. (And note that in the above dialogue the child preserved his double negative to the bitter end.)

Actually, children correct themselves (as adults do), a fact which suggests that they work linguistically with some kind of implicit regularities – *rules* – 'in mind'. This question of rules should now receive our attention. It would be all too easy to regard children's speech as a grossly deviant, reduced, inefficient imitation of adult patterns; to think that children's language is no more than an error-riddled reproduction of the sentences they hear. The evidence does not support this interpretation; rather, it leads one to believe that children construct their *own* grammars ('grammar$_1$'), that they induce regularities in mature speech and express them in organizing their own utterances. The rules of child grammars enable their possessors to form constructions which they could not have heard in other people's linguistic performance (and also tend to make children's grammars resistant to adult influence). One classic study of children's linguistic rules was carried out by Jean Berko. Working with pre-schoolers and first-grade children, aged between five-and-a-half and seven, she required them to inflect specially constructed nonsense words, 'nouns', 'verbs' and 'adjectives'. The children performed the task confidently and with a high level of success. For example, presented with a noun *wug* and a context in which the plural was required, they provided *wugs* (/wʌgz/); the verb *rick* yielded the past tense *ricked*; and so on. Clearly, *wugs* was not learnt by imitation – it's not part of adult language – so it must be assumed that these children formed plurals by rule rather than learning, memorizing and reproducing instances of whole words inflected for plural. Certainly, the possession of rules is the most acceptable explanation for the production of utterances which children *could not have heard* in adult speech. Perhaps *Adam make tower* is credibly explained as an erroneous reproduction of the adult *Adam is making a tower*: the 'omitted' elements are softly stressed in adult speech, and the child might just not hear them. But what are we to make of *allgone vitamins*? What perceptual or cognitive interference could possibly cause the child to invert the adult order *the vitamins are all gone*, if this were really nothing more than an inefficient imitation of an adult model? Negative sentences of the type *No singing song* are equally implausibly considered as incompetent imitations. Similarly, the much later sentences *What he can ride in?*, *Why kitty can't stand up?* do not seem sensibly explicable as inefficient versions of sentences copied from parents. It is much more likely that these are sentences *created* by the child on the basis of his own rules for that stage – rules which (to refer only to the last two examples) do not include the facility for inverting subject and auxiliary in this kind of interrogative structure.

Support for the theory that children talk by rule rather than by reproduction, with mistakes, of the utterances of their parents, comes from the kind of errors they make. The early sentences are not simply ungrammatical, but *systematically* ungrammatical. *What he can ride in?* and *Why kitty can't stand up?* depart from the adult grammar, but they agree with one another (and with other sentences from the same phase of this child's development): they exhibit syntactic regularities unrelated to the adult's language – generated presumably by the rules of the child's own temporary, but productive, grammar. The child has formed rules of his own, as it happens rules which are ultimately incorrect, and he uses them to create his own sentences. Many other examples of rule-governed, independent, language behaviour could be given, from the regularity of the 'Pivot/

Open' grammar onwards. One well-known case concerns the inflex-ion of verbs and nouns. The verbs of English (and the other Ger-manic languages) fall into two classes, depending on how they inflect for past tense: 'strong' or 'irregular' verbs which change the root vowel or even use a quite different word – *ride/rode, come/came, hide/hid, go/went*; and 'weak' or 'regular' verbs which preserve the vowel and add an alveolar plosive suffix – *laugh/laughed, call/called, wait/waited.* Children learn certain irregular past tense inflexions first: *came, went, did;* this probably happens because, although such irregular verbs are very few in number, they occur extremely fre-quently, and their past tense forms are assimilated as separate vocabulary items. The regular verbs (past tense *-ed*) are individually infrequent in linguistic performance, but very considerable in num-ber – they make up the bulk of the English verb predicate vocabulary. Because there are so many of them, they (unlike the irregular verbs) yield a pattern. When children get to the stage of being able to induce regularities in adult speech, they learn this pattern: add *-ed* (pho-netically, [t], [d] or [ɪd] depending on the phonetic form of the verb) to a verb root to form its past tense. Having acquired this rule, they overgeneralize it, producing forms like *comed, buyed, goed, doed, fighted.* Obviously *comed*, etc., were not learnt by imitation: they are created by rule. A similar thing happens with noun inflexions: for example, the plural *foots* is said to be almost universal among English-learning children. In the cases of both nouns and verbs, we see that the productiveness of an acquired pattern – a rule – is more influential than the pressure to 'copy' which a frequently repeated, but intrinsically irregular, lexical item exerts.

When I began this section of the present chapter (p. 206) I mentioned that although a linguistically rich environment is beneficial, it is not essential; that exposure to *some* speech is the minimal prerequisite; that teaching or coaching is not required. These observations give an impression of the child working actively, out of his inborn resour-ces, to construct a grammar compatible with that of his mature exemplars. The facts about the rule-governed character of children's language – rule-governed even when it is ungrammatical – which I have just reported also suggest that children progress by active, even creative, endeavour. They exercise their growing linguistic facility prolifically, and there is some evidence that they engage in fairly formal *practice* sessions: trying out, consolidating, the patterns of their language at each particular stage, using the syntactic regu-larities they have mastered as they accommodate new words into their language. Linguistic play, making and repeating syntactic patterns with variation of vocabulary, has been noticed by many students of child language. The most extensive documentation of this solo practice with language has been provided by the late Ruth Weir, who recorded samples of the pre-sleep monologues of her two-and-a-half-year-old son (see *Language in the Crib*). It seems very much as though the child works quite hard at developing his growing linguistic skill. But he does so on the basis of a native endowment – a faculty for language – which gives him a 'flying start'.

As yet, little is known about the growth of language after the earliest stages. Language in infancy seems to be predominantly the creation of the child; one suspects that at a later stage nurture plays a more prominent part than nature. The child going to school is subject to a battery of social forces which he did not experience in the relative privacy and simplicity of the home. His priority now is not to learn how to talk, but how to behave verbally according to the sociolinguistic conventions of his community. He has to learn *when* to talk and when to remain silent – this is not an authoritarian requirement but one of the fundamentals of linguistic 'tact' within a community. (In some communities, including ours, silence is a sign of unsociability; in others it is a sign of respect.) He has to learn to adjust the **style** of his utterances to the nature of the context of situation, by selecting some sentence-forms on some occasions, eschewing some types of construction totally at other times, and so on: some examples are given in the next chapter. He has to learn to distinguish, and exploit, the vast range of **functions** performed by language in a social setting. By the age of five or six he has proved himself a true speaking animal; in the following years, developing language is one of the chief forces in his becoming integrated as a social animal too.

Further reading

Dan I. Slobin's elementary text, *Psycholinguistics*, sets children's language development in the general context of psycholinguistic studies from the point of view of generative grammar. Philip S. Dale, *Language Development*, is a useful introductory textbook, more detailed than Slobin's, and compatible with the approach I have adopted here. A survey and interpretation of research and opinions in the areas discussed in this chapter is David McNeill's *The Acquisition of Language* (with an excellent bibliography to 1969); a shorter, earlier survey by the same author is 'Developmental psycholinguistics'.

Relevant biological facts are reported by Lenneberg, 'Biological perspective', Marshall, 'Biology of communication' and Campbell, 'The roots of language'. On human and animal communication see Brown, *Words and Things*, Hockett, 'Origin of speech'.

The best supporting reading for this chapter, however, would be two or three of the descriptive monographs concerned with child language; see particularly Jeremy M. Anglin, *The Growth of Word Meaning*, Lois Bloom, *Language Development*, Carol Chomsky, *The Acquisition of Syntax*, Paula Menyuk, *Sentences Children Use*, Ruth Weir, *Language in the Crib*. Additionally, there are a number of important articles (from which much of the material in this chapter is drawn); e.g. Braine, 'Ontogeny of English phrase structure', Berko, 'Child's learning of English morphology', Brown and Bellugi, 'Three processes', Ervin, 'Imitation and structural change', Klima and Bellugi, 'Syntactic regularities', Miller and Ervin, 'The development of grammar'.

Several important papers reporting the work of Roger Brown and his group are printed in Brown's *Psycholinguistics*; other interesting collections are Bellugi and Brown, *The Acquisition of Language*, Lyons and Wales, *Psycholinguistics Papers*, and Morton, *Biological and Social Factors in Psycholinguistics*.

The relationship between socio-economic background and linguistic achievement (in Britain) has been extensively discussed by Basil Bernstein; see his *Class, Codes and Control*. An anthology which reprints many papers revelant to this topic, as it appears in the American context, is Abrahams and Troike, *Language and Cultural Diversity*. Two other substantial anthologies are Ferguson and Slobin, *Studies in Child Language Development*, and Bar-Adon and Leopold, *Child Language*.

Three classic works to which I have not been able to do justice here are: Jakobson, *Child Language*, Piaget, *Language and Thought of the Child* and Vygotsky, *Thought and Language*.

ten

Language, society and the individual

Generative linguistics concentrates on those aspects of language which are abstract, formal and constant. 'Constant' applies in both of two senses. First, there are features shared by all speakers of the same language, by reference to which we are able to say that they speak the same language, and by virtue of which they communicate. Second, there are features shared by all languages, by reference to which we are able to decide whether a communication system is an instance of human language. An example of the second kind of constant would be the permitted transformation types (permutation, deletion, etc.; see p. 127 above); of the first, the language-specific transformations controlling agreement between subject and verb in English. As we have seen, these abstract qualities together comprise speakers' competence in their language, the tacitly known grammar which is reflected in the linguists' formalized written grammar.

Chomsky and Katz, who have argued this conception of grammar energetically, have frequently been criticized for an alleged excessive concentration on abstract qualities of language to the neglect of the variety, unpredictability and richness of texture of the actual facts of discourse. Chomsky's notion of 'competence' is said to be unduly restricted, in its degree of abstraction characterizing much less than a mature speaker would have to know in order to communicate. Certainly, some of the extensions of Chomsky's argument on competence are exaggerated: for instance, the claim that children 'know the language' by the age of five or six has been shown to be false. Moreover, the argument on competence and performance is conducted in an off-puttingly negative manner – 'performance' emerges as a sort of incompetent competence, failure on the part of a speaker to realize (through peripheral non-linguistic inadequacies

212

such as distraction, lapse of memory or attention) the norms of competence. I have argued elsewhere (for reference, see p. 239 below) that Chomsky is little interested in the theory of linguistic performance, and have asked whether such a theory cannot be given more positive motivation and design while preserving, if possible, the basic ideals of competence theory.

Linguists have good reasons for treating competence in a very abstract way, for placing clear and rather narrow limits around it: this strategy is meant to ensure that a grammar of a language is as simple and powerful as possible, and that it is readily comparable with grammars of other languages. Features relevant to the pairing of sounds and meanings are noted, while those which relate to other attributes of speech behaviour are ignored. No one denies the existence or the interest of aspects of language in use, though: they are simply referred to other branches of the linguistic sciences. This chapter is an introduction to one of these branches of linguistics concerned with linguistic performance, the branch called variously **sociolinguistics, ethnography of communication, ethnolinguistics, anthropological linguistics**, etc. (I will usually employ the first of these terms.) The subject has been given different titles in different periods and by different investigators, suggesting different angles and different focuses, but the interests of sociolinguists are generally much the same, whatever they call themselves. Sociolinguistics is the study of variation in the form of language in the light of non-linguistic dimensions of social structure; in particular, the correlation between grammatical choices and societal functions and situations; the correlation between the repertoire of language varieties available to an individual and the roles he performs in society; and the values a culture ascribes to its language – or its language*s* – and to the varieties of its language(s). Sociolinguistics also includes study of the ways language behaviour *determines* other kinds of social behaviour.

This is obviously an enormously wide and difficult brief, and it is not surprising that sociolinguistics still exists largely as a set of anecdotal observations and detailed field-studies. No agreed frame of reference or terminology has been constructed: the difficulty is that sociolinguists must invoke a great number of variables which interact in most complex ways. However, despite the frankly chaotic technical vocabulary, some attempts to sketch 'frameworks' for the study of language–society interaction match up quite well – for instance, the various elaborations of J. R. Firth's 'context of situation' and, say, Dell Hymes's independently conceived model for the analysis of 'communicative events'. Such correspondences suggest that at least the *objectives* of sociolinguistics, and to some extent the *expectations* of its practitioners, are much more homogeneous than might appear from the jungle of terminology.

Homogeneity of purpose goes with heterogeneity of materials. It might be said that sociolinguistics begins where linguistics leaves off: with data of speech which are unformalizable by traditional criteria of descriptive linguistics. Descriptive linguists are, I think rightly, unwilling to take account of facts about social behaviour, about physical context of utterance, about personal attributes of speakers – so there are many aspects of linguistic performance which go unexplained: aspects of style, for instance, or frequencies of words and sentence-types, or idiosyncratic qualities of pronunciation. The sociolinguist (and related students) takes on the diversity of performance features; he is able to do so because he is willing to entertain extra-linguistic causes for this diversity. So, as more than one sociolinguist has observed, aspects of language which to the linguist are variable, inconstant, irregular, assume pattern and rule – and *purpose* – under the sociolinguist's eye. He seeks to discover, and explain, patterns in variation, and as we shall see his materials exhibit a multiplicity of initially overwhelming complex and confusing structures. I cannot hope to give a complete or formal survey of sociolinguistic interests here; I will start with some illustrations of the sort of thing which engages the attention of sociolinguists, at the same time introducing a few of the basic concepts of the discipline, and finally consider the implications of sociolinguistic variety for an overall view of the communicative abilities of an individual speaker.

First, then, some examples.

Many European languages possess two second-person-singular pronouns, i.e. pronouns used to address one individual directly: French *tu* and *vous*, German *du* and *Sie*, Italian *tu* and *Lei*, Spanish *tu* and *usted*. The second member of each of these pairs (or its historically earlier version) was originally a *plural* form which, for complex reasons, came in the early middle ages to be used for singular as well as plural address. Let us symbolize these words as *T* and *V*, *T* applying to the historical singular, *V* the form used for plural and additionally as a singular form. (We are not concerned with plural here, so for our purposes *V* means '*vous*-in-the-singular'.) The choice between *T* and *V* is governed by cultural and personal, not linguistic, factors. Children are addressed as *T*, but adults receive *T* in certain conditions only. Employees, servants, waiters, etc. used to be addressed as *T* by their masters and employers, although this custom is dying in an increasingly egalitarian world culture. To address someone as *T* is to assert your power, superiority, etc., over him; in return, you expect him to address you as *V*. Until recently, for instance, a French officer would address a low-ranking soldier as *tu* and would receive *vous* in return. *T* then is the pronoun of power, *V* the pronoun of politeness, respect, deference. It is the pronoun of politeness in the additional sense that it is used *reciprocally* by people who are not sure of the power-relationship between them. People who have just met call each other *V* until they get to know each other well. On growing acquaintance, one of three things may happen: (a) both parties may continue using *V*, so *V* becomes a sign of distance, lack of intimacy; (b) one party may begin to use *T* and the other retain *V*, thus asserting an unequal relationship; (c) both parties may address each other as *T*. *T* then signals *intimacy*, not *power*: to put it more precisely, *T* announces intimacy or solidarity when used reciprocally, power when *V* is given in reply. Let us suppose a newly established employer–employee relationship in which both parties use *V* (which would be normal nowadays); the boss may subsequently address his subordinate as *T*. This move might signal an offer of solidarity, or it might be designed to put the employee in his place. The latter will not know which it is until he tries addressing his boss as *T*; then he will quickly find out!

A similar situation controls choice of what version of a person's *name* you address him by: first name alone (*FN*) or title plus last name (*TLN*): *Bill* versus *Dr Smith*. True to the conventions of power, I have addressed the secretaries who work in my Department as *Carol, Jane, Linda*, etc. from the moment of their employment; they automatically reciprocate with *Mr Fowler*. For new members of academic staff, the rules are different: I call them *Bill, Colin*, etc., and that is a gesture of solidarity – they are expected to reciprocate with *Roger*. But a new lecturer at a junior level, addressed by *FN* not by me but by a senior professor, might be forgiven for being in a quandary over this – does he reply with *FN* or with *TLN*? If the junior teacher misinterprets an expression of power as an expression of intimacy, calling the professor *FN* when *TLN* is expected, he will be rebuffed: the professor can announce the distance by reverting to the formal *TLN* in addressing the new man.

My first two examples, pronouns and names in addressing, illustrate two facts about the sociology of language. First, in the social context language is an object and instrument of *feeling*, or *value*, as well as a referential, propositional, communicative code. Second, there are *rules* for the use of language in culture. The *T/V* choice is highly schematized, depending on delicate factors of personal relationship. (Perhaps I should repeat that this choice is not now as sensitive as it used to be.) To go one stage further, the rules are rather powerful in the sense of 'general': the factors which govern choice between *T* and *V* are the same as those which control choice of *FN* or *TLN*. The social dimensions of *power* and *solidarity* (or *intimacy*) apply to both sets of linguistic facts – and to others, as we shall see.

My next series of examples concerns the sociolinguistic identity of cultural sub-groups. (I do *not* mean sub-cultures in the sense of disadvantaged low-status groups.) Many, perhaps all, societies distinguish the speech of women from that of men, the speech of children from that of adults. A pioneer study by Mary Haas showed that among the Koasati (an Amerindian culture) certain areas of vocabulary showed lexical, morphological and phonological differences as between men's and women's speech. These had been culturally 'institutionalized' to the extent that men would not use women's words, and vice versa; however, men would use women's words in reporting women's speech, so evidently the rules were clear and formal in that society. Mary Haas gave examples from other Indian languages, and there is no reason to believe that such patterns are not extremely common and pervasive.

Adults expect children to talk differently from themselves; adults talk differently to children than they do to other adults: many societies have developed elaborate and distinctive modes of 'baby talk'. Baby talk often has special phonological rules, special rules for the simplification and stylization of syntax, distinctive vocabulary items. It is only to a minimal extent a true reflection of the way infants do speak; it is more a projection on to the child of the adult's picture of infancy. Perhaps baby talk has an effect on the way children speak, for (in addition to the limitations of children's grammars detailed in the last chapter) their talk is 'stylistically' non-adult. Parents are surprised, even disappointed, when children speak continuously, with syntactic complexity and thematic unity, for several minutes, using proper technical vocabulary (e.g. *gramophone* rather than the childish periphrasis of 'the thing that makes the music'). There is something unnerving about a linguistic virtuoso of seven years, and it seems to me that children usually avoid this kind of role. Whatever the exact details of children's style – they remain to be analysed – it appears to be a cultural overlay, having little to do with cognitive and biological factors; the same judgment is relevant to the distinction between 'women's language' and 'men's language'. In all cases, a discrete social group has ascribed to it, and often co-operatively practises, a distinguishing mode of language. (Cf. more specialized groups such as disc jockeys, clergymen, teachers, whose styles are recognizable – even, serve primarily to promote recognition – rather than strictly functional. A group style is chiefly designed to be assertive, and confirmatory, of cultural expectations concerning the identity of the group.)

Dialects may be seen from a similar perspective. Any enclosed group of people, communicating predominantly among themselves and little with the members of other groups, develops a characteristic style of language, often with profoundly distinctive vocabulary, phonology and syntax. For groups which have little contact with others, this situation is normal, unremarkable. With movement and mixture of populations, however, the situation changes: a dialect which was originally brought into being by pure geographical factors, distinct in a merely mechanical and necessary way, becomes the focus for value-judgments and intense feelings. The peoples of Yorkshire and Lancashire, for instance, are keenly conscious of their separate dialectal characteristics, which are felt to express competing personal and communal attributes. In such situations one's own dialect is felt to embody qualities like warmth, homeliness, spontaneity, sincerity, fineness of sentiment while the competing dialect expresses coldness, brutalism, dullness, superficiality or slyness. (Similarly, other people's *national languages* may have non-linguistic qualities projected on them – musical Italian, logical French, passionate Spanish, etc.) One's own dialect may be asserted as a flag of cultural togetherness and of identity *vis-à-vis* the outside world: the prestige dialect of educated British Southerners is one such manifestation, as is the conservative dialect of polite (American) New England or the dialect of black militancy in the USA. Non-dialectal stereotypes may serve the same purpose. A woman may seek to affirm her femininity or femaleness by exaggerating the conventionally 'female' features of voice quality. Again, whole languages may be asserted in the same way, to consolidate and identify indigenous groups, particularly in colonized areas (e.g. Welsh, Irish, Basque), and to preserve close groups of expatriates (many American examples, e.g. Chinese, Filipinos, Puerto Ricans, Mexicans, Poles, even though they may be second or third generation American nationals).

Often two varieties – either dialects or distinct languages – co-exist in the same community but are carefully kept apart and of quite different statuses. One variety (e.g. Parisian French or standard educated British English) is an 'official', 'standard', 'received' code; opposed to this there may be several vernaculars, e.g. in England the various regional dialects such as Cockney and West Country. The 'standard' is the instrument of government, trade, education, intercourse with other nations; it accrues prestige and its acquisition is often necessary to personal advancement. The vernaculars tend to be despised and avoided in public circles. Many individuals respond to this value-system by becoming 'bi-dialectal'. A child born into a lower-class family naturally acquires the dialect of this region;

as he progresses through the educational system he discovers that his speech is not the dialect of his teachers, nor of the newsreaders on television, nor that of the majority of persons of high social, political, intellectual status. These people speak a non-regional 'Standard English'. In response to this situation, many children acquire Standard English in addition to their regional dialect, and switch between the two varieties as occasion demands. Standard English is their dialect for school, for speaking to 'outsiders', for 'polite' situations (i.e. it correlates with the *V* of politeness or deference); the regional variety is used for talk within the family and among schoolfriends (cf. the *T* of solidarity and intimacy). While the child remains in his home locale, the regional dialect must be preserved for fear that he will be accused of being 'stand-offish', for fear of alienation in home and in local peer-group. (The converse situation obtains: my two boys have become fluent in the Norwich dialect – syntax, morphology, intonation and some vocabulary – for the purpose of playing with their age-peers in the neighbourhood, but switch to their original Standard English for talk at home, or when addressing teachers, parents' friends, etc. In this case it is the regional code which is the super-added variety, rather than the Standard. In the past they have possessed East Yorkshire, Northern California and Providence-East Side varieties for the sake of solidarity with their friends at play.)

The relationship between a prestige variety and a low-status variety, which is rather fluidly expressed in the distinction between standard and regional versions of British English, is more formalized and recognizable in some other cultures which are said to be characterized by **diglossia**. A diglossic community is one which possesses two clearly distinct varieties, one High (*H*) and one Low (*L*). *H* is employed for government, trade, literature; it is the subject of grammar-writers and the instrument of education and advancement. *L* is the language of informal and domestic conversational interaction; it is usually not endowed with a writing system, is not thought worthy of the attention of native grammarians (though professional linguists from outside are avid students of *L* varieties!). Some transparent examples (studied in the pioneer article by Charles A. Ferguson, see p. 239 below) are Classical Arabic versus local vernacular Arabics (Cairo, Beirut, etc.), French versus Haitian Creole, High German versus Swiss German, Greek *katharévusa* versus *dhimotikí*. In all such communities, the bulk of the population knows both varieties: knowing *H* is not simply a key to advancement, as it is with Standard English, but a prerequisite for such ordinary activities as reading a newspaper.

It is a nice point whether the *H* and *L* varieties in situations such as those just mentioned are 'separate languages'; however, cases of diglossia with separate languages are by no means unknown. The standard example among sociolinguists is Paraguay, where a high proportion of the population are bilingual in Spanish and the local language Guaraní. Spanish is *H*, Guaraní *L*; Spanish connotes power, formality, distance, Guaraní solidarity, nativeness. Many ex-colonial African states must have substantial numbers of speakers whose choice between English/French/Portuguese and an indigenous language obeys similar patterns. In the United States, immigrant sub-communities are frequently diglossic: for Mexicans and Puerto Ricans, English is *H*, Spanish *L* (even though more positive feelings may generally be entertained towards Spanish by the speakers concerned – *L* is available for solidarity, remember).

Before passing on to some different types of examples, we may draw together some threads from the above materials, and consider some general concepts which have been implicit in discussing them.

It should be evident that sociolinguistics is not dependent on absolute lines being drawn between such concepts as 'language', 'dialect', 'idiolect', etc.; this is fortunate because these distinctions are notoriously hard to support in an empirical or a theoretical way. In fact, sociolinguistics would be actually hampered if it were forced to accept such distinctions as primary. Important generalizations would be missed or obscured; for instance the ideas of *H* and *L*, power, intimacy, distance, etc., are made more convincing, and clearer, once it is seen that their manifestation in a community may be realized by contrasts of dialect, of language, even of single features of a language (e.g. the *V* and *T* pronouns). For this reason, sociolinguists prefer the neutral term **variety** (or **code**). 'Variety' is not a taxonomic subordinate of 'language' (as 'dialect' is of 'language' and 'idiolect' of 'dialect'); it is *any consistent form of linguistic organization which answers to, and serves to express, some significant set of socio-cultural factors*. The 'factors' may be values, personal roles, communicative functions, topics, situations, media, and so on. Note that 'varieties' are not only brought into being by 'factors', and express 'factors', but also consolidate, identify and define 'factors'. Some examples of varieties are 'Swiss German', 'baby talk', 'women's language', 'television advertising language', 'hippie language', 'Belfast Protestant', 'pub conversation', 'ballad style', etc. etc. Since any act of communication is the product of a convergence of a number of simultaneously influencing sociocultural forces, every utterance is likely to belong to, or manifest, several varieties all at the same time. An educated Yorkshireman, male and of middle age, talking at a party in his own house to a young female employee about films, might present the eavesdropping sociolinguist with evidence of at least ten co-existent varieties! (He does not 'speak ten varieties all at once' of course; his speech contains features which might be referred to ten extrinsic varieties, some of them obviously rather trivial.)

The sociology of language has to assume, and often refer explicitly to, some notion of **speech-community**, an arena within which a set of rules for language variation is played. Defining speech-community is problematical in the extreme. Definitions involving 'country', 'race', 'nation' and the like are useless (as the reader may easily discover if he imagines definitions in such terms and then confronts them with counter-examples). Superficially 'community of speakers of the same language' looks a better bet, but is in fact no more useful, since it begs the question of what exactly a single language is – a precise notion would be needed here – ignores the premise that 'variety' has priority over 'language' in sociolinguistics, and neglects the empirical fact that some communities (e.g. Paraguay, Quebec) are structured on the interaction of clearly discrete tongues. I would hesitate to formulate a concise definition, but 'variety' seems to be the key. We are dealing in bodies of people who subscribe to, and employ, distinctive networks of varieties; these networks are neces- sitated by, express, and to a large extent create, modify and define, cultural patterns of a multiplicity of non-linguistic kinds. The relationship between sociolinguistic and cultural structure is integral, reciprocal and vital: so the sociolinguist may accommodate existing sociological observations within his framework (as William Labov does) so long as he remembers that the sociological insights may well be altered by linguistic findings.

The term 'speech-community' is variable in its scope of applica- tion. In some ways, it makes sense to think about the community of all speakers of English – we have feelings about American English, for instance, and there is no doubt that it is an influential pressure on the ways we use English and on our conception of the variety- structure of the English language. However, it is unlikely that description of a speech-community conceived on such a grand scale would be very illuminating. More typically, smaller units are selected: a village, an ethnic sub-group, a commuting population, a socio- economic or occupational stratum, a group with regular and inter- esting patterns of movement. (For example, in the last decades of the nineteenth century large numbers of East Anglian agricultural workers migrated every year, in the lean season, to Burton-on- Trent to work in the brewing industry. How did this movement affect their speech?) In all cases the investigator will begin with some sociocultural hypothesis concerning a speech-community of manage- able size, and look for a correlation between linguistic and non- linguistic variables. The size, number of languages, etc., of a community are not crucial to its sociolinguistic investigation: it is the overall communicative, interactional, network that makes it interesting.

'Speech-community' implies a cultural overview, a long focus revealing the patterning of varieties in a schematic, fairly abstract, meta-structure. This godlike perspective is not easy to attain, nor is it necessarily every sociolinguist's ultimate descriptive objective. (Though as I have said, the existence of a patterned speech-community is an *assumption* that has to be made.) There are two other points of entry into sociolinguistic structure. First, rather than looking at the community as a whole, asking what varieties it employs and how these are related, we might take the individual as our point of departure – or, indeed, as our centre of interest – and enquire into his own sociolinguistic abilities. What varieties does he command? On what occasions does he use one rather than another? What values does he attribute to the varieties he possesses? What varieties does he recognize in the language of other members of his community and how does he respond to them? The difference between the community focus and the individual focus will emerge if we take diglossia as an example. Diglossia is an attribute of a community: we would say that Haiti, the Swiss German cantons, Paraguay, are **diglossic**, but we would not talk of 'diglossic speakers'. **Bilingualism** and **bidialectalism** are attributes of individual speakers. Bilingualism and diglossia may coincide, as in Paraguay (for that part of the population which is bilingual) or in Puerto Rican communities in America. In these cases the speaker's bilingualism is culturally functional, for each of his languages is employed appropriately, in accord with the society's conventions for the contrasting values of the two tongues. But bilingualism need not imply diglossia. An educated Lebanese may know classical Arabic, his local vernacular and English; at home in Beirut he switches between the three varieties in his repertoire as circumstances dictate, so multi-lingualism and diglossia coincide. Living in England as a student, however, his two versions of Arabic cease to have any diglossic value. Similarly, an Englishman who also becomes fluent in French exemplifies bilingualism without diglossia so long as he lives in communities where French has no place in the sociolinguistic system. The Court in post-Conquest medieval England exemplified French/English bilingualism with diglossia (French *H*, English *L*); but if we consider the state of England as a whole at that time, we find diglossia *without* bilingualism. French and English were contrasted in the classic *H/L* fashion, and that was a potent cultural fact; but the vast majority of the people did not know French, and the monolingualism of the conquered population, with its corollary of possessing *L* only, was an important weapon for the Normans in their enforcement of a particular social and administrative structure.

In the last paragraph I used the terms **repertoire** and **switch**: these stand for essential concepts in any theory of the verbal behaviour of the individual. A speaker learns a repertoire of varieties; what the repertoire contains will depend on the characteristics of his speech-community and the position – position*s*, in fact – he occupies within the community. I will discuss the content and comparison of repertoires at the end of this chapter, and the psychological and sociological consequences for the individual of his own particular repertoire. The repertoire may contain varieties of quite different status: distinct languages and dialects, as we have seen, but much more besides. Languages and dialects were used above as obvious and graspable illustrations of choice of varieties within a community (or, we now see, within the personal repertoire), but in fact 'varieties' include modes of discourse much more delicately distinguished than dialects and languages. More complex choice situations may involve switching between several versions of several languages: for example, see Nancy Tanner's study of switching between stratified varieties of Indonesian, Javanese, English and Dutch among Indonesian intellectuals; or John Gumperz's analyses of complex variety-switching in communities in India and Norway (for references see p. 239 below). When we look even more closely at the facts of linguistic behaviour, we discover subtle and regular switches even within one version of a single dialect: differences of style appear as an individual talks to his children, his wife, his colleagues, his non-colleague friends, his superiors and his subordinates at work; when he talks about football and when he talks about economics; when he is addressing one person and when he speaks to a large audience; and so on. More attention will be paid to these kinds of switching below; for the moment, it is important to realize that they are all to be accommodated within a single framework that may also include culturally motivated switching between languages, for instance: hence the need for the neutral umbrella-term *variety*.

Switching between varieties is controlled by conditions of cultural appropriacy or 'decorum'. We select a style of language to suit the situation we find ourselves in; a variety which matches our assessment of the cultural significance of a context of discourse. 'Situation' leads me to the second alternative to a community-overview perspective on sociolinguistic facts: we can focus on particular instances of discourse in their social and physical settings. The central descriptive notion here is the **communicative event** (Hymes) or **context of situation** (Firth). This theory stresses a fact that the linguist (as opposed to sociolinguist) ignores: each piece of language is an integral component in the ongoing social and physical texture of life. The full value of an utterance, and the motivation for its specific form, can only be realized if it is seen as actively functioning within, and responding to, the framework of characteristics set by the situation in which it is produced. The most famous statement of this principle comes from the anthropologist, Malinowski, who insisted on it as a working rule in ethnographic fieldwork: unless one notes down what is going on at the time of utterance, he alleged, one cannot understand the utterances, and the point of the utterances, encountered in an unfamiliar society. Malinowski's 'context of situation' was taken over by J. R. Firth, who attempted to turn this practical recommendation into a theory of meaning and of the value of language in society. Firth's 'context of situation' is merely a sketch in his own writings (his followers have developed it considerably); but his conception is much more powerful and abstract than Malinowski's. Malinowski's features of context are extremely particularized and *ad hoc*: one is to note down as much local detail as possible, actual things, actions and circumstances surrounding the discourse. Firth recognized that the characteristics of speech contexts are recurrent: speech situations resemble each other in conventional ways, so a number of standard dimensions of variation may be extracted from them and used for the purpose of classifying types of context of situation. Hymes's 'communicative events' are descriptive schemes which elaborate and formalize dimensions of variation like those mentioned by Firth.

Factors such as the following seem to be particularly relevant to choice of variety:

- nature of participants; their relationship (socio-economic, sexual, occupational, etc.)
- number of participants (two face-to-face, one addressing large audience, etc.)
- roles of participants (teacher/student, priest/parishioner, etc.)
- function of speech event (persuasion, request for information, ritual, verbal play, etc.)
- nature of medium (speech, writing, scripted speech, speech reinforced by gesture, etc.)
- *genre* of discourse (political speech, epic poem, newspaper leader, dirty joke, etc.)
- topic of discourse (scientific experiment, sport, art, religion, etc.)
- physical setting (noisy/quiet, public/private, familiar/unfamiliar, appropriate for speech (e.g. sitting-room)/inappropriate (e.g. church, concert hall), etc.)

The above is by no means a full or properly organized list of socio-linguistically pertinent features of speech events; there is as yet no agreed set. But I think it will be obvious even from this informal presentation how readily speech events lend themselves to description in terms of simple, recurrent, features. Notice how many of the attributes place themselves into binary oppositions; no doubt the scheme could be expressed in a distinctive-feature notation (cf. pp. 56–64 and 178–83 above) but I am not going to attempt it here. The point is that contexts of situation are not unique and fortuitous (as Malinowski's approach suggests) but recurrent and classifiable according to a few simple variables recognized as significant within a culture. And a certain *type* of speech event requires a conventional *type* of linguistic behaviour.

It is to be expected that most of the situational variables needed for connecting speech events with the varieties they elicit will be specific to a particular culture. However, I think our materials already suggest some possible universals. Choice between T and V, between *FN* and *TLN*, between H and L varieties in diglossia, has been illustrated with reference to a number of unrelated languages. And notice that the *linguistic* variables involved in the choices (choice of pronoun, choice of title, choice of language) are quite different in each case. Nevertheless, the same kinds of situational factor are at issue in all these diverse examples; a contrast of intimacy and distance in the relationship between participants, a principle of 'superior/subordinate' characterization (equal or unequal), a contrast of formality. It is reasonable to expect that such contrasts will recur in other societies. Of course, the facts of particular societies will determine just who is acknowledged as superior to who; just what constitutes a 'formal' situation, etc. In one society the aged, as a group, may receive special dignity and status; in another, the wealthy or landed; in another, the professional classes (witch doctors, lawyers, teachers, etc.). Granted that categories may be filled by quite different types of person, according to the material structure, values, etc., of particular societies, it may well be true that in any society certain combinations of factors will recur, with predictable linguistic results. For instance, *intimacy, equality, informality* may be a recurrent cluster, and its expressions may include (among many others) the following: choice of mutual T (e.g. children of the same age and class, at play; lovers; equal-ranked colleagues relaxing); choice of mutual *FN* (the same examples would apply); choice of L variety (same examples, expatriates for solidarity, family circle, etc.). *Distance, equality, formality* together might select V, *TLN*, H (e.g. adults of the same social group at a polite party). The linguistic facts, and the social facts, are going to vary a great deal from one speech-community to another; yet the relevant dimensions of abstract structure in communicative situations may be fairly constant. In the present state of sociolinguistics we must confess that any statements about communicative universals are quite speculative, of course.

We now turn to varieties which are neither separate languages nor involve selection between a standard and a vernacular (e.g. choice between *H* and *L* dialects). By adjustment of style of utterance, within his own dialect, a speaker suits his language quite precisely to context of situation. I am thinking of the more or less delicate switches of style by which a speaker responds to changing situations through, say, the course of an ordinary day; also the variations in style he encounters in language to which he is exposed – e.g. the morning weather forecast on the radio, the style of the leader in his own newspaper, that of the editorial comment in some other paper he may pick up in the train, the television advertisements, and so on. Some of these differences we are conscious of, for instance TV advert language versus the language of news reporting in the same medium; or, in our own productive repertoire, letters to our parents versus chat in pub or club. In such cases we are aware that roles are being assumed, that conventional expectations of format, topic, level of seriousness, etc., are being fulfilled. Possibly we do not realize so clearly that all of our speech makes (or ought to make!) fine concessions to context of situation. We may think that, except for various 'specialized' uses, all of our discourse is conducted in some kind of neutral vein, a consistent all-purpose style. In fact, only people who are socially very insensitive behave in this way (or foreigners, or people whose experience is limited, or young children).

The problem for the maturing child is to learn this style-switching flexibility; for the sociolinguist, how to describe its patterning in the fluent adult. Rather than confront these problems directly, we may first look at some simpler instances of sociolinguistic adaptation.

If discourse is adapted to situation, then mode of utterance, and to some extent content of utterance, ought to be predictable from context. In fact, some of the most interesting and socially vital adaptations are relatively unpredictable (e.g. conversational styles). At the other extreme there are highly predictable kinds of talk, which we may call **routines**. Among these are greetings, which are very much institutionalized. They occur under set physical circumstances and allow very little choice of language (and very *little* language – greetings are short routines). The choice of language is circumscribed by the routine on which the first interlocutor embarks: if A says 'Morning, Jim' B is virtually bound to respond 'Morning, Tom' (or 'Mr Smith', depending on the status-relationship). A's 'Hi' virtually requires 'Hi' in reply. If A begins 'How are you this morning?' B will give back 'Just fine'; this routine can be expanded by B offering 'Just fine; how's yourself?' in which case A will complete the exchange with 'Oh, pretty good, thanks' or something of the kind. This sort of exchange is notable for its lack of real semantic content. A and B are not actually asking after the state of each other's health – if they were, they would choose a form of words which has *not* been conventionalized – but merely making a gesture of concern or acknowledgment. This is 'contact language', not 'content language' (it is often called **phatic communion**). Language which is superficially, but not actually, about personal health is a typically American greeting formula; the British counterpart is 'the weather'. An exchange of the type A 'Lovely/miserable day, isn't it?' B 'Yes, isn't it' serves exactly the same function as the 'How are you?' routine. The English use the weather as a peg on which to hang a greeting.

Conventionalized topics, spoken of in predictable language, define routine greetings of the kind illustrated. Any departure from the stylized verbal formulae signals a change of genre. If A says 'How are you this morning?' and B replies 'I feel a bit queasy', what has happened is that B has re-interpreted A's initial phatic utterance as a genuine request for information. The genre has been changed from 'greeting' (which is routine) to 'conversation' (which is not). From this point on the constraints on the form of linguistic performance are removed, or at least very substantially relaxed. B has changed the nature of the speech event, and different, more fluid, rules apply.

Very like routines, and subject to the same tendency to sudden metamorphosis, are instances of **transactional** language. Transactional language is a stylistically restricted form of communication employed between individuals for whom (on this occasion) speech is simply an instrument to the completion of some limited non-verbal interaction. Relevant events include asking for directions, purchasing goods, giving instructions, agreeing on a plan, etc. The archetypal situation is the customer–salesman relationship: A 'Pint of milk, please', B 'Five-and-a-half pence, please', A 'Thank you', B 'Thank you'. Transactional language resembles routines in its closed character, its avoidance of expansiveness, the fixity of its rules (so that any departure announces a desire, on the part of one of the participants, to abandon the genre and begin a new form). It is unlike routine in that it is genuinely referential, i.e. it is genuinely 'about' the objects of discussion; and in that it is designed to secure a *particular* effect (e.g. the transfer of goods or information) rather than a generalized reaction ('I acknowledge you; we belong to the same community').

Routines are presumably an inventory of closed formulae learnt by rote and withdrawn from memory as occasion demands; transactional language is also highly formulaic, but because it is specifically purposive, each instance of its use has to be constructed for the particular occasion. The two forms have in common an absence of 'creativity', in fact a stringent avoidance of creativity: when the language user steps outside the prescribed linguistic forms, he relinquishes the genre. An interesting half-way-house between routine and the openness of language at large is the phenomenon known as **restricted language**: this covers all uses of language in which, under standardized sociolinguistic conditions, some section of the grammatical rules of the language goes unused, or (producing the same effect) some *extra* linguistic rule is obligatory and consistently applied. Hypothetical examples would be: a convention whereby one deleted all nasal consonants in conversations about religion; or a rule which specified that every sentence in a discourse about war must contain at least one lexical item drawn from a special 'heroic' vocabulary otherwise unused. Thus a 'restricted language' does not lack the facility for unlimited inventiveness, creativity in sentence construction: it is a form of discourse which is marked by continuous and openly recognizable reiterated features, and in that discourse an unlimited number of sentences is possible. The kind of language associated with English parsons (particularly in their sermons) would count as a restricted language: the overall pitch level of the voice is high, and the frequency band through which the voice ranges is artificially narrowed, resulting in distortion of the normal intonation tunes of the language. Impressionistically, the effect is a distinctive combination of monotony and sing-song. Through a quite different linguistic cause, the language of legal documents is 'restricted', too. Here, to reduce the risk of misinterpretation, statements and conditions are run together in one continuous syntax; what strikes one visually is the lack of punctuation, but something 'deeper' is happening: certain modes of syntactic connection are repeatedly used, others avoided completely.

The mechanical reason for this syntactic curtailment in legal language is avoidance of ambiguity, but a by-product is just as important: legal documents are unmistakably legal documents, just as some parsons are inescapably parsons. The restricted language *advertises* distinctiveness, is an overt banner of belonging to a certain genre. (This self-announcement is the manifest purpose of the Gothic 𝔚𝔥𝔢𝔯𝔢𝔞𝔰 with which so many legal documents begin.) Proclamation of genre is an important function of the many and various forms of restricted language found in literature. Metrical compositions are 'restricted' by the superimposition of extra rules controlling the distribution of prominent syllables in the line – e.g.

the iambic pentameter obeys a restricting rule that even-numbered syllables in a line should be heavier than odd syllables. The initial impact of such a restriction is that the reader is invited to see the verse as a special kind of language requiring a special kind of response – 'I am a poem, you must behave differently towards me'. To give one example, ancient Germanic heroic poetry (which was originally oral) is composed in a severely formalized language which is, as far as we can see, very different from ordinary speech or from written prose. Each line is shaped around four strongly prominent syllables, the first three of which alliterate (begin with the same sound). The syntax is formulaic: certain types of short phrase and clause constantly recur, arranged in such a way as to cut the poetic line into two halves of two strong stresses each. The syntax is also repetitious, with lots of 'chiming' parallel structures. Finally, the diction of Germanic verse is highly distinctive, built upon a set of special poetic words which do not occur in the prose (and concomitantly, avoidance of prose words) and a set of morphological and semantic formulae for constructing distinctive compound words. The effect of the whole set of restrictions is extremely distinctive, to the extent that a student of Anglo-Saxon feels that he is compelled to learn virtually a new language when he comes on to *Beowulf*. The 'skaldic' verse of the Old Icelandic tradition is even more stringently restricted and distant from 'ordinary language'.

Routines, transactional language and restricted language are all somewhat special forms of language: they involve the learning of special constructional techniques and/or are rather inflexibly tied to specific contexts of situation. But this is not to say that there is some bland, neutral 'ordinary language' to which they are opposed. Rather, 'language at large' comprises a set of varieties, each with identifying context-determined characteristics, but these characteristics more diffusely spread than those of the more limited varieties I have just discussed. Two items which have been applied to sociolinguistic variation in this non-marginal sense (usually independently of concepts of diglossia, dialect, etc.) are **register** and **style**. I have to say at once that these two notions, though probably indispensable to sociolinguistics, have up to now proved more troublesome than any others in the entire subject. 'Register' (a term originating with British linguistics but now used internationally) has never been precisely defined, has sometimes been equated with 'any variety' – so an individual's repertoire would consist of a set of registers – and has been applied to varieties of many different kinds and statuses. 'Style' is equally elusive of definition, and has the mixed advantage/disadvantage that it has been an important and controversial term in literary studies for many centuries: it thus carries with it a multiplicity of competing definitions. However, it is a vital and useful term readily adaptable to certain sociolinguistic purposes.

'Register' is most commonly used in connection with varieties of language associated with culturally distinctive *types* and *fields* of activity of a rather general kind. By 'general' I mean that, say, 'scientific English' would be considered a register because it is productive, widely disseminated and formally unrestricted (yet recognizable) but 'greetings English' would not be thought of as a register because, although it is important and frequently uttered, it is unproductive and narrow in scope. (The dividing line is of course hard to draw: I do not think a formal definition of 'register' can be achieved at the moment.) Scientific English would also illustrate the idea of a 'field' of activity: a register is a form of language linked to one area of human experience and endeavour. (Compare the idea of **domain** in Fishman, **province** in Crystal and Davy: references p. 239 below.) A number of separate situational factors enter into the definition of 'fields'. Subject-matter is one: we would expect the register of science to differ from that of religion or sport. Another is the sort of milieu or social institution within which the register functions and to which it refers: education, the home, government, etc. Subject-matter and milieu often overlap, of course, as the category 'religion' illustrates: religion is an institution and an activity, and also a prominent subject of discourse among subscribers to the institution. But these two dimensions are not inevitably overlapping: *science* may be the subject-matter in an *educational* milieu, resulting in a distinctive register. (Contrast the language of technical papers with that of school textbooks.)

Field, domain or province is the basis of registers such as sport, science, religion, education, politics, domestic life, etc.: the distinctive modes of talk and writing proper to different spheres of action. I also mentioned *type* of activity as a determinant of register, and this means both the nature of any action which *accompanies* the use of language and the nature of the action *performed by* language (in so far as these are separable). As an example of the former influence, consider cocktail party conversation. Talk at such a party occurs between pairs of people who are usually standing up in a crowded room. It tends to be loud, fast, and fragmented, switching rapidly from topic to topic and from speaker to speaker, frequently interrupted. These characteristics reflect the physical circumstances of the scene: lots of people are talking at once, there is a good deal of movement as drinks are passed around, pairings of individuals change, people arrive and leave. The latter type of influence (the activity being performed by the speech) relates to the rhetorical function of speech events. Language may be used to inform, rebuke, persuade, cajole, flatter, woo, and so on. Linguists tend to forget that speech is action as well as communication; sociolinguists must keep themselves aware of this fact. The categories of verbal action are partly universal (e.g. persuasion) and partly determined by the structure of society. Verbal rituals (typically but by no means exclusively in religious ceremonies), for instance, are likely to diverge widely from culture to culture. Many other functional adaptations, specific to particular societies, must be noticed: some relevant categories for developed western societies, with sub-types for the individual cultures concerned, would be advertising, simultaneous commentary, journalism, verbal humour, reporting, instruction.

A final influence on register is the *medium* used for a speech event. A television commentary on a football or boxing match is dramatically different from its sound radio counterpart; the language of a newspaper advertisement differs substantially from that used to sing the same product's praises on a billboard, and again from the language of a TV commercial. A telephone conversation is structured quite differently from an exchange of letters on the same subject.

At present the theory of 'registers' is at a primitive and informal stage of development. It is not easy to pin down the exact meaning of the concept. Furthermore, very little exact descriptive work has yet been carried out, so the examples one offers are largely putative. Native speakers generally have confident intuitions about the kinds of variation subsumed under 'register', and these intuitions provide eminently researchable hypotheses. In advance of empirical study, nevertheless, the factors determining choice of register are of a fairly obvious kind.

Like register, *style* is an apparently useful but very imprecise concept in sociolinguistics. Crystal and Davy's *Investigating English Style* is about registers, and elsewhere 'style' simply equals 'variety'. Given the semantic history of this term in literary criticism and popular usage, it would be hopeless to try for one single meaning, but there are two senses of the word which may provide good service. (An evaluative sense can be discarded straight away: I am not concerned with characterizations like 'He has style' or 'He's stylish' where style means 'a gratifyingly dignified or striking manner of self-expression'.) My first use of 'style' exploits the breadth of application of this term and its established position in common usage. At the end of chapter 4 (pp. 91–4 above) I defended the notion of 'paraphrase', proposing that it is possible for the same semantic structure to be expressed, i.e. transformationally realized, in different ways. Thus the concept 'transformation' may be attached to the less formal idea of 'manner of expression'.

Style in its most general sense is 'manner of expression'; a particular style is a distinctive, recognizable manner of expression, and a text or discourse comes to be in a particular style as a result of consistent use or 'foregrounding' of a certain set of transformations. For instance, the style of legal documents derives partly from a consistent and distinctive use of certain types of syntactic conjoining. An important style of magazine advertising foregrounds personal and demonstrative pronouns and makes extensive use of short verb-less sentences: 'Smith's cruises. For that holiday you always promised yourself. Those lazy days in the sun. Superb cuisine prepared just for you. Visits to exotic ports of call. All this at our special low February rates. Escape the winter *this* winter!'

The term 'style' is useful, it seems to me, when one wishes to talk about a patently distinctive manner of expression without committing oneself to establishing the exact status of the variety to which a text manifesting this style belongs. Referring to a certain style of magazine advertising as a 'style' invokes its distinctiveness without either demanding, or precluding, its identification as, say, a particular sub-register. I have used 'style' in just this way several times in the present chapter: see for example the paragraph beginning 'We now turn to varieties . . .' on p. 225 above.

A second, more restricted, sense of 'style' occurs in sociolinguistics; like the first, it has its basis in traditional literary theory. Classical rhetoric regarded style in hierarchical terms. There were 'High', 'Middle' and 'Low' styles, and an author or orator selected an appropriate level in the hierarchy according to conventional rules of decorum. (Princes speak 'High', peasants 'Low', etc. Shakespeare has great fun with these rules in *Love's Labour's Lost*.) That this sort of hierarchy is not merely an artificial literary construct is suggested by the above discussion of diglossia and of pronouns of address: factors of formality, politeness and status govern comparable patterns of non-literary usage, leading to choice of more or less formal linguistic stances. Some linguists (e.g. H. A. Gleason, Martin Joos, Geoffrey Leech) have entertained ideas of an organized scale of degrees of stylistic formality. Joos, for instance, proposes five stylistic ranks – 'intimate', 'casual', 'consultative', 'formal' and 'frozen', and Gleason follows him with a less extravagantly named set of five. It seems to me unlikely that languages are sociolinguistically structured on a finite set of discrete levels (except in overtly diglossic cultures); yet a more loosely graduated scale of formality would seem a very realistic idea. An individual adopts a more formal manner of speech when addressing a stranger than when talking to an intimate friend; a more casual style talking to a colleague over coffee than talking to the same colleague on a business matter in the office. British national newspapers seem to be finely graded on the formality dimension of style, so that reports of the same event, advertisements for the same product, editorial comments on the latest governmental atrocity, are expressed in language of a degree of formality specifically tailored to the publishers' conception of the audience for the particular paper.

Medieval literary theory assumed that people of different social classes speak on different and mutually exclusive levels of formality; humourists have long proposed that people of different occupations (parsons, policemen, servants, criminals) each conform to their own stylistic stereotype. Doubtless there is some truth in both premises: as we have seen, the dominant role of a speaker, his place in the network of societal functions, leaves an impress on his mode of discourse; and individuals characteristically employ 'expected' styles of speech to confirm their membership of social or occupational groups. However, we must not exaggerate the degree of homogeneity which is to be found in the 'sociolinguistic' dimension of an individual's speech. It is an over-simplification, a caricature, to assume that the individual's speech reflects merely one single function, i.e. 'the' place of the individual within his society. The implications of all that has been said in this chapter are that the individual plays a multiplicity of roles as he interacts with his social group(s), and that the pressure of contexts of situation, continually changing in kind and in intensity, force him constantly to modify the character of his linguistic output. So the speaker is called upon to acquire a range of styles of speech, and to be able to switch between them smoothly – automatically, in fact – as communicative situations change.

Taking into account everything we can observe about the way a speaker *uses* language, how shall we think about that which he *knows* which underlies his use of language? This theoretical problem was raised in the concluding pages of chapter 2 and has been touched on at several other places in the book. A traditional starting-point is Saussure's division of *langue* from *parole*, Chomsky's of *competence* from *performance*. These two distinctions are not exactly parallel, but their purpose is much the same: to delimit the area of knowledge which is shared by all speakers of one language and which is responsible for the narrowly communicative aspect of linguistic performance – the information-channelling function, the pairing of sounds and meanings: this restricted category of knowledge is *langue*, competence. When a speaker expresses an intended meaning and a hearer retrieves the message from the acoustic signal, we explain this event by hypothesizing common possession of linguistic knowledge ('grammatical competence', cf. p. 38 above) of the special kind that is the subject of grammars ('grammar$_1$' represented in 'grammar$_2$'). How we go about describing this knowledge, according to one linguistic theory, was illustrated in chapters 3 to 8. From time to time I have expressed various cautions about the way the notion of grammatical competence is to be construed: that it is a theoretical category necessitated by the linguist's desire to go about his job in an orderly way; that the 'rules' of grammar$_2$ are not explicitly known by speakers, but are just the most workable mode of representation devised by linguists to capture regularities or patterns in speech; that grammatical competence does not pretend to exhaust all the areas of knowledge which underlie speech; and so on. It is now time to point out that the grammatical competence represented in a linguistic description of (say) English is not necessarily the property of every speaker of the language. There will be a large core of rules common to all speakers, and the possession of these rules will account for mutual intelligibility across the language-community. Outside this core, there are dialect divergences, so that the linguist must either choose a single dialect and reject variant forms in certain areas of structure, or list dialect variants in parallel. To see what is entailed by these alternatives, let us consider some concrete examples from dialects of British English.

Some discrepancies between dialects are (linguistically) very local indeed, affecting only a small part of the structure of the language. For instance, some regional dialects do not change the vowel when forming the past tense of certain strong verbs: instead of present tense *I come, I see* and past tense *I came, I saw*, we find *I come, I see* in past tense – 'I come yesterday', 'I see him yesterday'. Other dialect differences cut deeper. For example, native Norfolk speakers do not have a suffix *-s* on the third person singular, present tense, of verbs: they produce *he wait, she go*, etc., where other dialects have *he waits, she goes*. This is a productive pattern, in the sense that it is found in all relevant sentences of pure dialect speakers (but the situation is more complicated in speakers who switch stylistically between more pronounced (*L*) and less pronounced (*H*) varieties of the dialect depending on who they are speaking to; younger people supply the suffix when talking to speakers of standard English). To add an even more far-reaching example, there are substantial phonological differences between the vowel patterns of English dialects. In some cases vowels are realized with very different tongue positions: the phoneme /æ/ (as in *man*) will illustrate this. In northern England generally this is a *low* or 'open' front vowel, very like the German counterpart of this English vowel. Standard southern English articulates the phoneme with the tongue slightly higher; and in upper- and middle-class south-eastern speech, the tongue is held higher still, almost obliterating the distinction between *man* and *men*, *mat* and *met*, etc. These differences are marginal, in theory, because they are merely differences in the allophonic realization of a single phoneme (phonetic rather than phonological variants). A grammar of English can ignore these discrepancies, and give just one phoneme /æ/. However, there are complications in actual use: northern speakers, accustomed to a low /æ/, tend to hear the southern, higher, variety as /e/: they hear a different word from that intended – *men* where *man* is intended, *mention* for *mansion*, and so on. So although, as far as this point is concerned, the competence of Yorkshire speaker A and Hampstead speaker B is in principle the same, in practice A misunderstands B.

One final example. Most speakers of northern English regional accents do not distinguish between the vowels of *book* and *buck*, *look* and *luck*, etc. Southern English has the contrasting phonemes /ʊ/ and /ʌ/; northern dialects have only /ʊ/, and this replaces /ʌ/, *buck* being pronounced like *book*: /bʊk/ in both cases. (In some varieties the phonemic contrast is reinstated by the use of the vowel /u/ in places where /ʊ/ would contrast with /ʌ/ in southern dialects – *look* is then pronounced /luk/ (like southern *Luke*), *luck* /lʊk/ (like southern *look*) so that confusable words are kept apart.) Here we have, quite obviously, competing phonological rules: the grammar is different for the sets of speakers concerned. All the examples in the previous paragraph might be accommodated in 'footnotes', as it were, to a grammar of standard English; but here distinct phoneme-systems must be shown in parallel.

Consider the situation of someone living in a densely populated multi-dialect country such as England. His language displays a number of more or less permanent traits which together characterize him as an individual speaker (his friends recognize his voice even through the distortion of the telephone). He speaks English; his dominant variety of English is a particular dialect, which reflects his general position in the English community as a result of a complex of regional, socio-economic, and educational factors; he speaks with a distinctive **voice quality**, the product of his biological make-up. All this adds up to his own **idiolect**, the peculiar complex which is Smith's or Brown's speech. It ought to be clear by now that descriptive linguistics is very little concerned with idiolect: though idiolect may be vitally important to personal and social transactions in which Smith takes part (being interviewed for a job, delivering a political speech), it is a distraction as far as the grammarian is concerned. The latter is interested in those aspects of language which allow Smith and Brown to communicate, not those which set them apart.

Now judging from my remarks on phonological disparities between dialects, it would appear that Smith and Brown may understand each other despite blatantly competing features in their respective grammars: if Smith lacks the phoneme /ʌ/, substituting /ʊ/ for /ʌ/ and then /u/ for /ʊ/, Brown nevertheless understands him. The 'Received Pronunciation' accent of British English, common to educated southerners, widely used in broadcasting and standard in the speech of most prominent public figures, is intelligible to all non-RP speakers, and vice versa (though it may take time for a Londoner to accustom himself to the speech of a Cornishman or a Tynesider). The point is that a grammar cannot work on the lowest common denominator principle, reporting only those features which are shared by dialects, for that would not account for mutual intelligibility across dialects. If we want to represent the basis of a speaker's command of English, the competence which allows him to communicate productively and receptively with others (including those who speak different dialects from his own) we must recognize that his language powers are flexible and complex: in some sense speakers know other dialects 'passively', and that fact must suggest the necessity for a multi-dialect grammar. The individual's linguistic competence would be 'located' in one 'section' of such a grammar (or he would switch among several 'sections' if he was himself multi-dialectal for diglossic purposes); and the overall structure of the grammar would allow him to exploit the rules of other dialect 'sections' (sets of variant rules) for receptive communication with speakers of dialects outside his own active range.

The question arises: is linguistic competence quantifiable? does it vary measurably from speaker to speaker? Just how standards of measurement might be devised is a little difficult to imagine at present, but it seems clear that linguistic capacities differ from individual to individual. Some people are literate, others not, of course; some people's language is distorted by pathological or other biological causes (deafness, dyslexia): I am referring to more subtle variations, however. A person who travels a lot, has a wide range of acquaintances, occupies a professional role demanding much verbalization, is likely to command many varieties (styles and dialects), to be at ease in the transitions between them, to be very ready to perform linguistically on any occasion, to possess a large vocabulary, to speak continuously without preparation if called upon to do so, to exhibit a good range of syntactic constructions and lexical variants in most instances of his speaking, and so on. He is fluent, articulate, talkative. We have all met such people; also, people who do not possess such qualities, and people whose linguistic abilities seem to fall in between the two extremes. If, as seems likely, there is a scale of degrees of linguistic 'capability' (to use a deliberately non-technical term), it correlates closely with such well-known influential factors as social class, educational history, openness of community, etc. And since the point which an individual occupies on the scale has very powerful implications for his career opportunities, possibilities for social and geographical mobility, and the like, this matter ought to be of great practical concern to linguists, sociolinguists, educationists, psychologists. Of course, the problems of the linguistically disadvantaged are well known to teachers and to employers, and both remedial programmes and school courses to develop general stylistic capability and awareness of the potentialities of language are now available (after a long period of neglect of native language teaching, because 'school grammar' became prescriptive and disreputable). But here we are interested in this matter of 'variable capability' from the point of view of linguistic theory, not pedagogy.

The standard answer provided by strict followers of Chomsky would be roughly as follows. Variations of the kind discussed in the present chapter, including those mentioned in the last paragraph, are to be described at the level of linguistic performance. Competence remains untouched by variations in people's actual linguistic behaviour. The kernel of this doctrine is expressed right at the beginning of *Aspects of the Theory of Syntax*:

> Linguistic theory is concerned primarily with an ideal speaker-listener, in a completely homogeneous speech-community, who knows its language perfectly and is unaffected by such grammatically irrelevant conditions as memory limitations, distractions, shifts of attention and interest, and errors (random or characteristic) in applying his knowledge of the language in actual performance.

(I assume that it is intended that grammatical theory should also idealize away from the brute facts of stylistic behaviour, i.e. that the complete set of performance factors contains many that are by no means as negative as those instanced by Chomsky.) We must accept that some such simplification is essential if formal grammars are to be written at all – otherwise we are faced with a vast complex of data, some linguistic and some non-linguistic and in the former category some grammatical (having to do with the pairing of sounds and meanings) and some sociolinguistic (etc.). It is also reasonable to suppose, as generative grammarians do, that a grammar in this deliberately and necessarily narrowed sense 'has psychological reality': it represents knowledge which speakers have internalized. The difficulty is matching up this ideal competence with the actual capability of any *one* speaker. Judging from some statements by generative grammarians, competence is not simply the competence of an ideal speaker, but that of all speakers beneath the skin of their variable linguistic performance, as it were. For instance, in the earlier and stronger claims for an innate 'Language Acquisition Device' (e.g. Katz, McNeill) it is patently suggested that such a device is present in all normal children and causes them to achieve complete command of language by the age of five or six. We are asked to agree that the reasons why six-year-old children do not speak like adults are not linguistic reasons: i.e. they have the capacity, but fail to actualize it. In the previous chapter I argued that young children have more linguistic competence than they are usually credited with, and that they possess the basic semantic relationships and a great deal of syntactic knowledge by the time they enter school; also, that any under-use of these abilities is to be ascribed to cognitive immaturity and socio-cultural innocence (and/or deprivation). However, I think it would be at least an exaggeration, and certainly a piece of question-begging, to claim 'complete' achievement of language by this stage. Carol Chomsky's work has shown that some constructions are still being consolidated well into the school years, and she speculates on the possibility that some speakers never attain certain parts of linguistic structure.

We all know some adults who are 'bad speakers'. Bloomfield's well-known report of one such is worth quoting here:

White-Thunder, a man around forty, speaks less English than Menomini, and that is a strong indictment, for his Menomini is atrocious. His vocabulary is small; his inflections are often barbarous; he constructs sentences of a few threadbare models. He may be said to speak no language tolerably.

Faced with such instances of persistent and severe language deficiency, we surely cannot entertain an explanation which allows ideal linguistic competence inhibited by non-linguistic circumstances. White-Thunder (like many acquaintances of our own) seems not to possess the competence in language which would be represented in a generative grammar of English or Menomini. His competence is both deviant from the ideal and less than the ideal. Equally, we know speakers whose command of a language is very good, and speakers who are only middling. So the reality appears to be that speakers command *langue* to varying extents; that the linguist's grammar represents not that which all people ('really', 'despite appearances') know, but that which some people know and other people only approximate. The justification for Chomsky's (and, *mutatis mutandis*, Saussure's) idealization is, then, to be sought not in the abilities of the individual speaker but in the linguist's necessary compromise: in order to explain what it is that enables speakers to communicate, he constructs a grammar covering what the aggregate of linguistically skilled speakers know. No single speaker knows the whole of the grammar, for, as we have seen, it should be multi-dialectal; skilled speakers presumably know all of that part of the grammar which covers their productive dialect(s), plus other dialects receptively. Less skilled speakers exist who know less and/or know what they do know badly. It is this concept of variable linguistic competence which is absent from the Chomskyan model of grammar. But once we begin considering *socio*linguistic competence, as we have in the present chapter, the idea of varying degrees of competence becomes entirely natural. Depending on a vast range of personal and social factors – intelligence, memory, education, experience, outgoingness, degree of exposure to language, etc., etc. – the language of the individual at any one time will be more or less rich, flexible, effective. We may accept this fact and still be willing to assume the Chomskyan simplification of grammatical competence for the procedural reason that without it generative grammars just cannot be written. However, we must acknowledge that grammatical competence, translated into the sphere of the single individual's personal abilities, is a relative concept. Some people 'have less grammar' than others. And 'grammar' in the necessarily restricted sense of generative linguistics is only one component of the individual's linguistic faculties. If we look at linguistic performance in the light of the individual's activity within the whole social framework, we are bound to become convinced that a theory of *parole* must be very complicated indeed – so must a complete psychological theory of language users – and that it must presuppose a great and complexly interacting range of 'competences', only one of them 'grammatical' in our strict sense.

Further reading

There is as yet no single book which offers a unified, agreed, general sociolinguistic theory, and the most valuable access to the subject will come through sampling the many practical studies to be found in anthologies. Some selections: Ardener, *Social Anthropology and Language*; Bright, *Sociolinguistics*; Fishman, *Readings in the Sociology of Language*; Gumperz and Hymes, *Directions in Sociolinguistics* and *The Ethnography of Communication*; Hymes, *Language in Culture and Society*. These contain most of the classic field studies drawn on in the present chapter, which are as follows (in order of mention): Brown and Gilman, 'The pronouns of power and solidarity'; Brown and Ford, 'Address in American English'; Haas, 'Men's and women's speech in Koasati'; Ferguson, 'Diglossia'; Rubin, *National Bilingualism in Paraguay*; Bloomfield, 'Literate and illiterate speech'; Labov, *Social Stratification of English in New York City*; Tanner, 'Speech and society'; Gumperz, 'Linguistic and social interaction'.

Three elementary textbooks: Fishman, *Sociolinguistics*; Greenberg, *Anthropological Linguistics*; Pride, *The Social Meaning of Language*.

'Frameworks' are sketched in Hymes, 'Toward ethnographies of communication'; Firth, 'Personality and language in society'. Firth's 'context of situation' derives from Malinowski: see the latter's 'The problem of meaning in primitive languages'.

'Register' is discussed in Halliday, McIntosh and Strevens, *The Linguistic Sciences*; Leech, *English in Advertising*. The concept (though the name is rejected) governs Crystal and Davy's *Investigating English Style*. Most discussions of 'style' are literary-critical, but general observations can be extrapolated from, e.g., Enkvist, 'On defining style' and 'Style in some linguistic theories' or Fowler, *The Languages of Literature*. For the hierarchical sense of 'style', see Gleason, *Linguistics and English Grammar*; Joos, *The Five Clocks*; Leech, *English in Advertising*.

The question of variable competence is explored in Hymes, 'On communicative competence'; Basil Bernstein's work is of course relevant; see his *Class, Codes and Control*. On multiple competences, see Fowler, 'Against idealization' and several of the contributions to Lyons and Wales, *Psycholinguistics Papers*.

eleven

Uses of language

If we attempt seriously to achieve an understanding of language, of the nature of language, we ought to ask many different kinds of questions about it; to focus our curiosity from many different viewpoints. What are its structural characteristics (its 'algebra')? What media does it employ? Who possesses language? How do people come to possess language? How does it relate to social structure? to biological structure? What is its relationship with 'reality'? How do other communication devices compare with it? What are its uses? etc. etc. These questions overlap, and their answers interpenetrate, but we ought to try to answer all of them, and many more, in order to attain the richest possible perspective upon language.

Almost inevitably, a linguist asked to define his subject-matter will provide an answer which reflects the partiality of his own approach. This outcome results from the very wide range of possible attitudes to language and the diversity of special branches of linguistics. It is understandable that a phonetician should see language as a different kind of thing from, say, the sociolinguist. For the first the physical dimension must assume overwhelming prominence, whereas the second must regard language primarily as a code providing the materials for the construction of 'varieties'. A lexicologist will view language as a collection of words; a theorist in semantics will stress the capacity of language to supply a structured representation of our experience. Each focuses on a part of language rather than the whole: the whole structure contains a great many components, and linguistics breeds many very distinct specialists.

Just as one's speciality within language studies may encourage a limited perspective on language, so one's general conception of the

240

characteristics of the code may be coloured by general prejudice. The use of the word 'code' in the last sentence, for instance, might betray a limitation of viewpoint: emphasis on the capacity of language to transfer ideas from person to person by means of conventional symbols. Such a characterization would be consistent with the pre-occupation with the system of grammar which has been at the centre of the present book, and we must check any tendency to think of language as *only* a coding device for the transmission of messages. Someone else, less interested in the formal properties of the system than in the way it affects interpersonal transactions, might present language as a means of getting things done, of controlling the behaviour of others, of managing the division of labour within society. This would stress the **instrumental** powers of language. Leonard Bloomfield (*Language*, chapter 2) takes just such a line. He presents a story of Jack and Jill, Jill wanting an apple which she cannot reach and securing it by asking Jack to act on her behalf. Bloomfield generalizes: 'Language enables one person to make a reaction (R) when another person has the stimulus (S) .... The division of labor, and, with it, the whole working of human society, is due to language.' This quality of language gives human beings the edge over other species in the fight for survival: it allows co-operation, reliance on other people's skills when one's own are inadequate to some necessary task. Certainly, language is available for this function – indeed, performs the function constantly – but Bloomfield is wrong to stress this one function to the exclusion of others (his chapter is called 'The use of language'). Equally, my emphasis on the information-channelling function of language must be qualified by acknowledging the many other qualities and functions of the phenomenon.

In this chapter I shall consider some of the uses, functions and effects of language: in short, what it *does* (in contrast to other chapters in which I have discussed what language is like, how it works). Let us first think about 'uses of language' in an informal way. Here is a fairly simple speech-situation, simple because it has a strong element of ritual about it. I and a number of my colleagues quite often have lunch at a pub five minutes' walk away from the university. On a sample occasion, I arrive before anyone else:

1. Manager: Morning, sir.
2. R.F.: Morning. Not a bad morning, either. It's quite hot.
3. Manager: Yes, the forecast said it would be warm. What can I get you?
4. R.F.: Pint of bitter, please.
5. Manager (*pouring*): You like the Adnams, don't you (?)
6. R.F.: How are they getting on with decorating the other bar?

241

7. Manager: Oh, shouldn't be long now. They've finished the ceiling and are on the windows now. End of the week, they say. I'll be glad to see the back of them, makes such a ruddy mess – dust all over the glasses and that.
8. R.F.: Still, it'll be nice when it's done. It was very scruffy before.
9. Manager: Oh, yes, but it's an upheaval. Sixteen pence, please.
10. R.F.: Thank you.
11. Manager (*giving change*): Thank you. Do you want to order anything?
12. R.F.: No, I'll wait a bit.

This is probably a characteristic example of our ordinary mundane discourse. It is stylized, predictable (he and I have had dozens of similar conversations) and functional; it is also rigidly constrained by physical conditions, principally the time it takes to pour a pint of beer, to give change, etc. Despite these situational restrictions, the participants' language moves through several functions, at some points several at once. In 1–3 language is used for greeting. *Morning* does not have its dictionary meaning in 1; however, in 2–3 it is re-interpreted, restored to its usual lexical meaning: we are genuinely commenting on the weather, as the reference *the forecast* makes clear. It is relevant to exchange ideas on this topic, because at this pub customers sit out on the terrace when it is warm enough. But 2–3 are not primarily referential; they remain within the framework of the greetings sub-discourse 1–3. The expansion of 1 in 2–3 serves the purpose of 'softening' the whole exchange, avoiding abruptness, crudely transactional language. 4 is an instrumental utterance, of course: the response is the action of serving the drink. 5 also looks functional, since it concerns a choice between two types of beer; however, the barman doesn't wait for an answer, and I don't give one. It seems most likely that this is 'contact language' intended primarily to signal one person's knowledge of the other's tastes. The exchange 6–9, though more concretely referential than any other part of the dialogue (it clearly communicates information and opinions), still continues the social dimension of the conversation. Though I may earnestly wish to learn about the progress of the painting, I initiate the sub-conversation principally for social reasons – silence, in our culture, being regarded as a sign of unsociability; one keeps the talk going in this sort of situation. Social gesture is everywhere reflected in the style, too. Both parties aim at a style of 'polite familiarity' (if that is not a contradiction!). The language is neither really casual nor intimate; it could not be so because it is constrained by the rules of a stereotyped transactional context,

242

buying and selling with the mechanical activities which those operations entail. Additionally, there are contrasts of role between the
interlocutors to be maintained: customer versus provider of a
service, intellectual versus publican. Yet because I visit the place two
or three times a week I practise the studied familiarity of the 'regular', and my interlocutor also tints his speech with that style: note
the ellipsis throughout the conversation (*Morning, Pint of bitter,
shouldn't be long now, End of the week*, etc.); the loose syntactic
transitions, e.g. the last sentence in 7; the cheerful euphemism
ruddy; the assumption that the other party will interpret inexplicit
references on the basis of past experience – *bitter* in 4 means a
particular bitter; *anything* in 11 refers to sandwiches; note also the
use of *they* without antecedent in 6–7.

There is the archetype of the child who says 'I want a drink
of water' but is 'really saying' 'I'm not going to bed yet'. That
story does *not* show that the semantic interpretation 'I want a drink
of water' is not to be attached to the child's utterance. It would be
more accurate to say that the child *uses* the utterance for a purpose
which is not announced in the semantic content. The unco-operative
child at bedtime does not present an extreme or untypical case;
my analysis of the pub conversation in the previous paragraph is
meant to suggest that, as we speak (and write, read, etc.) we continuously put our language to a multitude of separate uses, these
uses being relatively unpredictable in terms of the content and
structure of sentences. Linguistic performance is not merely the
formation of utterances: it is personal, or interpersonal, behaviour
for which language is the communicative means. In particular
circumstances we use language to make statements, ask questions,
command, persuade, threaten, cajole, entertain; to proclaim our
feelings and individual identities; to work out problems and to
increase and stabilize our command over the world of things and
ideas; to amuse ourselves (literature is, among other things, a
sophisticated form of verbal play); to record and preserve experience;
to perform rituals (marriage, legal sentence, cursing, etc.); to assist
and co-ordinate physical work (sea shanties, children's skipping
rhymes); to explore and to translate experiences; and so on. These
are particular actions which may be performed by language, separate speech acts; they may be inventorized indefinitely, or, as we
shall see, arranged into categories, since they fall into a limited number of types. In addition, language fulfils certain more generalized
functions, to which I shall return later in this chapter: continuous
expression of group identity, ordering of experiences, etc.

Linguists are on the whole reluctant to think of speech as *action*;
language is seen as expression rather than action; a speaking person

is 'communicating', not 'doing'. The philosopher J. L. Austin did much to redress the balance in a series of lectures, posthumously a book, with the challenging title *How to Do Things with Words*. He interested himself particularly in the class of verbs which includes, for instance, *warn, promise, welcome, apologize,* etc., the utterance of which in a first-person sentence actually counts as a performance of the action which the verb describes. If I say 'I promise to pay you back on Friday', my utterance *is* an act of promising (contrast 'He promised to pay me back last Friday' which is not an act of promising although it is an account of an act of promising). Compare 'I pronounce you man and wife', 'I declare this supermarket open', 'I name this ship The Skylark'. In all these cases, the deed referred to by the verb is, if conditions are favourable, actually achieved by the utterance itself. Such utterances do not refer to objects and events outside of themselves; they are performances, they are independent actions of a self-fulfilling kind (if appropriately performed). Austin, followed by John R. Searle, who has refined Austin's analysis, called them **illocutionary acts**. It is necessary to add the condition 'if appropriately performed' because an illocutionary act may be unsuccessful, 'infelicitous', if relevant conventions are not observed: for instance, 'I pronounce you man and wife' only succeeds in formalizing a marriage if the person who utters it is recognized by his society as someone authorized to conduct this linguistic ritual (a priest, or the captain of a ship at sea, etc.).

The utterances which most obviously have illocutionary force are those which contain explicit performative verbs such as *declare, warn, command,* etc. But an illocutionary act does not require the presence of a verb of this type: such an act results from a particular use of an utterance, not from its internal lexical content. Employing an explicit performative allows one to perform an illocutionary act in a particularly formal way (and adding *hereby* makes it even more formal and more evidently illocutionary: 'I hereby bequeath all my property to my children'); however, the performative verb is clearly not demanded by an illocutionary act. 'I order you to shut the door' is only a colder and more insistent variant of 'Shut the door!': the latter as well as the former carries out the illocutionary act of ordering. But 'Shut the door!' contains no performative verb. This lack of a performative is generally true of questions as well as commands: we would normally say 'What's the time?' rather than 'I ask you what the time is', the latter implying a mood of exceptional formality, even severity. Now if one says 'I asked you what the time is' (expanding a mis-heard 'What's the time?') he is not performing the illocutionary act of asking, despite the presence of the performative *ask*. What is the illocutionary act here? Compare

'He asked me what the time was', which raises the same question. We could say that these utterances have no illocutionary force; that they are 'just statements'. But why should a statement be regarded as 'just' a statement? The speaker is engaging in an illocutionary act, the act of *stating*: this can legitimately be regarded as one selection from a range of choices in the illocutionary system. It would be a mistake to ignore the most frequently occurring type of speech-act simply because it is the most neutral or because its illocutionary force is not openly displayed in surface structure.

We need to say, surely, that every utterance has illocutionary force. (Whether or not it counts as a *successful* illocutionary act, is another matter altogether.) In fact, we must acknowledge that a speaker exercising his linguistic competence is doing something which is simultaneously several kinds of action, or, to put it another way, is effecting a complex action the several facets of which may be characterized in different ways. A speech act is first of all a linguistic structure, and may be described as a sentence or sentences, a pairing of sounds and meanings, in terms of the apparatus of descriptive linguistics as sketched in the present book. Incidentally, it must also be a physical act, of course, typically a sequence of events in the speech musculature. Then it also has a *propositional* dimension: a speaker not merely emits signals which are describable as sentences, he also refers to objects and concepts, and he predicates properties, actions and states of them. The semantic organization of a sentence, although describable autonomously within the framework provided by linguistics, is, we must remember, the means of connection by which language is related to the world of ideas. In seeing an utterance as a propositional act – a communication of ideational content and structure – the linguist moves towards a *rapprochement* with his natural colleague, the logician.

At this point one must be clear that a proposition is not the same as a statement. A statement is one particular illocutionary use of a proposition or set of propositions; and propositions necessarily figure in other kinds of illocutionary acts. Thus, the utterances 'Kingfishers fly' and 'Do kingfishers fly?' are manifestly different sentences, and typically will achieve distinct illocutionary ends (stating and questioning respectively), but they may quite reasonably be said to contain the same proposition. In both, the word *kingfishers* is used in such a way as to refer to the class of all kingfishers, and the predicate *fly* is tied to that category of referents. The differences are linguistic and illocutionary, and we must not confuse qualities at those levels with the properties of the propositional dimension of an utterance.

To the above three aspects of linguistic performance – linguistic (shaping sentences), illocutionary (using sentences purposively) and propositional (referring and predicating) – we might add a fourth, **perlocutionary**. The notion of illocution takes no account of the consequences of a speech act. One may successfully perform the illocutionary act of commanding – 'Shut the door!' – by fulfilling all the necessary conditions pertinent to that act (e.g. one must address someone who may reasonably be expected to close the door, there must be an open door to be closed, etc.) and after the command the door may be closed, or it may not. The point is that the *effect* of most illocutionary acts is not under the speaker's control; success is measured in relation to his performance, not its effects. (This distinction does not apply to such speech-acts as marrying, naming ships, promising, of course.) If I tell someone to shut the door and he does so, I have performed the illocutionary act of ordering and the perlocutionary act of persuading (or whatever one wishes to call it). 'Statement' is an illocutionary concept, since it is defined wholly in terms of the speaker's behaviour in relation to appropriate conventions. In the perlocutionary domain, a statement may have many different implications and results. If I say to X 'Your son's a criminal' I may be *informing* him, *insulting* him, *enraging* him, *amusing* him, etc. Or there may be no perlocutionary act here: he may receive this simply as an assertion, and I may follow up with some more statements which may *convince* him of the truth of my first statement.

'Illocution' is an apparently formal concept: it seems that there is a set range of illocutionary acts one of which each utterance must fulfil (or may infelicitously approximate) and which seems to be closely linked to the Mood system under *Aux* in linguistic description. 'Perlocution', however, is much less determinate, and is indeed the least convincing aspect of the Austin–Searle theory of speech-acts. That is to say, 'least convincing' in terms of that particular theory of linguistic functions: designed to elucidate 'illocution', it is not well adapted to defining linguistic functions according to the nature of their effects. We need to enrich the theory so that it can classify 'uses of language' from the point of view of what is *achieved* by linguistic acts. Clearly, in any account of 'uses of language' we must be able to accommodate notions such as 'informing', 'persuading', 'expressing', 'entertaining' and the like.

A traditional distinction is expressed thus by I. A. Richards:

A statement may be used for the sake of the *reference*, true or false, which it causes. This is the *scientific* use of language. But it may also be used for the sake of the effects in emotion and attitude produced by the reference it occasions. This is the *emotive* use of language.

246

'Reference' is intended in the sense provided by the Ogden–Richards semantic theory, i.e. 'act of reference' (see above, p. 46). But the distinction does not depend on 'meaning' being conceived of in referential terms. In essence, Richards is drawing a line between language used for the transfer of ideas and information from one person to others, and language used to promote responses – verbal, actional, attitudinal – in an audience. The paradigm examples would be, on the one hand, an article in a scientific journal reporting the technique and results of an experiment, or a chapter in a history book; on the other, a lyric poem or a piece of political oratory designed to capture votes or to sway people to action. This is an illuminating and necessary distinction, though it needs careful qualification and elaboration. It is essential to an understanding of the nature of literary fiction, since the 'emotive' category, whatever its deficiencies, does at least underline the fact that there are some texts the proper response to which requires suspension of our normal standards of truth and falsehood; on the other hand, 'scientific' texts positively demand exercise of our faculty of dis-belief – scepticism is invited, we are under an obligation to scrutinize the observations presented in a scientific report so as to convince ourselves of their validity.

But Richards draws the line too sharply. Our discussion of illo-cutionary acts in the preceding paragraphs ought to suggest that the functions of language cannot be sorted into two mutually exclusive classes (which is the clear implication of Richards's assertion). We cannot say that an utterance is (for instance) either purely scien-tific or purely emotive. Take the case of newspaper reporting. The majority of newspaper articles purport to record facts and events, but only the most naïve of readers would regard them as unfiltered representations of 'reality'. We know that different newspapers, and individual reporters, have distinct styles, and that these styles are functional: the manner of representation is *expressive* in announcing the ideals and preoccupations of the paper or journalist, *persuasive* in seeking to create and reinforce a readership which will sympathize with a point of view and perhaps act in conformity with its implica-tions. Comparison of the front pages of two papers of different political persuasions purchased the day after some major event of domestic politics will instantly confirm this observation. As for written history, this is closer to referential transparency only in degree: consciously or not, the historian colours his account, reflect-ing his methodological practice, his ideological inclinations, etc. Finally, scientific writing, though perhaps affecting a plainness of style, is almost invariably conducted in an argumentative conven-tion: the author seeks to persuade his audience of the rightness of his insights and interpretations and the fallaciousness of rival theories. Standards of judgment with respect to empirical phenomena are important here, but that is not to say that scientific discourse is purely referential.

Nor can the exclusiveness of the 'emotive' category be supported in the fashion that Richards apparently intends it. Even the crudest demagogue rants about *something*: he sways his audience by the way he treats his subject, but he has a subject; that is to say, his emotive utterances at least have propositional content. As for literature, it is extremely difficult to discover more than a handful of poems, other than so-called 'sound-poetry', which throw the referential dimension overboard. It is a matter of prominence, not an absolute choice. In poetry, particularly lyric poetry, formal aspects of language – especially phonetic structure and to a large extent syntax – are prominently foregrounded: we perceive the propositional content through the structuring grid of form. However, a poem is a propositional act, not merely a phonetic act; statement as well as pattern, even if primarily pattern. In some kinds of discourse, presumably the ones which Richards would put in the 'scientific' box, content takes precedence over form: form is arranged so that propositions can be conveyed as neutrally as possible.

We see, then, that Richards's distinction between 'two uses' reflects a difference of degree, not of kind. It would be possible to regard 'scientific' and 'emotive' as the end points on a continuous scale, texts at the 'scientific' end laying particular emphasis on the propositional dimension, those at the 'emotive' extreme attaching less importance to the illocutionary act of stating than to the perlocutionary effects that discourse may achieve. This re-wording of Richards's distinction allows us to preserve certain dramatic contrasts (instruction versus curse, the language of textbooks versus the language of love-making, literary history versus poetry) while remaining faithful to the principle that every utterance is an admixture of functions, of which one or other is often relatively prominent. Such a revision also enables us to account naturally for the fact that many pieces of discourse shift through subtle transitions from function to function as they unfold through time: ordinary relaxed conversation, for instance, may move imperceptibly from informing to arguing to persuading to abusing, etc. (and other functions, in other sequences, etc.). When we participate in talk of this kind, we are not conscious of strict or exclusive changes in purpose; what takes place is a series of gradually fluctuating alterations of emphasis. A theory which claims that different *uses* of language depend on the highlighting of distinct *functions* latent within the composition of language itself is the most natural way of explaining minute shifts in the modes of language in action.

I said that Richards's dichotomy needs elaborating, as well as qualifying. It has been qualified, above, by the suggestion that it is not a sharp dichotomy: that there is no possibility of sorting all linguistic acts on to one side or the other of a distinct boundary; the edges are blurred, the functional differences between speech-acts (on Richards's criterion) being attributable to relative differences of emphasis which 'reference' receives. The scheme can be elaborated by noticing other dimensions of the communication situation which may be foregrounded in different uses of language. The most famous of existing elaborated schemes is the one offered by Roman Jakobson, and I shall adapt it here, altering his terms for the sake of consistency with terminology elsewhere in this book and providing different definitions for some of the features he mentions.

The vast majority of utterances are 'about' something – excepting Jabberwocky, they are generally founded on recognizable lexical items from which a *subject-matter* can be retrieved by the audience. When language invites primary attention to the subject-matter, it fulfils the **referential** function, which I have already discussed. Other terms are 'cognitive', 'descriptive', 'denotative'. Now language can hardly escape being referential, since it is at base propositional. A referential *use* of language is one in which language is employed primarily to indicate objects outside of itself; to put it another way, this use subordinates all other aspects of the communication situation to the transfer of ideas which are felt to exist independently of language. (Whether concepts, or categories of referents, do in fact enjoy such independent existence is a moot point; but its resolution is immaterial to the functional speculations of the present part of this chapter.) Granted that all texts must have a rhetorical (persuasive) element, and that none can exist without the normal formal components which are the linguist's main concern, examples which heighten the referential over other dimensions would include: expository prose, e.g. descriptive guidebooks, textbooks, instruction handbooks on cars and other complex machines, specifications, job descriptions; records, e.g. reports of parliamentary debates, registers of births, marriages and deaths, diaries, chronicles; narration, e.g. verbal retelling of a day's events or of the conduct of an assignment.

Often the 'reference' in a referential use of language is language itself: we say things like '"Dog" is a noun'; 'I can't stand Americanisms such as "escalation" or "stenographer"'; '"Tutankhamen" should be pronounced "toot-onk-ah-moon"'. This is the **metalinguistic** use of language: 'language about language'. The technical vocabulary of linguistics is metalinguistic, as is the notational system of logic.

In Richards's division of the uses of language, the 'emotive' is the less convincing of the two classes because it is the more mixed and woolly. Jakobson's scheme allows us to separate several distinct uses which are muddled together under 'emotive' in the more primitive plan. First, emphasis may be on the *form* of a text rather than its subject-matter, and this is the **poetic** use of language. Particular care is lavished on the structure of expression; for instance, in the case of verse composition extra phonological rules operate (their character varying from language-type to language-type and from one verse convention to another) to produce an exceptional regularity in phonetic structure. Verse, then, is literally more highly structured than non-verse: linguistic structure is perceptibly more prominent. What aspect of linguistic form is foregrounded depends on the tradition concerned and the design of the poet. Metre is a presence which cannot be ignored; syntax may be rendered specially prominent, as in Pope; attention to pure structure of sound may be demanded, as in French Symbolist poetry or in Hopkins. The poetic use extends to what is, technically, prose: most obviously in a writer like Virginia Woolf, but also in syntactic craftsmen such as Henry James. The reader is directly engaged, even challenged, by the highly wrought syntax: the focus on form is strongly enforced. But the syntax is not merely decorative; it serves to build, in the reader, a particular perspective on the world depicted in the novel – to control the reader's attitudes. Thus the 'poetic' use of language is not simply language used in an extremely 'physical' way (though that is the case with some verse) but a foregrounding of the formal elements of language in the service of building an aesthetic structure which is unique and independent of the 'real' world (non-referential, in a sense, but nevertheless propositional).

So far I have mentioned, under the 'elaborated' scheme, uses of language which focus particular attention on content (reference, concern with things outside language), on language itself as a topic (metalinguistic) and on the form of a particular utterance or text (poetic). Other uses of language are directed specifically to the role of the speaker/writer, or to demands on the audience, or to the relationship between these participants. The last has already been alluded to. There are many situations in which language is used almost exclusively for the sake of interpersonal contact: the 'Hello', 'Nice day', 'How's yourself' type of language which is no more referential than a handshake or a kiss. This is the **phatic** use of language, essentially non-propositional, functioning entirely to enforce links between individuals on specific occasions of contact.

As we have seen, if addressee B interprets the phatic utterance of addresser A as referential (e.g. responds to 'How are you this morning?' with 'I've got a terrible headache'), there is a momentary communicative discord. (Such an occurrence is a dramatic confirmation of the theory of contrasting uses of language.) 'Phatic' is the most recognizable and formally circumscribed of the uses of language, being largely announced in a set of 'routines' (see p. 225 above) abandonment of which upsets the function; it is a function which we associate with particular occasions, most especially mutual greeting when acquaintances meet one another. But we must remember that there is also a constant and inevitable phatic use of language (just as language is never totally unpoetic in its expository uses, and vice versa): when we speak, we are bound to make known our cultural (social, geographical, etc.) affiliations by our characteristic accent, vocabulary, phonetic gestures, and so on. These are unconsciously assimilated conventions and on the whole immutable or at least very slow to change; they suffuse our speech, and by them we 'know' each other – we sort each other into contact groups.

Phatic communication is mutual on local occasions of its manifestation, universal in the generalized form to which I have just referred. Language in interpersonal functions may also be one-sided, with dominant focus on either the speaker or the audience. The former use is the **expressive**, the latter the **conative**. Expressive language highlights the role of the speaker/writer. The pure expressive utterance would be exemplified by a shriek of pain, emanating from the sufferer with no care for a listener: to borrow Bloomfield's terminology, this is a response to an inner stimulus, but not designed to stimulate a reaction in a hearer – there is no consideration of an audience, no intention to communicate anything or to move anyone to action. But screams (likewise most other exclamations) are not linguistic, since they are non-propositional and do not fall into any structural system. Expressive language proper is *language* proper, that is to say well-formed utterances happening to function expressively. The speaker talks of himself, his preoccupations and concerns, or he talks of other topics in such a way as to be simultaneously revealing 'information' about his character or life-style or mood. Certain obvious grammatical markers, such as the repeated use of the first person pronoun with present tense verbs, are associated with expressive language, though they are of course not essential. Some verse traditions, for instance the convention of first-person lyric love-poetry in the European Renaissance, developed formalized linguistic routines for the expression of individual sentiment. The self-indulgent 'complaint' form provides a particularly clear example.

251

One sonnet of Sir Philip Sidney's begins

> My words I know do well set forth my mind

Another

> Come, let me write. And to what end? To ease
> A burthened heart.

Such lines announce the expressive convention; others appear to wallow in verbal celebration of the grieving heart:

> Marvel no more although
> The songs I sing do moan,
> For other life than woe
> I never proved none.
> And in my heart also
> Is graven with letters deep,
> A thousand sighs and mo,
> A flood of tears to weep.   (WYATT)

Personal letters are characteristically expressive in function (love letters, a conventional genre, particularly so); so are patients' speeches in psychiatric interviews – but not reports on physical symptoms in medical consultations: this is referential language. Autobiography is referential as far as subject-matter is concerned, frequently expressive in style.

In spoken language expressive function is signalled not only by grammatical choices, but also by **paralinguistic** devices: phonetic gestures. Phonetic devices such as tempo, rhythm, pitch range (e.g. abnormal contrasts between high and low pitches), tremolo, drawl, huskiness, creakiness, nasality, where they are not organized in the phonological system of the language or an inevitable physical attribute of the speaker (e.g. nasality due to cleft palate) are extensively employed for expressive purposes. A speaker can employ such devices to declare that he is angry, bored, tired, excited, authoritarian, nervous, submissive, self-pitying, etc., etc. Or, he can make known his character or his occupational or assumed role – 'make known' consciously or unconsciously. We are all familiar with the parson's monotone, the politician's studied pauses, the demure lisp of the stage dumb blonde. All these paralinguistic phenomena are of course conventional rather than natural: one can be expressive phonetically only within a society which has (tacitly) agreed to recognize the signs. Characteristically, the conventions of expressive language are relatively unstable, fluctuating rapidly and differing from one cultural sub-group to another. (Compare the speed with which acting styles change from generation to generation and the extent to which they differ from company to company.) An individual who feels that he is projecting his personality as a friendly chap in some social context with which he is only partly cognizant may in fact discover to his discomfiture that the conventions of that group establish him as a pushing fellow, or an insinuating creep, or worse. It is at moments when expressive language misfires that we dramatically realize its power.

Finally, Richards's 'emotive' category includes what others have called the 'conative' function of language: language directed primarily at an audience or listener. Since it is only the purest expressive language which does not assume an audience (and the purity of that category might be questioned – compare suicide attempts, which are in very many cases other-directed rather than self-directed: pleas for help), virtually all language is conative, and the type might be thought to be superfluous. However, there are undoubtedly some uses of language which make particular calls upon the audience's attention. All utterances which incorporate the second-person pronoun singular or plural, the vocative case if the language has it, or the imperative mood or the interrogative, automatically belong to the conative type (reported speech excepted, of course). Questions by definition assume the existence of an audience available for questioning; even 'rhetorical questions', to which there is no answer, are audience-directed in the sense that they demand an awareness on the part of the audience of the rhetorical force implicit in the question, the intention in posing it.

Language primarily oriented to an addressee may be more or less neutral in the demands it is designed to impose upon him. 'Address' itself is apparently the most neutral type, assuming passivity in the audience: 'Dear Sir' at the beginning of letters, 'Good morning, Jane' in greetings. Related usages are the calling of names to catch people's attention – 'Tom! wait for me!' – or to single out someone from a group – 'I'd like *you* to translate the next paragraph, Alan'. In classical and neo-classical literature, address is stylized into set literary formats, one of which is *apostrophe*, a set speech addressed to a person, divinity or even object; the *invocation* (of a poet's Muse) is also familiar: a calling-up or an appeal for assistance. The *ode* is a traditional genre, a highly formal, celebratory address, containing many vocatives, presented to a public figure of heroic stature, addressed to a personified moral quality or even (as in Keats) to a psychological abstraction or a physical object, generally an art object. These formal modes of address carry with them emotive tones, especially in extended versions, which it is relevant to notice in a discussion of functions of language. I referred to the ode as 'celebratory' in purpose; in ordinary language the counterpart is flattery, of course, the verbal equivalent of physical caress. We use language to let people know that they are intelligent, beautiful, strong, influential and so on and so forth. (In so far as such statements usually mean '*I think* that you are intelligent . . .' they are also expressive; and since flattery is almost always directed to securing some end through the co-operation of the person being subjected to flattery, there is an implicit persuasive function in this mode.) The counterpart to flattery is abuse, the verbal equivalent of physical assault. This too is expressive as well as conative, since we swear at someone to let off steam, and probably instrumental also, to the extent that we hope the person we insult will suffer as a result. Ritual cursing, as practised by superstitious people and institutions, is intended to bring down the evil influence of some omnipotent force upon the head of the unfortunate cursee. Happily, curses are less harmful than sticks and stones, but they may have a profoundly depressive or intimidating effect on the person cursed, since we all tend to the primitive belief that words are inherently potent.

What appears at first to be purely expressive language or purely 'addressing' language may, then, turn out on closer inspection to have a pronounced persuasive or instrumental side; to be 'causative' in intention and perhaps in effect. Once again it is demonstrated that to attribute a particular function to an instance of language use is to say that that is the *primary* function of the utterance and does not exclude its fulfilling other uses at the same time. We now turn to uses of language in which preoccupation with the addressee is dominant and in which the design is fundamentally persuasive. Bloomfield, we recall (p. 241 above), regarded all language as basically or essentially instrumental, seeing its purpose as the manipulation of other people's actions in the interest of an economic division of human labour. This is undoubtedly a slanted perspective upon language (encouraged by the behaviourist psychological theory Bloomfield held at that time), but it is distorted rather than absolutely untrue. It is not easy to pinpoint uses of language which have no conative value, and indeed it is difficult to find utterances which are not instrumental in intention or in incidental effect; and there are many uses which are explicitly manipulative. The existence of the imperative mood as distinct grammatical category argues the fundamental importance of the instrumental function. Although it is not the only grammatical structure available for commanding, it is a dramatically direct structure for that function: 'Shut the door!' is unequivocal – no one could doubt the speaker's intention. Politer versions are available: 'Please shut the door', 'Would you please shut the door?' etc.

The existence of imperative mood epitomizes the instrumental function of language, but it is by no means essential to the linguistic

254

control of others. Persuasion can be effected by discourses using all kinds of linguistic structure; and 'persuasion' subsumes many different processes. It can aim at, and may result in, a change of behaviour or of attitude. In the case of behaviour persuasion can cause an individual to perform a particular action at a particular time at the persuader's instigation, or it can cause him to modify his typical behaviour in the long term. In the case of attitudes an individual may be persuaded to accept the existence or the truth of observations of which he had previously been ignorant or sceptical. Scientific argument is persuasion, though superficially it may look like mere factual reporting. Novels are persuasive in the sense that, if successful, they cause their readers to 'believe in' the existence of a fictional world which is generally a set of imaginary people inter- acting in an unreal setting at the period of the novelist's choosing. They are further persuasive in that their language embodies a specific viewpoint on the actions and places represented, a 'world-view' which is local to that one novel and which the reader may be moved to apprehend and subscribe to. (It is an axiom in literary theory that a work of art moves its audience to a change in world-view (attitude) but not a change in real-life behaviour. A novel may, for instance, be erotic in the sense that it presents its readers with new occasions of sexual arousal, but a serious novelist does not, pre- sumably, intend to cause his readers to go out and commit sexual offences. But as the experience of the courts has shown, it is a delicate matter to distinguish between harmless fiction and persuasion to depravity.)

Scientific writing, historical report, novels, etc., do not appear to be persuasive writing, although as I have shown the persuasive element is inescapably present, despite the usual lack of grammatical witness to that element. When we think of persuasive language, we generally turn our minds to obvious forms such as advertising and propaganda. These are 'obvious' in the sense that they are known to be prominent institutions within some cultures – or at least suspected of being prominent: Americans particularly tend to be alarmist about the possibility of contamination by propaganda within their society. The dividing line between advertising and propaganda is difficult to draw: although the former is devoted to the commercial objective of causing people to buy a product, it works through the creation of a favourable attitude towards the product, and propaganda is of course directed to the modification of attitudes and ultimately to the generation of action. Possibly the distinction is of no interest to linguistics, since it is formulatable only in terms of the intention of the propagandist/advertiser and of such factors as the cynicism with which he regards the process: does he believe that the effect on the persuadee is beneficial, or does he seek to persuade only for his own, selfish, ends? Is product X (soap powder, God or totalitarianism) good for humanity or is its promotion beneficial only to its promoter? Opinion on such questions is likely to differ predictably and uninterestingly.

A student of the ways language works within the matrix of human society can make certain revealing observations about the nature of persuasive language without involving himself in judgment on the process or the persuader, however. Central to his observations must be the tension between two opposing tendencies in the shaping of predominantly persuasive language: on the one hand the tendency to develop specialized types of construction particularly adapted to the task of persuasion; on the other the attempt to *conceal* one's intention to persuade. It is well known that certain forms of persuasion tend to settle into conventional formats of linguistic expression: one has only to think of sermons or of television advertisements, both of which utilize large numbers of repetitive set formulae – phonological, syntactic and lexical – of proven effectiveness. Addressing a naïve and uncritical audience (as churchgoers and viewers of television tend to be), an advertiser can exploit successful formulae to the limit and remain undetected. But as the level of education and critical attentiveness increases, the advertiser is forced to vary the rhetoric of advertising (or to change the product gratuitously, a distracting trick practised by car manufacturers); if he does not do so, the advertisement loses its message because the audience reacts to its style as commonplace or becomes merely entertained by the style – commercials become boring or self-destructively beautiful. To combat this process of diminishing returns the persuader can respond by changing the product; by devising new and attention-catching linguistic formulae; or by pretending that it is not persuasive language at all. The last of these three ways out is the typical way of propaganda: for instance vote-catching attempts by major political parties claim to be factual analyses of their own achievements and of the disasters engineered by their opponents. Persuasive language dressed as referential discourse is a common device in political communications, and more sinister than the TV commercial analogue of the pharmaceutical salesman dressed up as research chemist (complete with white coat and appropriate glasses) because less easily exposed by ridicule. But pseudo-referential commercial advertising certainly needs watching closely. Newspaper and magazine advertisements, particularly in prestige publications, are especially interesting from this point of view: they adopt an immaculate parody of the typography and prose style of the journal and the reader is protected from deception only by the mandatory warning

Uses of language

'Advertisement' or 'Advertising Feature' printed small at the top of the page.

To summarize: language serves a multiplicity of functions; on any specific occasion, a piece of language may be assigned a certain function according to which part of the total communicative situation is highlighted in the specific language event – expressive if the speaker or writer assumes a prominent role, poetic if the form of the text is foregrounded, and so on. And this is a relative, not absolute, matter: to say that a particular utterance is 'persuasive' is not to deny it all expressive value. It would be difficult to discover a piece of language in which all functions could not be detected, even though some might be severely diminished.

So far, this chapter has been mainly concerned with the range of specific actions a speaker may perform through the medium of language, considering the subject in terms of particular language events. Another perspective is available: we may enquire into the general benefits and values which accrue to the individual through the fact of possessing language. I do not want to give the impression that language is simply a conveniently adaptable tool which a speaker chooses to adjust for specific jobs as occasion demands, something separate from his total identity and which can be laid aside and then taken up for mechanical use when needed. The fact is that language is an integral part of the identity of the human animal: once the infant masters this faculty, it is a continuously active force in determining his cognitive and social existence. In chapter 1 (pp. 15–16) I suggested that a person without language would be unimaginably handicapped. Most people, even if they have no direct experience of such a condition, can conceive of the difficulties of the adult who cannot read or write (in the midst of a society saturated with the printed word); the isolation of the deaf person, particularly of someone who also cannot speak because he cannot hear. Teachers know how educational difficulties are compounded with children who suffer from any kind of language defect; physicians and psychiatrists, how humiliating and disabling speech defects can be. If deficiencies in language cause severe problems, how would *absence of language* affect the human being? Of course, we cannot really answer this question: the closest we could get to an insight on this state would perhaps be speculation on the effects of the terrifying psychological disorder known as 'autism'. Autistic children fluctuate unpredictably between desperate passivity and violent uncontrollability. They are destructive both of themselves and of their families. Above all they are isolated, contained within themselves, apparently uninterested in others and impenetrable to the observer. Typically there is no evidence of language – and

257

significantly therapists strive to build up contact through building up language.

Without intending to be cruel or callous, we might say that autistic children hardly qualify as human beings; and I suspect that the parents of normal children often nervously await the onset of speech as confirmation of the humanity of their offspring. What I am trying to suggest is that a humanoid without language could not be a human being; that having language is an essential qualification for being human. Language gives us powers that no other human monopoly – the wheel, fire, explosives or whatever – can equal. Through language we order the world, sort our experience into manageable categories in stable relationships. I do not assert that thought is silent speech; but it seems justifiable to claim that thought presupposes language. It is quite likely (one may concede) that human beings are disposed to organize – mentally – the universe they inhabit in particular categories and relationships, language or no; but the successful *realization* or *achievement* of this 'natural' cognitive structure is almost certainly dependent upon language. At the very least, we know empirically that language development facilitates learning; and that personality disintegration, the breakdown of contact with the world, is very often accompanied by the loss of language.

There are grounds for strongly suspecting – to put it modestly – that language determines humanness. Anyone who is prepared to entertain that suspicion has good reason to try to attain an understanding of the nature of language. Linguistics may contribute centrally to our realization of what makes man man.

Further reading

Bloomfield, *Language*, chapter 2; Austin, *How to Do Things with Words*; Searle, *Speech Acts*; Richards, *Principles of Literary Criticism*, chapter 34; Jakobson, 'Linguistics and poetics'; Brown, *Words and Things*, chapter 9; Leech, *English in Advertising*; Crystal and Quirk, *Systems of Prosodic and Paralinguistic Features in English*; Mukařovský, 'Standard language and poetic language'.

Bibliography

The following list of books and articles is designed to provide full bibliographical references for the works cited at the end of each chapter. It is *not* intended as a list of elementary writings in linguistics; the works cited here should be read in the contexts provided by a chapter-by-chapter reading of *Understanding Language*.

ABERCROMBIE, DAVID, *Elements of General Phonetics* (Edinburgh, 1967).

ABRAHAMS, ROGER D. and TROIKE, RUDOLPH C. (eds), *Language and Cultural Diversity in American Education* (Englewood Cliffs, N.J., 1972).

ADAMS, PARVEEN (ed.), *Language in Thinking* (Harmondsworth, 1972).

ALLEN, J. P. B. and VAN BUREN, P. (eds), *Chomsky: Selected Readings* (London, 1971).

ANGLIN, JEREMY M., *The Growth of Word Meaning* (Cambridge, Mass., 1970).

ANTTILA, RAIMO, *An Introduction to Historical and Comparative Linguistics* (New York, 1972).

ARDENER, EDWIN (ed.), *Social Anthropology and Language* (London, 1971).

AUSTIN, J. L., *How to Do Things with Words* (London, 1962).

BACH, EMMON, *Introduction to Phonological Theory* (New York, 1968).

BACH, EMMON, *An Introduction to Transformational Grammars* (New York, 1964).

BACH, EMMON, 'Nouns and noun phrases', in Bach and Harms (eds), *Universals in Linguistic Theory*, pp. 91–122.

BACH, EMMON, and HARMS, R. T. (eds), *Universals in Linguistic Theory* (New York, 1968).

BAR-ADON, AARON, and LEOPOLD, WERNER F. (eds), *Child Language: A Book of Readings* (Englewood Cliffs, N.J., 1971).

BARTHES, ROLAND, *Elements of Semiology*, trans. Annette Lavers and Colin Smith (London, 1967).

259

BASTIAN, J. R., 'Primate signalling systems and human languages', in DeVore (ed.), *Primate Behavior*, pp. 285–606.

BELLUGI, URSULA, and BROWN, ROGER (eds), *The Acquisition of Language* (Chicago, 1964).

BENDIX, E. H., *Componential Analysis of General Vocabulary* (Bloomington, 1966).

BERKO, JEAN, 'The child's learning of English morphology', *Word*, **14** (1958), pp. 150–77.

BERNSTEIN, BASIL, *Class, Codes and Control* (London, 1972).

BIERWISCH, MANFRED, 'Semantics', in Lyons (ed.), *New Horizons in Linguistics*, pp. 162–84.

BLOOM, LOIS, *Language Development: Form and Function in Emerging Grammars* (Cambridge, Mass., 1970).

BLOOMFIELD, LEONARD, *Language* (New York, 1933).

BLOOMFIELD, LEONARD, 'Literate and illiterate speech', *American Speech*, **10** (1927), pp. 432–9; reprinted in Hymes (ed.), *Language in Culture and Society*, pp. 391–6.

BRAINE, MARTIN D. S., 'The ontogeny of English phrase structure: the first phase', *Language*, 39 (1963), pp. 1–13.

BRÉAL, MICHEL, *Semantics: Studies in the Science of Meaning* (first published 1897, trans. New York, 1964).

BRIGHT, WILLIAM (ed.), *Sociolinguistics* (The Hague, 1966).

BROWN, ROGER, 'The first sentences of child and chimpanzee', in *Psycholinguistics, Selected Papers*, pp. 208–34.

BROWN, ROGER, *Psycholinguistics, Selected Papers* (New York, 1970).

BROWN, ROGER, *Words and Things* (Glencoe, Ill., 1958).

BROWN, ROGER, and BELLUGI, URSULA, 'Three processes in the child's acquisition of syntax', in Lenneberg (ed.), *New Directions in the Study of Language*, pp. 131–61.

BROWN, ROGER, and FORD, M., 'Address in American English', *Journal of Abnormal and Social Psychology*, 1961, pp. 375–85; reprinted in Hymes (ed.), *Language in Culture and Society*, pp. 234–44.

BROWN, ROGER, and GILMAN, A., 'The pronouns of power and solidarity', in Sebeok (ed.), *Style in Language*, pp. 253–76.

CAMPBELL, BERNARD, 'The roots of language', in Morton (ed.), *Biological and Social Factors in Psycholinguistics*, pp. 10–23.

CARROLL, J. B., *Language and Thought* (Englewood Cliffs, N.J., 1964).

CHAFE, WALLACE, L., *Meaning and the Structure of Language* (Chicago, 1970).

CHATMAN, SEYMOUR B. (ed.), *Literary Style: A Symposium* (London and New York, 1971).

CHOMSKY, CAROL, *The Acquisition of Syntax in Children from 5 to 10* (Cambridge, Mass., 1969).

CHOMSKY, NOAM, *Aspects of the Theory of Syntax* (Cambridge, Mass., 1965).

CHOMSKY, NOAM, *Selected Readings*, eds J. P. B. Allen and P. Van Buren (London, 1971).

CHOMSKY, NOAM, *Studies on Semantics in Generative Grammar* (The Hague, 1972).

Bibliography

CHOMSKY, NOAM, *Syntactic Structures* (The Hague, 1957).

CHOMSKY, NOAM, and HALLE, MORRIS, *The Sound Pattern of English* (New York, 1968).

CRYSTAL, DAVID, and DAVY, DEREK, *Investigating English Style* (London, 1969).

CRYSTAL, DAVID, and QUIRK, RANDOLPH, *Systems of Prosodic and Paralinguistic Features in English* (The Hague, 1964).

CURME, G. O., *A Grammar of the English Language* (Boston and New York, 1931, 1935).

DALE, PHILIP S., *Language Development* (Hinsdale, Illinois, 1972).

DE CECCO, J. P. (ed.), *The Psychology of Language, Thought, and Instruction* (New York, 1967).

DEVORE, I. (ed.), *Primate Behavior: Field Studies of Monkeys and Apes* (New York, 1965).

ENKVIST, NILS-ERIK, 'On defining style', in Spencer and Gregory (eds), *Linguistics and Style*, pp. 3–56.

ENKVIST, NILS-ERIK, 'Style in some linguistic theories', in Chatman (ed.), *Literary Style*, pp. 47–61.

ERVIN, SUSAN, 'Imitation and structural change in children's language', in Lenneberg (ed.), *New Directions in the Study of Language*, pp. 162–89.

FERGUSON, CHARLES A., 'Diglossia', in Hymes (ed.), *Language in Culture and Society*, pp. 429–37.

FERGUSON, CHARLES A., and SLOBIN, DAN I. (eds), *Studies in Child Language Development* (New York, 1973).

FILLMORE, CHARLES J., 'The case for case', in Bach and Harms (eds), *Universals in Linguistic Theory*, pp. 1–88.

FILLMORE, CHARLES J., 'Lexical entries for verbs', *Foundations of Language*, 4 (1968), pp. 373–93.

FILLMORE, CHARLES J., and LANGENDOEN, D. TERENCE (eds), *Studies in Linguistic Semantics* (New York, 1971).

FIRTH, J. R., 'Personality and language in society', *Sociological Review*, 42 (1950); reprinted in Firth, *Papers in Linguistics, 1934–1951* (London, 1952), pp. 177–89.

FISHMAN, J. A. (ed.), *Readings in the Sociology of Language* (The Hague, 1968).

FISHMAN, J. A., *Sociolinguistics* (New York, 1970).

FODOR, J. A., and KATZ, J. J. (eds), *The Structure of Language* (Englewood Cliffs, N.J., 1964).

FOWLER, ROGER, 'Against idealization: some speculations on the theory of linguistic performance', *Linguistics*, 63 (1970), pp. 19–50.

FOWLER, ROGER (ed.), *Essays on Style and Language* (London, 1966).

FOWLER, ROGER, *An Introduction to Transformational Syntax* (London, 1971).

FOWLER, ROGER, *The Languages of Literature* (London, 1971).

FOWLER, ROGER, 'Style and the concept of deep structure', *Journal of Literary Semantics*, 1 (1972).

FRANCIS, W. NELSON, *The Structure of American English* (New York, 1958).

FREEMAN, DONALD C. (ed.), *Linguistics and Literary Style* (New York, 1970).

Bibliography

FREGE, GOTTLOB, 'On sense and reference', in Peter Geach and Max Black, *Translations from the Philosophical Writings of Gottlob Frege* (Oxford, 1952).

FRIES, C. C., *The Structure of English* (New York, 1952).

FRISCH, KARL VON, *Bees: Their Vision, Chemical Sense, and Language* (Ithaca, N.Y., 1950).

GARDNER, R. A., and GARDNER, B. T., 'Teaching sign language to a chimpanzee', *Science*, 165 (1969), pp. 664–72.

GARVIN, PAUL L. (ed. and trans.), *A Prague School Reader on Esthetics, Literary Structure, and Style* (Washington, D.C., 1964).

GIGLIOLI, P. P. (ed.), *Language and Social Context* (Harmondsworth, 1972).

GIMSON, A. C., *An Introduction to the Pronunciation of English* (2nd ed., London, 1970).

GLEASON, H. A., JR., *An Introduction to Descriptive Linguistics* (2nd ed., New York, 1961).

GLEASON, H. A., JR., *Linguistics and English Grammar* (New York, 1965).

GREENBERG, JOSEPH H., *Anthropological Linguistics: An Introduction* (New York, 1968).

GUMPERZ, JOHN J., 'Linguistic and social interaction in two communities', in Gumperz and Hymes (eds), *The Ethnography of Communication*, pp. 137–53.

GUMPERZ, JOHN J., and HYMES, DELL (eds), *Directions in Sociolinguistics* (New York, 1971).

GUMPERZ, JOHN J., and HYMES, DELL (eds), *The Ethnography of Communication*, Special issue, *American Anthropologist*, 66 (1964).

HAAS, MARY, 'Men's and women's speech in Koasati', *Language*, 20 (1944), pp. 142–9; reprinted in Hymes (ed.), *Language in Culture and Society*, pp. 228–33.

HALLE, MORRIS, *The Sound Pattern of Russian* (The Hague, 1959).

HALLE, MORRIS, and KEYSER, SAMUEL J., *English Stress: Its Form, its Growth, and its Role in Verse* (New York, 1971).

HALLIDAY, M. A. K., MCINTOSH, ANGUS, and STREVENS, PETER, *The Linguistic Sciences and Language Teaching* (London, 1964).

HEFFNER, R.-M. S., *General Phonetics* (Madison, 1950).

HILL, A. A., *Introduction to Linguistic Structures: From Sound to Sentence in English* (New York, 1958).

HOCKETT, C. F., *A Course in Modern Linguistics* (New York, 1958).

HOCKETT, C. F., 'The origin of speech', *Scientific American* (September, 1960).

HYMES, DELL, 'On communicative competence', in Gumperz and Hymes (eds), *Directions in Sociolinguistics*.

HYMES, DELL (ed.), *Language in Culture and Society* (New York, 1964).

HYMES, DELL, 'Toward ethnographies of communication' in Gumperz and Hymes (eds), *The Ethnography of Communication*, pp. 1–34; reprinted in part in Giglioli (ed.), *Language and Social Context*, pp. 21–44.

JACOBS, R., and ROSENBAUM, P. S., *English Transformational Grammar* (Waltham, Mass., 1968).

JACOBS, R., and ROSENBAUM, P. S. (eds), *Readings in English Transformational Grammar* (Waltham, Mass., 1970).

Bibliography

JAKOBSON, ROMAN, *Child Language, Aphasia and Phonological Universals* (The Hague, 1969; first published in German, 1941).

JAKOBSON, ROMAN, 'Linguistics and poetics', in Sebeok (ed.), *Style in Language*, pp. 350–77.

JAKOBSON, ROMAN, FANT, GUNNAR, and HALLE, MORRIS, *Preliminaries to Speech Analysis* (2nd ed., Cambridge, Mass., 1963).

JAKOBSON, ROMAN, and HALLE, MORRIS, *Fundamentals of Language* (The Hague, 1956).

JESPERSEN, OTTO, *A Modern English Grammar on Historical Principles*, 7 vols (Copenhagen, 1909–49).

JONES, DANIEL, *An Outline of English Phonetics* (8th ed., Cambridge, 1956).

JOOS, MARTIN, *The English Verb* (Madison, 1964).

JOOS, MARTIN, *The Five Clocks* (Bloomington, 1962).

JOOS, MARTIN (ed.), *Readings in Linguistics* (Washington, D.C., 1957).

KATZ, JERROLD J., *Semantic Theory* (New York, 1972).

KATZ, J. J., and FODOR, J. A., 'The structure of a semantic theory', *Language*, 39 (1963), pp. 170–210; reprinted in Fodor and Katz (eds), *The Structure of Language*.

KATZ, J. J., and POSTAL, P. M., *An Integrated Theory of Linguistic Descriptions* (Cambridge, Mass., 1964).

KENNY, ANTHONY, *Action, Emotion and Will* (London, 1963).

KING, ROBERT D., *Historical Linguistics and Generative Grammar* (Englewood Cliffs, N.J., 1969).

KLIMA, E., and BELLUGI, URSULA, 'Syntactic regularities in the speech of children', in Lyons and Wales (eds), *Psycholinguistics Papers*, pp. 183–208.

KOUTSOUDAS, ANDREAS, *Writing Transformational Grammars* (New York, 1967).

KRUISINGA, E., *A Handbook of Present-day English* (first publ. 1909; 4th ed., Utrecht, 1925–32).

LABOV, WILLIAM, *The Social Stratification of English in New York City* (Washington, D.C., 1966).

LADEFOGED, PETER, *Elements of Acoustic Phonetics* (Edinburgh, 1962).

LADEFOGED, PETER, *Preliminaries to Linguistic Phonetics* (Chicago, 1971).

LADEFOGED, PETER, *Three Areas of Experimental Phonetics* (London, 1967).

LAKOFF, GEORGE, *Irregularity in Syntax* (New York, 1970).

LAKOFF, GEORGE, 'Stative adjectives and verbs in English', *Report No. NSF-17* [of Harvard University Computational Laboratory, ed. Anthony Oettinger] (Cambridge, Mass., 1966).

LANGACKER, RONALD W., *Fundamentals of Linguistic Analysis* (New York, 1972).

LANGACKER, RONALD W., *Language and its Structure* (New York, 1968).

LANGENDOEN, D. TERENCE, *Essentials of English Grammar* (New York, 1970).

LANGENDOEN, D. TERENCE, *The Study of Syntax* (New York, 1969).

LEECH, GEOFFREY N., *English in Advertising* (London, 1966).

Bibliography

LEECH, GEOFFREY N., *Towards a Semantic Description of English* (London, 1966).

LEES, ROBERT B., *The Grammar of English Nominalizations* (Bloomington and The Hague, 1960).

LEHMANN, WINFRED P., *Historical Linguistics: An Introduction* (New York, 1962).

LENNEBERG, E. H., 'A biological perspective of language', in Lenneberg (ed.), *New Directions in the Study of Language*, pp. 65–88.

LENNEBERG, E. H. (ed.), *New Directions in the Study of Language* (Cambridge, Mass., 1964).

LONG, R. B., *The Sentence and its Parts* (Chicago, 1961).

LYONS, JOHN, *Chomsky* (London, 1970).

LYONS, JOHN, 'Generative syntax', in Lyons (ed.), *New Horizons in Linguistics*, pp. 115–39.

LYONS, JOHN, *Introduction to Theoretical Linguistics* (London, 1968).

LYONS, JOHN (ed.), *New Horizons in Linguistics* (Harmondsworth, 1970).

LYONS, JOHN, *Structural Semantics* (Oxford, 1963).

LYONS, JOHN, and WALES, R. J. (eds), *Psycholinguistics Papers* (Edinburgh, 1966).

MCCAWLEY, JAMES D., 'The role of semantics in a grammar', in Bach and Harms (eds), *Universals in Linguistic Theory*, pp. 124–69.

MACLAY, HOWARD, 'Overview' [to the 'Linguistics' section of] Steinberg and Jakobovits (eds), *Semantics*, pp. 157–82.

MCNEILL, DAVID, *The Acquisition of Language* (New York, 1970).

MCNEILL, DAVID, 'Developmental psycholinguistics' in Smith and Miller (eds), *The Genesis of Language*, pp. 15–84.

MALINOWSKI, BRONISLAW, 'The problem of meaning in primitive languages' in Ogden and Richards, *The Meaning of Meaning* (2nd ed., 1936).

MALMBERG, BERTIL, *Phonetics* (New York, 1963).

MARCHAND, HANS, *The Categories and Types of Present-day English Word-formation* (Wiesbaden, 1960).

MARLER, P., 'Communication in monkeys and apes', in DeVore, *Primate Behavior*.

MARSHALL, J. C., 'The biology of communication in man and animals', in Lyons (ed.), *New Horizons in Linguistics*, pp. 229–41.

MENYUK, PAULA, *Sentences Children Use* (Cambridge, Mass., 1969).

MILLER, WICK, and ERVIN, SUSAN, 'The development of grammar in child language', in Bellugi and Brown (eds), *The Acquisition of Language*, pp. 9–34.

MORTON, JOHN (ed.), *Biological and Social Factors in Psycholinguistics* (London, 1971).

MUKAŘOVSKÝ, JAN, 'Standard language and poetic language', in Garvin (ed.), *A Prague School Reader*, pp. 17–30.

NIDA, E. A., *Morphology* (2nd ed., Ann Arbor, 1949).

NIDA, E. A., *A Synopsis of English Syntax* (first published 1960, reprinted, The Hague, 1966).

OGDEN, C. K., and RICHARDS, I. A., *The Meaning of Meaning* (London, 1923).

Bibliography

OLDFIELD, R. C., and MARSHALL, J. C. (eds), *Language: Selected Readings* (Harmondsworth, 1968).

PALMER, F. R., *A Linguistic Study of the English Verb* (London, 1965).

PARKINSON, G. H. R. (ed.), *The Theory of Meaning* (London, 1968).

PEDERSEN, HOLGER, *Linguistic Science in the Nineteenth Century*, trans. J. W. Spargo (Cambridge, Mass., 1931; reprinted as *The Discovery of Language*, Bloomington, 1959).

PIAGET, JEAN, *The Language and Thought of the Child* (New York, 1926).

PIKE, KENNETH L., *Phonemics* (Ann Arbor, 1947).

PIKE, KENNETH L., *Phonetics* (Ann Arbor, 1943).

POTTER, R. K., KOPP, G. A., and GREEN, H. C., *Visible Speech* (New York, 1947).

POUTSMA, H., *A Grammar of Late Modern English* (Groningen, 1914–29).

PRIDE, J. B., *The Social Meaning of Language* (London, 1971).

PULGRAM, E., *Introduction to the Spectrography of Speech* (The Hague, 1959).

QUIRK, RANDOLPH, GREENBAUM, S., LEECH, G. N., and SVARTVIK, J., *A Grammar of Contemporary English* (London, 1972).

REIBEL, D. A., and SCHANE, S. A. (eds), *Modern Studies in English* (Englewood Cliffs, N.J., 1969).

RICHARDS, I. A., *Principles of Literary Criticism* (London, 1924).

ROBINS, R. H., *A Short History of Linguistics* (London, 1967).

ROSENBAUM, PETER S., *The Grammar of English Predicate Complement Constructions* (Cambridge, Mass., 1967).

RUBIN, JOAN, *National Bilingualism in Paraguay* (The Hague, 1968).

SAPIR, EDWARD, *Language: An Introduction to the Study of Speech* (New York, 1921).

SAPIR, EDWARD, 'Sound patterns in language', *Language*, 1 (1925), pp. 37–51; reprinted in Joos (ed.), *Readings in Linguistics*, pp. 19–25.

SAUSSURE, FERDINAND DE, *Cours de linguistique générale* (1916), translated by Wade Baskin as *Course in General Linguistics* (New York, 1959).

SCHANE, SANFORD A., *Generative Phonology* (Englewood Cliffs, N.J., 1973).

SEARLE, JOHN R., *Speech Acts* (London, 1968).

SEBEOK, T. A. (ed.), *Current Trends in Linguistics*, III (The Hague, 1966).

SEBEOK, T. A. (ed.), *Style in Language* (Cambridge, Mass., 1960).

SLEDD, JAMES, *A Short Introduction to English Grammar* (Chicago, 1959).

SLOBIN, DAN I., *Psycholinguistics* (Glenview, Illinois, 1971).

SMITH, FRANK, and MILLER, G. A. (eds), *The Genesis of Language* (Cambridge, Mass., 1966).

SPENCER, JOHN, and GREGORY, MICHAEL (eds), *Linguistics and Style* (London, 1964).

STAGEBERG, NORMAN C., *Introductory English Grammar* (New York, 1965).

STEINBERG, D. D., and JAKOBOVITS, L. A. (eds), *Semantics: an Interdisciplinary Reader* (London, 1971).

STERN, GUSTAV, *Meaning and Change of Meaning* (Gothenburg, 1931).

STOCKWELL, ROBERT P., SCHACHTER, PAUL, and PARTEE, BARBARA HALL, *The Major Syntactic Structures of English* (New York, 1973).

STRANG, BARBARA M. H., *Modern English Structure* (London, 1962).

265

SVARTVIK, JAN, *On Voice in the English Verb* (The Hague, 1966).

TANNER, NANCY, 'Speech and society among the Indonesian elite: a case study of a multilingual society', *Anthropological Linguistics*, 9 (1967), pp. 15–40.

THOMAS, OWEN, *Transformational Grammar and the Teacher of English* (New York, 1965).

TRAGER, G. L., and SMITH, H. L., *An Outline of English Structure* (Norman, Okla., 1951).

TRAUGOTT, ELIZABETH CLOSS, *A History of English Syntax* (New York, 1972).

TRUBETZKOY, N. S., *Introduction to the Principles of Phonological Description*, trans. L. A. Murray (The Hague, 1968). (First edition, *Grundzüge der Phonologie*, Prague, 1939; French trans., *Principes de phonologie*, Paris, 1949.)

ULLMANN, STEPHEN, *Semantics: An Introduction to the Science of Meaning* (Oxford, 1962).

VYGOTSKY, L. S., *Thought and Language* (Cambridge, Mass., 1962).

WATERMAN, JOHN T., *Perspectives in Linguistics* (Chicago, 1963).

WEINREICH, URIEL, 'Explorations in semantic theory', in Sebeok (ed.), *Current Trends in Linguistics*, III, pp. 395–477.

WEIR, RUTH H., *Language in the Crib* (The Hague, 1962).

WHORF, B. L., *Language, Thought, and Reality: Selected Papers* (New York, 1956).

ZANDVOORT, R. W., *A Handbook of English Grammar* (2nd ed., London, 1962).

Main symbols used in phonetic transcription of English

a first element in diphthong [aɪ] (*write*)

æ short front vowel as in Southern English *hat*

ɑ long vowel as in *farm*; first element in diphthong [ɑʊ] (*house*)

ɒ short back vowel as in *dog*

ɔ long back vowel as in *caught*

e short front vowel as in *let*

ə short central vowel occurring in lightly stressed syllables, e.g. the first syllable of *above*, the second syllable of *china*

ɛ first element in diphthong [ɛə] (*air*)

ɜ long central vowel as in *bird*

i long front vowel as in *see*

ɪ short front vowel as in *bit*

u long back vowel as in *boot*

ʊ short back vowel as in *put*

ʌ short back vowel as in *luck*

aɪ diphthong as in *light*

ɑʊ diphthong as in *house*

eɪ diphthong as in *hate*

əʊ diphthong as in *show*

ɔɪ diphthong as in *boy*

ɛə diphthong as in *fair*

b voiced bilabial plosive as in *buy*

d voiced alveolar plosive as in *die*

f voiceless labio-dental fricative as in *foe*

g voiced palatal plosive as in *go*

h voiceless fricative as in *hit*

ʰ aspiration following voiceless initial plosives, as in [pʰɪn] (*pin*)

j semi-vowel as in *you, yacht*

k voiceless palatal plosive as in *kin*

l voiced lateral as in *leap* ('clear *l*')

ł voiced lateral as in *peal* ('dark *l*')

m voiced bilabial nasal as in *me*

n voiced alveolar nasal as in *no*

ŋ voiced palatal nasal as in *sing*

p voiceless bilabial plosive as in *pie*

r voiced continuant as in *rip, marrow*

s voiceless alveolar fricative as in *sigh*

ʃ voiceless palatal fricative as in *shy*

ʒ voiced palatal fricative as in *measure, rouge*

t voiceless alveolar plosive as in *tie*

θ voiceless dental fricative as in *thigh*

ð voiced dental fricative as in *thy*

z voiced alveolar fricative as in *zoo*

tʃ voiceless alveolar affricate as in *choose, leech*

dʒ voiced alveolar affricate as in *jar, large*

Index

This is designed chiefly as a subject index. The only proper names listed are those mentioned in the text itself; authors of references cited in the reading lists are not included.